And the Band Played On...

And the Band Played On...

CHRISTOPHER WARD

HODDER &
STOUGHTON

First published in Great Britain in 2011 by Hodder & Stoughton
An Hachette UK company

1

A CIP catalogue record for this title is available from the British Library

Hardback ISBN 978 1 444 70794 6
Trade Paperback ISBN 978 1 444 70795 3
eBook ISBN 978 1 444 70797 7

Typeset in Albertina MT by Hewer Text UK Ltd, Edinburgh

Printed and bound in the UK by CPI Mackays, Chatham ME5 8TD

Hodder & Stoughton policy is to use papers that are natural, renewable and r
ecyclable products and made from wood grown in sustainable forests.
The logging and manufacturing processes are expected to conform to
the environmental regulations of the country of origin.

Hodder & Stoughton Ltd
338 Euston Road
London NW1 3BH

www.hodder.co.uk

For my mother, Johnann Law Hume Costin,
known to all her friends as Jackie

And for Jock, the father she never knew

Contents

'I found a new hope today in the most unexpected of all places – in the cemetery at Halifax at the grave of a man named Jock Law Hume. The Jock Humes of this world were immediately apparent [on 9/11 at the World Trade Center] helping to keep the crowds calm and prevent panic . . . asking nothing for themselves. Hume – to me he came to represent all of them. They will come out again, if they are needed. And it's enough for me to know that they are near us, though we don't always see them there. They are hope. They are the future.'

Charles Pellegrino, writing about the collapse of the twin towers of the World Trade Center in *Ghosts of Vesuvius*.

'No one was a greater favourite at school than Jock. Indeed everyone who knew the happy-faced lad will have felt a catch in their breath and a lump in their throat when they read that poor Jock had, 'like the Wanderer', gone through the darkness to his rest. Yet, withal, pride masters our grief, for the lad died a hero, his beloved violin clasped to his breast, playing in that last requiem for the passing soul of others and for his own.'

From 'The Last Hymn' – an anonymous appreciation of Jock Law Hume published in the *Dumfries & Galloway Standard*, 24 April 1912.

Introduction

On the night of 14–15 April 1912, the White Star liner *Titanic* sank on its maiden voyage from Southampton to New York after colliding with an iceberg. Of the 1,497 passengers and crew who died in the North Atlantic that night only 306 bodies were recovered. One of them was my grandfather, Jock Hume, a violinist in the *Titanic*'s band. He was twenty-one.

His pay was stopped the moment the ship went down and two weeks later, his father received a bill for the White Star Line brass buttons and epaulettes on his uniform.

Many hundreds of books have been written about the *Titanic*. Nearly all of them, like films of the disaster, end with the ship, its stern vertical in the water, disappearing beneath the waves. This book begins where the lives of the passengers and crew end: with the aftermath. It is a shocking story of corporate callousness and cover-up, with powerful contemporary parallels. It is set in the context of a corrosive class system that was as ruthless in its discrimination in death as it was in life.

This book started out at the beginning of 2010 as one of those *Who Do You Think You Are?* family history projects intended only for my children and grandchildren and for my sister's family – not as a book about the *Titanic*. My sister had died four years earlier, our mother dying ten years before that. With a growing sense of my own mortality, I realised I was now the only person who knew anything about the family, the only one able to put names to faces on the faded sepia pictures in the battered old suitcase in the attic.

It is a human story about the catastrophic consequences of the *Titanic* for two ordinary families in Dumfries, south-west Scotland, and how the tragedy has resonated down through generations of the families involved for nearly one hundred years. My mother, who was born six months after Jock's death and lived into her eighties, was never able to escape the shadow of the *Titanic*. This is also true of the family of the American millionaire Colonel J. J. Astor who, like Jock, died leaving behind an unborn child. It must be the same for other 'Titanic families', too.

My grandmother, Mary Costin, was engaged to Jock Hume and they were to be married when the *Titanic* returned from its maiden voyage. Last year, I spent many days in Dumfries gathering information about the Costins and the Humes, who lived a few hundred yards away from each other. In the Ewart Library in Dumfries I delved through yellowing local newspapers and other records. In the National Archives of Scotland in Edinburgh I sifted through hundreds of bundles of old court records, each neatly tied with a pink silk ribbon. At night, I went online, accessing births, deaths and marriage registers and checking census records. I had to clear shelves in my study to make space for still more books on the *Titanic*, adding several feet to my already substantial *Titanic* library.

My part-time interest developed into a full-time fixation, my research project into a detective inquiry. What made Jock, a child prodigy, decide to leave home at fourteen to play in orchestras on passenger liners? The teenage violinist had seen most of the world before he was twenty, sailing across the Atlantic at least three times in the year before his death. I had not known this. The answers to these questions – and so many more – lay in the complex character of Jock's father, Andrew Hume. I had spent my life thinking of myself as a Ward and a Costin. It took my publisher to remind me that Andrew Hume was my great-grandfather and that I shared some DNA with him, an unwelcome discovery.

Another surprise was to meet a cousin I did not know I had: Yvonne Hume, granddaughter of Jock's younger brother, Andrew, who had just written *Dinner Is Served*, a book of *Titanic* recipes. There was a useful exchange of family memorabilia and a new friendship formed.

In August last year I flew to Halifax, Nova Scotia, where all the bodies recovered from the *Titanic* were brought by the cablelaying ship, *Mackay-Bennett*. It is in Halifax that Jock is buried in the beautiful Fairview Lawn Cemetery, along with 121 other *Titanic* dead. The Nova Scotia Archives and Records in University Avenue, Halifax, contain all the original coroner's reports on the dead. During my time in the archives, and in the Museum of the Atlantic, I discovered the answers to more uncomfortable questions and at the Nova Scotia Maritime Museum I was given the privilege of reading the log of the *Mackay-Bennett*, which gives a detailed account of the voyage of 'the ship of death', as it became known.

Researching and writing this book has been a painful personal journey and, although the book is now completed, I suspect the journey will continue, as many questions remain unanswered. And I feel at last that I know my grandfather, Jock. I found it difficult to picture him while I was growing up, not least because my mother never knew him, either. Everything one was told was second or third-hand.

Thousands who lost fathers and grandfathers in the two world wars must share this alienating experience.

But I know now what good fun Jock was. I can see his smile and hear his laugh. A charming young man. And brave, too. Brave not only in the manner of his dying but, more important, in the manner of his living. For going to sea with his fiddle, aged fourteen, and playing so well that by the time he was twenty-one he had had the chance to play on the greatest ocean liner ever built.

It was his bad luck that it was the *Titanic*.

Christopher Ward, January 2011

1

The Band Who Stayed Together

15 April 1912, 2.05 a.m.: on board the SS *Titanic*

Many brave things were done that night, but none more brave than by those few men playing minute after minute as the ship settled quietly lower and lower in the sea and the sea rose higher and higher to where they stood; the music they played serving alike as their own immortal requiem and their right to be recorded on the rolls of undying fame.

Lawrence Beesley, survivor, from *The Loss of the S.S. Titanic*

The moment eventually came when all eight members of the band knew that they could no longer play on. It wasn't because of the bitter cold, even though they had been on deck for almost an hour, overcoats and scarves thrown hastily over their bandsmen's tunics to provide some additional warmth. My grandfather, Jock Hume, at twenty-one the second youngest member of the orchestra, had only been able to lay his hands on a light raincoat in the desperate rush to reconvene the band on deck. He must have been pleasantly surprised to discover that, despite the lack of feeling in his hands and the difficulty of playing a violin while wearing a cork lifejacket and a purple muffler, he had managed to complete all five verses of 'Nearer My God To Thee' without missing a single note. Nor did the band stop playing even when most of the audience attending this impromptu performance had left – the usual indication to a band that it is time to pack up and go home. The women and children had been the first to leave – in the lifeboats. That was an hour ago. The remaining 1,500 passengers and crew were now carrying out the last order that Captain Smith would give in his long career at sea, namely to abandon ship. A nicety, this, when one considers that the only alternatives were being washed overboard or drowning below decks. Some delayed their departure to receive the last rites on the sloping deck from Father Thomas Byles, kneeling before him in the Act of Contrition as he gave them general absolution and exhorted them to meet their God. Only a mutinous few decided to stay with the ship, retiring to the First Class lounge to await their death with a large brandy in their hand.

Nor was the band intimidated by the relentless advance of the cold sea edging ever closer. None of them had given a moment's thought to their own safety when they came up on deck, and they did not do so now. They were not afraid. They were in this to the end.

The band stopped playing because, as the stricken ship reached its tipping point, even they could no longer hear themselves play above the deafening sound of the *Titanic*'s death throes. 'It was a noise no one had heard before and no one wishes to hear again,' said Colonel Archibald Gracie, a survivor who was in the water as the ship went down. 'It was stupefying, stupendous.'

The symphony of cacophony opened with the sound of breaking glass as the finest Waterford crystal goblets slid from polished mahogany shelves and smashed into a million pieces, covering the floors of the saloons with shards like diamonds. Then, seconds later, came the crash of breaking china as ten thousand plates broke away from their anchor points in the galleys of the First and Second Class kitchens and dining rooms: Royal Crown Derby in First Class (the White Star Line had haggled for weeks over the price), plain white china in Steerage. Not that such distinctions were important any more, the deafening noise drowning even the cries for help from the poor souls already in the water.

Now tables and chairs were on the move, some flying through the windows of the saloon, showering the band from behind with broken glass. In the dining saloon on D Deck a Steinway grand piano – one of six pianos on the ship – snapped its chains, killing a steward as it gathered speed across the dance floor, ending its last waltz upside down and broken in half, its guts spilling out in a final fortissimo of wire, wood and ivory.

But more frightening still was the death rattle of the ship itself. A reverberating rumble, followed by a deep groan louder than thunder and more terrifying than an earthquake, came from somewhere deep inside the bowels as, one by one, the *Titanic*'s twenty-nine boilers burst, tearing huge steel plates free from their rivets. Stokers were boiled alive where they stood, the ear-shattering blast of the superheated steam that engulfed them sparing them the sound of their own short shrieks of death.

So huge and heavy were the *Titanic*'s three anchors that a year before it had taken two teams of eight shire horses to pull each one on low-loaders to the Harland and Wolff shipyard. Now they were on the move again, straining their great chains to breaking point, with no assistance required this time from shire horses.

Distress rockets exploded high in the starlit sky above the ship; now an explosion as loud as an artillery barrage announced the collapse of the forward funnel as the guy wires, unable to stand the extra strain, snapped, the steel hawsers snaking menacingly across the bridge deck. The whole ship shuddered again as the force of gravity ripped its steam turbine engine from its hardened steel mountings, sending it shrieking on an unstoppable journey through the ship on the first leg of its 8,500ft journey to the bottom of the Atlantic.

Wallace Hartley, the band master, just nodded at the musicians, which was his usual signal that they should stop playing now and put away their instruments; he followed this with his customary short respectful bow. Leaning forward, he had difficulty keeping his balance as the deck was now at a steep angle. The band huddled round their leader. 'Gentlemen, thank you all. A most commendable performance. Good night and good luck.' It is what he always said at the end of a performance and tonight would be no different. They shook hands with each other, according to witnesses. Hartley loosened the bow of his violin, placed it firmly in its case next to the instrument, and closed the lid. Then he wound the strap round his body until it was tight against his lifejacket, looping his belt through the strap. The extra buoyancy would increase his chances and, all being well, he would also save his favourite instrument. Jock Hume did the same with his violin, first putting a cloth over the strings to protect the polished wood, slipping the violin mute into his pocket. He kept his hand there for a few moments to warm his fingers, long enough to feel his watch and look at the time. It was 2.11 a.m. The bow of the ship was completely under water now, the icy water slapping the musicians' thighs. They moved further back towards the stern so that they could jump clear of the side.

It would have been Jock's style to volunteer to jump first, joking that it would be like a dip in the Mediterranean compared to swimming in a Scottish burn in summer. But Hartley, would have led the way, a leader to the last, hugging his violin case tightly against him to prevent it slipping off him as he leaped over the side. 'Good luck, boys,' he would have shouted. 'Keep close together, we'll have more chance that way.'

They had no chance at all, of course. But they did stay together.

As our brave bandsmen join the other 1,500 passengers and crew in the water, we must pause for a moment to understand what will now happen to them, in the last minutes of their lives. Contrary to the findings of two official inquiries, and the statements issued later in Halifax, Nova Scotia, by Dr W. D. Finn, the provincial coroner, very few people drowned that night. Most died from hypothermia. A few lucky ones died almost immediately from what is now known as CSR – 'cold shock response'. Charles Lightoller, the most senior officer to survive the sinking, described the experience of entering the water as 'like being stabbed by 1,000 knives'. He was in the sea for only a short time but it is clear he came close to dying from CSR.

Two world wars have increased our understanding of the effects of cold water on the human body as scientists searched for ways to save the lives of sailors and airmen who found themselves 'in the drink'. The Nazis set about their research with their usual precision and ruthlessness, building experimental cold water tanks in concentration camps to record the precise time it took someone to die depending on the temperature of the water and the body weight of the victim. There were no survivors among those selected for these experiments, just a slow, agonising death recorded by the click of a stopwatch and a small ink mark on a sheet of graph paper.

More research has been carried out in the years since the war. Life expectancy in cold water is now measured across a band of six temperature ranges, from the warmest water, 27 degrees Centigrade, to the coldest, zero degrees Centigrade and below. The temperature of the North Atlantic that night was at the very bottom of the survival scale: 28° Fahrenheit or -2.2°C. A grid entitled 'Expected Survival Time in Cold Water' provides a simple guide to the life expectancy of the *Titanic*'s passengers and crew once they entered the freezing water of the North Atlantic. Within fifteen minutes they would have lost consciousness. Ten minutes later they would be dead.

Survivors of cold water accidents have reported how their breath was driven from them on the first impact with the water. If your first gasp for air is under water, you are on a fast track to drowning. If you succeed in holding your breath for long enough, the deadly combination of lack of oxygen and sudden drop in temperature places a severe strain on the body: surface blood vessels constrict, heart rate increases, blood pressure rises and hyperventilation takes over. This can trigger an immediate 'cold shock response' – effectively a fatal heart attack. This is the best you can hope for. It's your lucky day.

If you are still alive two minutes after falling into the water you enter the first of three stages of death by hypothermia. You lose all feeling in your arms and legs, your body temperature plummets and you start shivering so violently that your teeth chatter. Your pupils dilate. The worst thing you can do now is start swimming – you will shorten your survival time by up to 50 per cent as your body loses heat at a much faster rate when you move. All the *Titanic* victims were desperately trying to get as far away from the sinking ship as possible for fear of being sucked down with it, but they were unknowingly hastening their deaths. You may suddenly start to feel warmer. This is a cruel deception. Your body temperature is still dropping like a stone. When you are unable to touch your thumb with your little finger, you are about to enter stage two.

In stage two, movement becomes slower and confusion sets in. Surface blood vessels contract further as the body focuses its remaining resources on keeping the vital organs warm. Lips, ears, fingers and toes turn blue. Pulse rate drops further but heart rate increases. Breathing becomes erratic and shallow.

Stage three kicks in when the body temperature drops below 32°C (89.6°F). Shivering usually stops. At 30°C (86°F) you lose consciousness as cellular metabolic processes, essential for maintaining life, shut down. Major organs fail. Clinical death occurs at 26°C (79°F) but brain death follows later because of the decreased cellular activity. No one in the water would have been alive after 2.45 a.m.

It is hard to imagine two more different lives than those of the American millionaire Colonel J. J. Astor and my grandfather Jock Hume, a music teacher's son from Dumfries. But fate would bind them together that night, not only by throwing them together in the final minutes of their lives, but with what the two men left behind. For both Astor's young wife Madeleine and Jock's fiancée Mary Costin were pregnant and, later that year, would give birth to children who would grow up never having known their fathers. The *Titanic* would cast a dark shadow over both families for a hundred years.

My mother had a clear childhood memory of a postcard of the *Titanic* propped up on the mantelpiece at her home in Buccleuch Street, Dumfries; it stayed there for many years. From time to time it would be taken down to be dusted, or to be shown to a visitor. Jock would have sent it from Southampton on the morning of Wednesday 10 April before the ship sailed.

Jock had found out only a week earlier that Mary was expecting his baby, although she had suspected for a week or more that she might be pregnant. Mary broke the news to him the night before he left to join the ship. They had been saving up to be married at Greyfriars Church, Dumfries in May, after the *Titanic* returned from its maiden voyage and she had been nervous about how Jock would take the news that she was expecting his child. It was a relief to find that he was as thrilled as she was.

Mary went with Jock early next morning, 9 April, to Dumfries railway station where he was to catch a

Caledonian Railway train to Carlisle for a connection to Liverpool, the first leg of his journey to Southampton where he would join the *Titanic*. They had left home late and had to run the last thirty yards to the station as they heard the train approach, Jock boarding the train and slamming shut the door as the stationmaster blew his whistle. They kissed briefly through the open window then, as the locomotive built up steam and pulled slowly out of the station, they waved frantically behind a billowing curtain of smoke and steam. It would be the last time they saw each other.

In Liverpool, Jock headed straight for Lord Street where he was fitted for his bandsman's uniform by J. J. Rayner, the naval outfitters, who sewed on the brass White Star Line buttons and epaulettes. From there he walked the short distance to Castle Street to the offices of C. W. and F. N. Black, the musical agents who employed him and all the other members of the band. Here he collected a rail warrant for the last leg of the journey to Southampton to board the ship. Rayner's had an arrangement with the Black brothers and would send the bill for Jock's uniform to them. Then it was back to Lime Street station.

Jock caught an afternoon train to London arriving in time to take a late train from Waterloo to Southampton. It was 10 p.m. by the time he knocked on the door of number 140 St Mary's Road, Southampton, where he was welcomed by his landlady Mrs King. She kept rooms for five lodgers, most of them crew on passenger liners. Jock was one of her regulars and Mrs King was used to late arrivals. The following morning he boarded the *Titanic* early at Southampton's Berth 44, the dockside already swarming with people. The band were travelling on a Second Class ticket and Jock entered the ship aft on C Deck via the Second Class gangway. Two cabins on E Deck had been made available for the eight musicians.

Jock had never minded leaving Mary before – in truth, he had spent much of the past two years away from Dumfries, playing on passenger ships, and they had both come to terms with separations. But this time it was different. For the first time in his life, Jock's thoughts were on what he had left behind rather than what lay ahead. He normally waited until he reached his destination before writing a postcard or a letter to Mary but this time he sent a postcard of the *Titanic* with some reassuring, well-chosen words.

The Astors boarded the *Titanic* at Cherbourg, accompanied by Astor's valet Victor Robbins, Madeleine's maid Rosalie Bidois and her nurse Caroline Endres. Astor's much-loved Airedale dog Kitty, who had accompanied them to Egypt, was with them.

Astor could not have been looking forward to the reception that awaited him and his young bride Madeleine in New York. The couple, who had been on an extended honeymoon lasting several months, had been the focus of fascination and gossip since Astor's acrimonious divorce from his wife Ava the previous year, a divorce that had scandalised society and divided loyalties. Aged just eighteen, Madeleine Talmage Force was twenty-seven years her husband's junior and a year younger than his son Vincent. 'A rather tall, graceful girl with brown hair and strong clean-cut features', according to the *New York Times*,

Madeleine had only just left finishing school when she had been inadvertently introduced to Astor by her parents, who thought him a suitably wealthy match for their older daughter, Katherine.

Astor had sensibly decided to put time and distance between himself and his critics while showing Madeleine the world. They had spent several weeks in Egypt and France and were now settled in one of the most luxurious state rooms on the ship. But the honeymoon was almost over; Madeleine was six months pregnant and when the *Titanic* docked in New York Astor would be facing the wrath of his family and the disapproval of his detractors as well as the scrutiny of investors.

Sunday 14 April was a beautiful starlit night, cold but pin-sharp clear, and it must have reminded Jock of the cold winter nights at home in Dumfries and Galloway. Survivors later recalled their separate encounters with Jock and with Astor, both of whom, before the end of the night, would demonstrate one other thing they had in common – courage. Violet Jessop, a stewardess on the ship, first ran into Jock during the band's interval during dinner, which was announced every evening at 6 p.m. with a blast on a horn by the ship's bugler. 'He was always so eager and full of life was Jock,' she said. 'He called out to me in his rich Scotch accent that he was about to give them a "real tune, a Scotch tune, to finish up with".'

Later that night, after the order to abandon ship had been given, she passed the band as they raced up the stairs carrying their instruments to resume playing on deck. Jock looked pale, she thought. 'We're just going to give them a tune to cheer things up a bit,' he told her.

First Class Passenger List

PER

ROYAL AND U.S. MAIL

S.S. "Titanic,"

From SOUTHAMPTON and CHERBOURG

to NEW YORK

(Via QUEENSTOWN).

Wednesday, 10th April, 1912.

Captain, E. J. Smith, R.D. (Commr. R.N.R.).

Surgeon, W. F. N. O'Loughlin.　　　　　Pursers { H. W. McElroy
Asst. Surgeon, J. E. Simpson.　　　　　　　　　　　 { R. L. Barker.

Chief Steward, A. Latimer.

Allen, Miss Elizabeth
　　　　　Walton

Allison, Mr. H. J.

Allison, Mrs. H. J.
　and Maid

Allison, Miss

Allison, Master
　and Nurse

Anderson, Mr. Harry

Andrews, Miss Cornelia I.

Andrews, Mr. Thomas

Appleton, Mrs. E. D.

Artagaveytia, Mr. Ramon

Astor, Colonel J. J.
　and Manservant

Astor, Mrs. J. J.
　and Maid

Aubert, Mrs. N.
　and Maid

There were conflicting accounts of Astor's last moments, as there were disagreements about just about everything that happened that night. But several people independently saw him kiss Madeleine on both cheeks before helping her into lifeboat number 4, and then stand back and salute her. The best and probably most accurate account is that of Colonel Archibald Gracie, one of the last to leave the ship, who wrote a dramatic eyewitness account of the sinking before dying a year later as a result of his exposure in the sea. Colonel Gracie helped Astor lift Madeleine over the 4ft high rail into a lifeboat:

Her husband held her left arm as we carefully passed her to Lightoller (Charles Lightoller, Second Officer) who seated her in the boat. A dialogue now ensued between Colonel Astor and the officer, every word of which I listened to with intense interest. Astor was close to me in the adjoining window frame, to the left of mine. Leaning out over the rail he asked permission of Lightoller to enter the boat to protect his wife which, in view of her delicate condition, seems to have been a reasonable request, but the officer, intent upon his duty, and obeying orders, and not knowing the millionaire from the rest of us replied: 'No, sir, no men are allowed in these boats until women are loaded first'. Col Astor did not demur, but bore the refusal bravely and resignedly, simply asking the number of the boat to help find his wife later, in case he also was rescued. 'Number 4' was Lightoller's reply. Nothing more was said.

It seems that one of Colonel Astor's last acts was to go below decks to retrieve his Airedale dog Kitty from the *Titanic's* kennels. Madeleine never spoke publicly about what happened that night except to say that as lifeboat number 4 pulled away from the sinking ship, the band was still playing and the last thing she saw was Kitty pacing the deck.

Of the 1,497 passengers and crew who died that night, more than 1,000 were never seen again, their bodies disappearing for ever, their families, loved ones and friends left in an eternal state of not knowing, with no body to grieve over.

Yet the bodies of three out of the eight bandsmen *were* recovered and – even more remarkably – were found together. For the next eight days and nights, kept upright and buoyant by their cork lifejackets, Hartley's violin case still strapped firmly to his chest, they were carried forty miles from the *Titanic's* last resting place by winds and currents.

We will never know how, in the last minutes of their lives, numb with cold, they managed to achieve this, or how or when the other five slipped away from the rest of the band. But on 23 April the three dead bandsmen had a rendezvous with a ship as remarkable in its own way as the *Titanic*: the cable ship *Mackay-Bennett*. One of the three was my grandfather, Jock.

2

The Agony of Not Knowing

16 April, 35 Buccleuch Street, Dumfries

Two thousand miles away in Dumfries, the Humes and the Costins waited anxiously for news of Jock. In the absence of any statement from the White Star Line, conflicting newspaper reports fuelled hope and despair. The *Daily Mirror*, for instance, assured its readers that all 2,209 passengers and crew on board the *Titanic* had been saved and that 'the hapless giant' was being towed safely to New York. The *Liverpool Courier*, whose offices were round the corner from the White Star Line headquarters in James Street, went one further by publishing a photograph of the Allan liner *Virginian* towing the *Titanic* into New York harbour – a miracle of montage and the airbrusher's art. Underneath the headline 'ALL PASSENGERS RESCUED' was a report of the 'remarkable rescue' of all those on board. 'News of the collision with an iceberg has been received with something akin to consternation,' said the *Courier*.

This story could not possibly have appeared without the collusion of the White Star Line. I worked in Liverpool for the *Daily Mirror* in the Sixties and enjoyed, along with all the other pressmen in the city, the closest relationship with the shipping companies. In 1912, when Liverpool was the

Empire's leading sea port, the press and the shipping lines would have been completely in each other's pockets.

Other newspapers sensibly put their trust in news coming from the wire services in the USA and Canada, based on Marconi intercepts from Cape Race. The *Daily Sketch* accurately reported that the liner had sunk with a 'Feared Loss of 1,700 Lives in Mid-Atlantic'.

My grandmother, Mary Costin, who had risen early and waited outside McMillan's, the newsagent's shop in Friar's Vennel, until it opened shortly before 6 a.m., knew at once which of the two conflicting accounts she believed. For as long as Mary could remember, the people she loved had died: her two young sisters Margaret and Elizabeth when she was five, both from cerebral meningitis; her father from a haemorrhage a year later; and then last year her beloved brother William, from appendicitis, aged twenty-four, leaving three more young Costin children fatherless. Now Jock had been taken from her.

It might have been some comfort to both families if they could have shared their grief, exchanged information and comforted each other. But to say that the Humes and the Costins did not speak would be an understatement. Ever since my grandparents Jock and Mary had fallen in love two years earlier, a state of war worthy of the Montagues and Capulets had existed between the families. Andrew Hume had instigated the hostilities, forbidding his son to see Mary on the grounds that Jock could 'do better' for himself. From that moment on Mary's mother Susan, a proud and determined woman who liked Jock and cared about her daughter's happiness, did everything possible to encourage the relationship, including inviting Jock to live under her own roof with Mary, which he did, between voyages, during the last year of his life.

To the Costins, it must have seemed as if Jock's father Andrew and his stepmother Alice were holding all the cards. As Jock's parents, the Humes were the next of kin with whom the White Star Line would communicate. But with the survivors still at sea on board the SS *Carpathia* and the company maintaining its blackout on news, both families were equally in the dark.

Although Mary had not slept, there was no question of not working as normal at the glove factory. But she decided to leave home early so that she could call on the Humes on her way to the mill and see if they had received any news of Jock. Her mother counselled her against doing this but Mary ignored her mother's advice and strode the 400 yards to 42 George Street, mounted the six York stone steps to the Humes' front door, grasped the heavy lion's claw doorknob and knocked twice. She saw an upstairs curtain flicker briefly. Two minutes passed, then she heard the sound of a woman's footsteps followed by the grating noise of a large key being turned in the lock.

Jock's stepmother, Alice, opened the door. She looked Mary up and down and before Mary had time to speak said, 'Please do not call here again, Miss Costin,' and shut the door in her face. Mary walked back down the steps and wondered what kind of reception she might receive when she called to tell the Humes she was expecting Jock's baby.

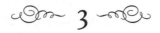

3

The *Mackay-Bennett* Sets Sail

17 April, Halifax, Nova Scotia

At exactly 12.45 p.m. on Wednesday 17 April 1912 the cable-laying ship *Mackay-Bennett* cast off from the wharf at Upper Water Street, Halifax, Nova Scotia. On the bridge deck of the 1,731-ton ship Captain Frederick Larnder, a tall handsome Englishman with a full brown beard and 'eyes of unnatural keenness', started a new page in the ship's leather-bound deck log. In capital letters he wrote in pencil: 'PROCEEDED TO SEA TOWARDS WRECK OF SS TITANIC' noting the conditions – 'foggy, gentle breeze' – before charting a south-easterly course which would take him the 680 miles to the last known position of the *Titanic*.

Larnder's orders were to recover the dead and bring the bodies back to Halifax, the nearest point of land to where the *Titanic* foundered. There had been no talk of survivors and no one, least of all Larnder, was under any illusion about finding anyone alive. He had seen men die of hypothermia within minutes of falling into these sub-zero waters. Even in a lifeboat you would be lucky to live for more than a few hours and the *Mackay-Bennett* would not reach the scene for four days, nearly a week after the great liner had sunk. Nor had anyone told him how many dead he was to expect. He had 103 coffins on board but he still had no idea of the horror that was waiting for them out there. Robert Hunston, the keen young wireless operator manning the new Marconi communication station at Cape Race, had kept a message log of all the signal traffic on Sunday night as the *Titanic's* wireless operator called for assistance from ships in the area. Hunston decoded the word S-I-N-K-I-N-G three times just to make sure he had understood it properly. Then the *Titanic* went off the air.

One person, however, knew exactly how many had died: Bruce Ismay, Chairman of the White Star Line. But he was remaining silent. For two days Ismay had been safely aboard the Cunard liner SS *Carpathia* sailing to New York with the 712 survivors. The arithmetic to calculate the death toll was so simple a child of five could do it: take 2,209 passengers and crew, subtract 712 survivors and you have . . . yes, 1,497 is the correct answer.

There were 1,497 passengers and crew dead in the sea somewhere out there in the North Atlantic. It would have been 1,498 if Ismay himself had not joined the women and children in one of the *Titanic's* lifeboats, from where he heard the screams and watched the desperate death throes of hundreds of men, women and children who had been entrusted to his corporate care. No wonder he could not bring himself to tell the world what had happened. Transmission problems thwarted an attempt by the SS *Carpathia's* wireless officer to transmit by Morse code a full list of those who had been saved, it is but no surprise that names such as Bruce Ismay and Mrs Astor were among the few to get through.

Yesterday. It seemed like a year ago to Larnder now. Only yesterday he had been preparing the 270-ft *Mackay-Bennett* for the task for which it was purpose built: to repair a cable break

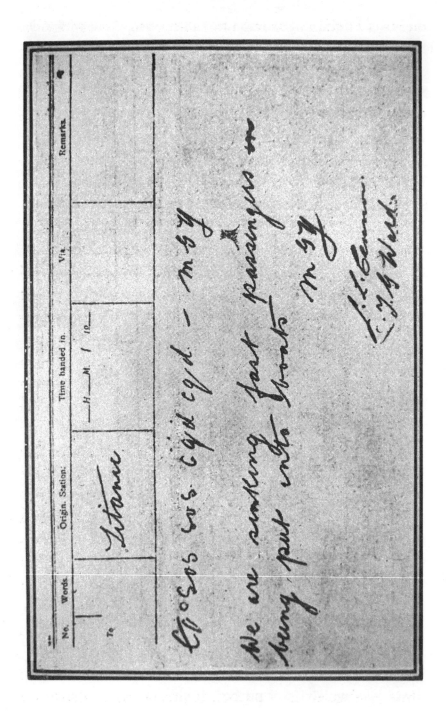

near Cape Cod in a transatlantic cable linking Europe and the United States. All day the crew had been flat out, filling the bunkers with coal, feeding miles of telegraph cable on to drums in the *Mackay-Bennett*'s three tanks, painting girders, taking in water and stores and scrubbing the decks while the ship's carpenter raced around making last-minute repairs.

Then, shortly before noon, Larnder was summoned to the office of his employers, the Commercial Cable Company, where he was introduced to Mr A.G. Jones, the White Star Line's agent in Halifax. Jones informed him that the White Star Line had chartered the *Mackay-Bennett* to recover bodies from the *Titanic*. Larnder's orders were to make ready for sea and sail tomorrow. Jones handed him a piece of paper with the last known position of the wreck, which Jack Phillips, *Titanic*'s wireless operator, had radioed shortly before the ship went down. The position was 41.46 N, 50.14 W but Larnder would have to make careful calculations based on wind and sea currents to determine where the bodies were likely to be by Sunday, the soonest the *Mackay-Bennett* was likely to reach the scene.

The White Star Line were paying the Commercial Cable Company $550 a day to charter their ship and would pay the crew, including Larnder, double wages after they completed their unpleasant mission. Everything that the *Mackay-Bennett* required would be on the quayside ready for loading tomorrow morning. Larnder would need to take on extra crew – probably ten men. In addition, they would be joined on board by Canon Kenneth Cameron Hind of All Saints Cathedral, Halifax and John R. Snow Jnr, chief embalmer with his father's firm of John Snow & Co, Nova Scotia's largest undertakers. Larnder knew the men well; both were at the top of their professions in the efficient processing of death: Mr

Snow attending to the bodies with all the skills of the mortician, Hind commending souls to the Almighty. Neither man
could have guessed what distressing scenes lay ahead for
them: Mr Snow running out of coffins and embalming fluid,
Hind standing in his vestment on the freezing deck chanting
'Forasmuch as it hath pleased Almighty God' time after time
as he commended the soul of yet another dearly departed to
the Good Lord.

Larnder returned to the *Mackay-Bennett*, where work began
at once to prepare the two-masted ship for its gruesome task.
The removal of non-essential equipment for their planned
voyage was done efficiently and with urgency yet it could have
given Larnder no pleasure to preside over the unwinding of
the submarine cable from the drums in the tanks. For five
years he had been master of the *Mackay-Bennett*, laying telegraph cables hundreds of miles along the ocean bed, often
– mostly – in the most inhospitable weather that the North
Atlantic could serve up. He had come to believe it was his calling to help move the world from the industrial revolution to
the new age of technology and communication, connecting
Europe to North America. Now he found himself in command
of an ocean-going mortuary, 'The Ship of Death' as it would
soon be called. But today the White Star Line were paying the
bills and by 5 p.m. the last of the cable had been unwound and
Larnder retired to his cabin after writing the last entry for that
day in the log: '5 p.m., Hands piped down.'

Larnder didn't get much sleep between the clatter of
horses' hooves and shouted instructions signalling every
new delivery throughout the night. Coffins, 103 in all, of
varying quality, the most that Halifax's funeral directors and
carpenters could knock together at such short notice, were

stacked so high on the dockside that they looked as if they might topple. Sheets of sailing canvas in which to wrap bodies were piled next to them. And grate iron, ten tons of it, to weight bodies that would be buried at sea. At midnight the purser woke Larnder to ask where they could safely stow the wooden cases containing fragile flasks of Mr Snow's embalming fluid. Meanwhile, the boatswain was trawling Halifax's inns in a frantic search to recruit men who would be sober enough to sail in the morning and who had the strength and stomach for the work ahead.

Loading started early next morning. Larnder noted in his log: 'Hands getting ice, old iron and coffins on board.' The ice had been Larnder's idea. As a boy, Larnder had served his time on trawlers and knew that this was the only way to keep the catch fresh until you returned to port. The *Mackay-Bennett* had three empty tanks below the deck where, until yesterday, three huge drums of submarine cable had been stored. Now the tanks became the containers for 20,000 tons of crushed ice, only it wouldn't be Newfoundland cod that was being tipped into the hold: it would be bodies. Many of the passengers and crew of the *Titanic* would end up there, First Class passengers and White Star Line officers excepted of course, lying frozen side by side like so many dead fish. It would become a transit area for the underdog when the *Mackay-Bennett* ran out of coffins and canvas.

Ten new crew members had to be accommodated – and cabins found for Larnder's VIP guests. Fortunately the Commercial Cable Company's owners, John William Mackay and James Gordon Bennett Jnr, had insisted on the *Mackay-Bennett* being built to the highest specifications by John Elder & Co. of Glasgow in 1884. It was exceptionally comfortable as well as leading edge in its engineering and equipment. The fact that it withstood its maiden voyage spoke volumes for it. On 17 February 1885 the *Mackay-Bennett* had left London, where it had been fitted out, for Halifax, where it was to be delivered to its owners. The following day it sailed into a series of gales and hurricanes 'never before experienced'. Four days out to sea it passed through 'a terrible hurricane' that lasted six hours, according to a *New York Times* report. On arrival in Halifax two weeks later, the four storm-battered officers, relieved to have survived the ordeal, declared the *Mackay-Bennett* 'a handsome craft . . . a magnificent sea boat and one of the finest specimens of modern marine architecture'.

Mrs Mackay, wife of the popular millionaire president of the company, had christened the ship when it was launched the previous year in Glasgow, and had taken a particular interest in the interior design when it had been fitted out. The captain's cabin, situated in a deckhouse forward of the poop, was unusually comfortable and on either side of the saloon on the main deck were state rooms for cable engineers, electricians or passengers. One of these, a large cabin handsomely panelled in mahogany, was reserved for the use of Mr Mackay and Mr Bennett. It was here, no doubt to his immense relief, that Canon Hind was shown after boarding the ship.

The *Mackay-Bennett* owed its name and existence to the brilliant business partnership of Mackay and Bennett, who had founded the Commercial Cable Company in 1884 to compete with Western Union's virtual monopoly on transatlantic telegraphy. Bennett was a madcap entrepreneur who had financed Henry Stanley's expedition in Africa to discover Dr Livingstone. After taking over management of the *New York Herald* from his father he had moved to Europe to build a newspaper empire there, with London and Paris editions of the *Herald* made possible by the recently developed technology of undersea cables. The *Mackay-Bennett* was built specifically as a cable repair ship to maintain CCC's undersea cables, which remained in use carrying telegraphic traffic until 1962.

In Halifax the *Mackay-Bennett* was particularly well regarded and its captain was as popular as he was well respected. Such reputations were not easily gained in the tough shipping community of Halifax. Reporters boarded the ship before its departure from Halifax, the *Evening Echo* publishing a large picture of the ship taken shortly before it sailed. The accompanying report said that

> . . . in the *Mackay-Bennett* the White Star Line have secured a ship especially well fitted for the task set her. Her commander, F. H. Larnder is a thoroughly trained navigator, careful and resourceful and he has under his command a crew of officers and men that might be classed as picked.

It was indeed good fortune for the White Star Line – and for the relatives of the dead whose bodies were recovered – that the *Mackay-Bennett* was available for charter by the White Star Line. Its cable-laying design and specialist equipment were exactly what was required for the job in hand: that is to say, retrieving dead bodies from the water. It was well equipped with grapnels and grappling hooks and manned by crew who knew how to throw them accurately and retrieve them quickly. For heavier weights there was a powerful capstan and two horizontal steam winches. Because of the nature of its work, it was a ship designed for drifting, with a rudder at each end of the ship for manoeuvring and two large cutters for working outside the ship. Twin generators drove powerful lamps, which allowed the ship's crew to work at night.

Larnder had sailed the *Mackay-Bennett* out of Halifax harbour a hundred times before. As always, he took the easterly channel past George's Island, passing McNab's Island on the port side. Even as the fog thickened he could make out the shapes of the familiar landmarks slipping past them, their names reflecting Halifax's rich history: Ferguson's Cove, Sleepy Cove, Sandwich Point, then Herring Cove where a pod of dolphins joined them, racing alongside the bow and leaping and diving, their welcoming grunts clearly audible above the chugging of the *Mackay-Bennett*'s engines.

The graceful escort raised Larnder's spirits. The proximity of the coffins on deck had made him morbidly preoccupied with the gruesome task ahead. The dolphins reminded him that for the moment anyway his priority must be the living, not the dead, the safety of his crew put above all else. The *Mackay-Bennett* had cast off less than an hour ago but already his wireless operator had brought warnings of three more sightings of hazards directly in the course: icebergs, pack ice and 'growlers' – small icebergs awash and floating just below the surface but no less deadly and almost impossible to see.

Larnder had already decided there was be a round-the-clock series of one-hour watches for ice and, later, for bodies. Bouderot had taken the first watch. Now Larnder noted his order in the deck log – Bouderot noon to 1 p.m., Sampson 1-2, Stratford 2-3, Carter 3-4, Patterson 4-5, Abbott 5-6 and 6-7, Carr 7-8 – and then Bouderot followed by Sampson again.

The ghostly shape of the lighthouse on Devil's Island loomed up, marking the south-east passage out of Halifax. Through the fog they could barely see Maugher's Beach, better known as 'Hangman's Beach', once a popular site for hanging mutineers and leaving them there as a warning to passing crew. From here it was a straight run to the open sea past Portuguese Cove and the Chebucto Head lighthouse.

Now they were in open water, leaving behind them a low slip of land and the Sambro Island lighthouse. The oldest lighthouse in North America, it burned brightly for years fuelled by whale oil but around 1900 was converted to burn kerosene. It had been painted with red stripes the previous summer to make it more visible in the winter snow.

The *Mackay-Bennett* was three days' sailing away from its destination but there was still much to be done and no time to be wasted. The ship's carpenter made an operating table for the undertaker which was 'strong enough to take a 20-stone man', according to Mr Snow's instructions. The undertaker also requested the carpenter to make three screens so that he could work in privacy away from curious eyes.

Other hands were put to work cutting up sailcloth to make small duck bags. This was the purser, Frank Higginson's idea. When the bodies were brought aboard, each corpse would be given a sequential number, a label bearing the number tied to the body. A description of each person, and their identity if known, would be entered in a book against the number. Any possessions found on their body would then be put in a duck bag, numbered by stencil, so that personal effects could be returned to the correct next of kin. At least two crew members would help in this process, in the presence of either Mr Snow, the purser Mr Higginson, or the ship's surgeon, Dr Thomas Armstrong, to prevent theft or other irregularities. The clothes of the dead would be removed, bagged separately and stored in the ship's hospital. When the *Mackay-Bennett* returned to Halifax the clothes were first taken to the mortuary to assist identification, and then burned to prevent them falling into the hands of ghoulish souvenir hunters. This system of numbering the dead proved to be so successful that it was adopted to identify the fatalities – nearly 2,000 of them – after the catastrophic explosion of an ammunition ship that ripped Halifax apart in 1917.

For the next two days Captain Larnder's log recorded only the barest of facts: wind, weather, sea temperature, names of lookouts, tasks undertaken – 'hands washed decks, etc.' The weather was deteriorating fast, the temperature dropping. As the *Mackay-Bennett* approached the area where ice had been reported, Larnder doubled the watch – four eyes being better than two. At the same time he gave the order to double the men's daily rum ration. They would need it to keep their spirits up. When the ship was at sea, it was customary for the Chief Steward to bring a pail of English rum at 6 p.m. every evening and dispense 3-4 ounces into each man's drinking mug. From today, they would get eight ounces. Larnder was a captain who knew how to get the best out of his crew.

On Saturday 20 April Larnder noted in his log that a lifebelt was sighted and a cutter lowered to retrieve it, but the lifebelt was found to belong to a ship from the Allan Line. The same day, two messages were sent from the *Mackay-Bennett* via the Cape Race radio station to Ismay at the offices of the White Star Line in New York. The first message reads: 'Steamer *Rhein* reports passing wreckage and bodies 42.10 north, 49.13 west, eight miles west of three big icebergs. Now making for that position. Expect to arrive 8 o'clock to-night.' The second tells Ismay, 'Received further information from (steamship) *Bremen* and arrived on ground at 8 o'clock p.m. Start on operation tomorrow. Have been considerably delayed on passage by dense fog.' The *Mackay-Bennett* hove to for the night to begin operations at first light.

But nowhere in the log does Captain Larnder report that he is in touch with Bruce Ismay, who was now safe in New York, where the *Carpathia* had docked three days earlier. After receiving these messages Mr Ismay issued the following statement through the White Star Line's New York office:

The cable ship *Mackay-Bennett* has been chartered by the White Star Line and ordered to proceed to the scene of the disaster and do all she could to recover the bodies and glean all information possible. Every effort will be made to identify bodies recovered, and any news will be sent through immediately by wireless. In addition to any such message as these, the *Mackay-Bennett* will make a report of its activities each morning by wireless, and such reports will be made public at the offices of the White Star Line.

The cable ship has orders to remain on the scene of the wreck for at least a week, but should a large number of bodies be recovered before that time she will return to Halifax with them. The search for bodies will not be abandoned until not a vestige of hope remains for any more recoveries.

Below deck, one of the cable engineers, Frederick Hamilton, had been keeping a diary with more colourful detail including wireless encounters with several passing ships. The original of the diary is in the National Maritime Museum in Greenwich.

April 19th: We spoke to the *Royal Edward* by wireless to-day, she lay east of us, and reported icebergs, and growlers . . .
April 20th: French liner *Rochambeau* near us last night,

reported icebergs, and the *Royal Edward* reported one thirty miles east of the *Titanic's* position. The *Rhine* [sic] passed us this afternoon, and reported having seen icebergs, wreckage and bodies, at 5.50 p.m. The *Bremen* passed near us, she reported having seen, one hour and a half before, bodies etc. This means about twenty-five miles to the east. 7 p.m. A large iceberg, faintly discernible to our north, we are now very near the area were [sic] lie the ruins of so many human hopes and prayers. The Embalmer becomes more and more cheerful as we approach the scene of his future professional activities, tomorrow will be a good day for him.

Early the next morning, Sunday 21 April, the *Mackay-Bennett*, having covered 669 miles since leaving Halifax, came upon an expanse of wreckage including an overturned lifeboat and dead bodies. Larnder cut all engines and ordered a cutter to be lowered. His log records the event without emotion and with few facts: 'Drifting. Wind WSW, force 4. Lat 41.59N, 49.25W. Picking up bodies. Logging icebergs, Considerable swell.' Later he described the scene as 'like nothing so much as a flock of sea gulls resting upon the water . . . all we could see at first would be the top of the life preservers. They were all floating face upwards, apparently standing in the water.'

Hamilton's diary entry that day provides an equally dramatic picture:

April 21st: Two icebergs now clearly in sight, the nearest is over a hundred feet high at the tallest peak, and an impressive sight, a solid mass of ice, against which the sea dashes furiously, throwing up geyser like columns of foam, high over the topmost summit, smothering the great mass at times completely in a cascade of spume as it pours over the snow and breaks into feathery crests on the polished surface of the berg, causing the whole ice mountain, which glints like a fairy building, to oscillate twenty to thirty feet from the vertical. The ocean is strewn with a litter of woodwork, chairs, and bodies, and there are several growlers about, all more or less dangerous, as they are often hidden in the swell. The cutter lowered, and work commenced and kept up continuously all day, picking up bodies. Hauling the soaked remains in saturated clothing over the side of the cutter is no light task. Fifty-one we have taken on board today, two children, three women, and forty-six men, and still the sea seems strewn. With the exception of ourselves, the bosum bird is the only living creature here.

When the crew in the cutters had recovered five or six corpses they would row back to the *Mackay-Bennett* where the cutter would be raised to the rail of the ship and the bodies passed by the seamen to their mates on the deck. The cutter would then be lowered to the sea again so that searching could continue. The fourth body hauled out of the sea was to be the youngest of all those recovered: a two-year-old boy who was found floating without a lifejacket, suggesting that he had been carried by his mother and slipped from her arms. The sight of the dead child was said to have so moved the seamen that they later paid for the boy's burial and a special gravestone, a lasting monument to the 'Unknown Child' of the *Titanic*, whose identity has been the source of controversy ever since. Thousands lay flowers at his grave in Fairview Lawn Cemetery, Halifax, every year.

The crew of the *Mackay-Bennett* had braced themselves for their unpleasant task but they were caught off balance by their distress at finding women and children. Men were easier to cope with. Sailors lived and died by the sea and the sight of a floating male corpse was not an unfamiliar one. Many of Larnder's men had worked on whalers or participated in mass seal culls. As one of them said, 'The first ten are difficult, after that it's just work.' They stopped seeing bodies as people – they were loads that had to be moved from one place to another.

Once on deck, bodies were undressed by the undertaker so that distinguishing body marks such as scars could be noted by the purser, Frank Higgison assisted by the ship's surgeon, Dr Armstrong, along with a general description of the person, to assist identification. The White Star Line would never concede that bodies recovered by the *Mackay-Bennett* were processed according to class and the issue has always been a sensitive one. But the fact remains that they were, whether intentionally or otherwise. In death as in life the passengers and crew would be treated in a way appropriate to their perceived 'position' in the world.

No one knew how many bodies the *Mackay-Bennett* would find when it arrived at the scene of the wreck. It could have been fifty. Or a thousand. As it turned out, they recovered 306, three times more bodies than they had coffins for, and also ran out of embalming fluid and canvas in which to wrap bodies for which there were no coffins. Decisions had to be taken, choices made. Society dictated that men of property or position would always take precedence. Captain Larnder would admit this later when defending himself from accusations that too many bodies were buried at sea.

All the evidence suggests that the bodies of those deemed to be First Class passengers were embalmed by Mr Snow and placed in coffins. Second Class passengers and officers were also embalmed before being sewn in canvas and stacked in rows on the deck. When supplies of embalming fluid and canvas ran out, steerage passengers and crew were consigned without embalming to the ice in the hold – the three tanks that held the *Mackay-Bennett*'s huge cable drums. Where no identification could be found, decisions on a body's 'class' seemed to have been a judgement based on a combination of what a person was wearing and their general appearance, tattoos quickly resolving any uncertainties.

There was no mistaking body number 124, quickly identified as John Jacob Astor from the silk initials inside his collar. Astor was wearing a gold watch, gold cufflinks with diamonds, a diamond ring with three stones – and carrying $3,000 in cash. Had coffins been allocated to victims on a 'first come, first served' basis, John Snow would have run out of coffins twenty-one bodies ago. But he had kept a coffin to one side for this moment and saved more than enough embalming fluid.

The Astor family had promised a $10,000 reward for the recovery of his body and would later keep their word. Although Captain Larnder received the lion's share of the reward it was a tremendous morale booster for the crew of the *Mackay-Bennett*, who generously used some of their share of this money to pay for the grave of the unknown child.

Within a day of arriving at the scene of the drifting wreckage it became clear that the number of bodies recovered would exceed the number that the *Mackay-Bennett* could accommodate on its decks. Disposing of bodies at sea thus

became an expedient solution. 'Hands sewed up 24 unidentified bodies and attached a 50lb weight to each,' Capt
Larnder noted in his log on Monday 22 April. This was to
become a source of much grief later among relatives of the
dead. Out of 306 bodies recovered by the *Mackay-Bennett* 116
were buried at sea, more than a third. All bodies brought on
board were seen at once by Canon Hind and Mr Snow. Those
that were to be buried at sea would be sewn up in canvas and
stored separately on deck to await burial that night. Frederick Hamilton's diary records the ritual:

> The tolling of the bell summoned all hands to the fore-
> castle where thirty bodies are ready to be committed to
> the deep, each carefully weighted and sewn up in canvas.
> It is a weird scene, this gathering. The crescent moon is
> shedding a faint light on us, as the ship lays wallowing in
> the great rollers. The funeral service is conducted by the
> Reverend Canon Hind, for nearly an hour the words 'For
> as much as it hath pleased . . . we therefore commit his
> body to the deep' are repeated and at each interval comes,
> splash! as the weighted body plunges into the sea, there
> to sink to a depth of about two miles. Splash, splash,
> splash.

It had been agreed in advance in Halifax that bodies judged
to be injured beyond recognition would be disposed of in
this way. This was why the grate iron had been brought on
board. Several bodies were indeed so crushed and blackened
by soot that it is thought they must have been in the water
directly below one of the *Titanic*'s mighty funnels as it
toppled. Others were hideously disfigured by preying

seagulls as they drifted dead in the sea, face up in their cork lifejackets. But Larnder needed to dispose of more bodies than those that had been disfigured beyond recognition.

Once again, the class system provided the solution to making what might have been difficult choices. Examining the 'Disposition of Bodies' list available at the Nova Scotia Archives in Halifax it is clear that one's chances of being buried at sea increased substantially if you had tattoos, were wearing a steward's jacket, looked foreign or, worse, *were* foreign. A combination of any two of these factors made it a virtual certainty. The double misfortune of body number 58, identified as Catavelas Vassillios, was to be foreign and a Third Class passenger. Body number 36 – a steward with tattoos – was also consigned to the deep that night, in spite of being one of the first to be recovered. Someone called Madge would surely have known who he was from the purser's notes: 'Unidentified male. Steward's uniform. Left arm tattooed all over; right arm, clasped hands and heart, breast, Japanese fans. Gold ring engraved "Madge".'

Women were not exempt from arbitrary disposal overboard either. Mary Mangan, thirty-two, from Carrowkehine, County Mayo, was buried at sea on the second night. The official record describes her simply as 'Third Class, Embarked Queenstown', suggesting that she was dismissed as another Irish immigrant. Yet she carried a gold watch with her name engraved on the back and could easily have been identified from the White Star Line passenger list. Mary had lived in America for some years and was on her way home to Chicago to marry her fiancé after visiting her parents. In 2002, ninety years after Mary died, her watch found its way to her nephew, Anthony Mangan, in County Mayo, but her body could never come home.

At some point, a halt must have been called on the practice of indiscriminate disposal because no bodies were buried at sea after the recovery of body number 201. Whether this was a decision made on board the *Mackay-Bennett* by Larnder, by Canon Hind or by John Snow because he was coping better with the workload, we will never know. It was most likely an instruction that came from New York late on 24 April as Larnder seems to have been in regular contact with the White Star Line via Cape Race. But the decision must have been taken quite suddenly because iron weights were still attached to the legs of several of the bodies sewn in canvas when the *Mackay-Bennett* docked in Halifax a week later and were hurriedly removed before the bodies were taken ashore. The controversy over sea burials continued for many months after the *Mackay-Bennett's* return.

When the scale of the task facing the *Mackay-Bennett* became clear, Larnder radioed for supplies and assistance. The White Star Line commissioned a second cable ship, the *Minia*, to sail at speed to assist the *Mackay-Bennett*. On Tuesday 23 April, after another 128 dead had been brought on board, bodies were piled high everywhere with no more canvas to wrap them in. A rendezvous was arranged with the Allan liner *Sardinian* that evening, during which the *Mackay-Bennett* winched on board all the supplies that the *Sardinian* could give them.

With so many bodies to process, no particular attention was paid that day to body number 193, a young man wearing a light raincoat over a green bandsman's tunic, a purple muffler tied under his chin. Like all the dead, when it came to his turn to be processed, number 193 had been stripped of his clothes so that Mr Snow could examine him for any unusual body marks which might later assist in his identification. As the young man lay grey and lifeless in his sodden underclothes on the mortician's trestle table, the purser entered this brief description into his register: '193: Male, height 5ft 9ins, weight 145lbs, age about 28; Hair, light curly, clean shaven'. Emptying the contents of the young man's pockets into the stencilled duck bag, he recorded each item carefully: 'Cigarette case, English lever watch, empty purse, knife with carved pearl handle, mute'. The purser dropped the young man's effects into the numbered mortuary bag, which was securely tied. The bandsman's tunic and purple muffler were bagged up and taken away. Two seamen carried him to the ice in the hold.

It was not long before Jock Hume, still in his underclothes, found himself among friends again. Less than an hour later, his pal, John 'Nobby' Clarke, body number 202, the bass player in the band, joined Jock in the ice. Their bandleader, Wallace Hartley, had been with them in the sea for eight days and was not far away, but for the moment the *Mackay-Bennett* had more bodies than it could cope with. Capt Larnder gave the order to let the ship drift with the wreckage and leave the bodies in the sea but keep sight of them while the crew dealt with the dead they had already recovered. On Thursday morning the cutters went out again and Wallace Hartley was brought on board, body number 224. He joined Jock and Nobby on the ice, the first and last reunion of the *Titanic* band.

It was an extraordinary coincidence, was it not? After ten days in the North Atlantic, despite wind and currents, the three men had drifted, staying together; and three out of the eight members of the band had been found while barely one in five of the bodies of other passengers and crew were recovered. Or perhaps it is not a coincidence at all. It can only mean that the band stayed together in the water, just as they played together – until the end and beyond.

By Saturday 27 April the *Mackay-Bennett* had recovered 306 bodies, leaving nearly 1,200 passengers and crew from the *Titanic* still unaccounted for. The *Minia* had now taken up the search, having brought more canvas and embalming fluid for the *Mackay-Bennett*, but already the gulf stream was carrying bodies and wreckage east and north-east away from the original search area. The search would continue for another three weeks but the *Minia* would find only seventeen more bodies before it was recalled on 3 May. Two other vessels sent out to join the search, the *Montmagny* and the *Algerine*, would find only five, one of them Jock's old school friend Thomas Mullin, who had joined the ship as a steward.

With 190 bodies stacked on the forward deck or stored on ice in the hold, the *Mackay-Bennett* could accommodate no more and the following morning Larnder headed for port. Starting a new page in his log he wrote in capital letters, 'TOWARDS HALIFAX'. Underneath he noted: 'Moderate breeze. Hands stowing corpses on bridge deck and securing coffins on poop.'

4

The Besieged Offices of the
White Star Line

17 April, Liverpool

Andrew Hume was a man who liked to contain his emotions. He had shed no tears at the funeral of his wife Grace six years earlier. The death of his mother the following year had left him similarly unaffected and, though he admitted this to no one, slightly relieved. Indeed, Andrew Hume could not remember the last time he felt emotional about anything, except possibly a performance in Edinburgh of Elgar's *Enigma Variations*, conducted by the composer himself.

But Jock's *disappearance* – he couldn't yet bring himself to contemplate the word death – had distressed and unsettled him, the roller-coaster of conflicting news raising, then dashing, his hopes.

In the two days that had passed since the *Titanic* had sunk, Andrew Hume had still received no word of what had happened to his son. His telegrams to White Star Line offices in Liverpool, Southampton, London and New York had gone unanswered. His local police station had referred him to the Foreign & Commonwealth Office, who referred him back to the White Star Line. His visit to the offices of the *Dumfries & Galloway Standard & Advertiser* had yielded no information, but had led instead to a request by the editor, Mr Dickie, for some background information on Jock's life for an obituary in next week's edition.

Meanwhile, the Revd James Strachan from the Congregational Chapel in Waterloo Place, where Jock had worshipped, called to express his condolences. These premature presumptions of his son's death annoyed and distressed Andrew. So far as he was concerned, Jock was alive until proven dead.

Andrew felt he was getting nowhere in Dumfries and decided he would confront the White Star Line in person. He was not alone in this. All over Britain anxious relatives and friends were besieging White Star Line offices in Liverpool, London and Southampton, demanding news of their loved ones. More than 700 of the *Titanic*'s crew had come from Southampton and hundreds of distraught family members staged distressing protests outside the White Star Line offices there in the days after the tragedy. In London, crowds stormed the White Star Line offices in Cockspur Street, just off Leicester Square, shouting, 'Murderers!'

Although the *Titanic* was built in Belfast and sailed from Southampton, she was registered in Liverpool – then still the British Empire's leading sea port – and carried the name of the city across the full width of her stern.

It had been Andrew's original intention to demand to see the chairman, the rich and famous J. Bruce Ismay, but newspaper reports had revealed that Ismay himself had been a passenger on the *Titanic* and might also be missing. Andrew drew some comfort from this: if they were searching the North Atlantic for their chairman, there might be more chance of finding Jock.

On his way to Dumfries station, Andrew called at McMillan's, the newsagent's shop in Friar's Vennel. He first scanned all the papers, looking for any mention of the band, then bought the

Dumfries & Galloway Standard. As it was printed locally, and Wednesday being one of its two publication days, Andrew hoped the *Standard* might have the most up-to-date report.

> A calamity involving a loss of life without parallel in the maritime archives of Great Britain occurred on Sabbath night when the latest built and most magnificent of the greyhounds of the Atlantic was engulfed on her maiden voyage. Only the Miracle of Marconi prevented it from being added to the long catalogue of unexplained mysteries of the deep.

Andrew nearly died with rage at the pomposity of it. In an article on another page however the *Standard* reported that Jock was among those missing and said that 'no news has yet been received as to whether Mr Hume is amongst the survivors'.

The national newspapers confirmed in more vivid prose the previous day's most pessimistic reports of the tragedy: that nearly 1,500 had lost their lives, with 'only 868 people saved'. The news that 'Mr Bruce Ismay is among those rescued' brought no encouragement to Andrew Hume. He wished him dead.

Andrew could not know it as he boarded the train at Dumfries but White Star Line officials in Britain, and to a lesser extent in New York, knew very little more than what they were reading in today's newspapers. The *Carpathia* had not yet reached New York with the survivors and no official statements had been received from the ship, Bruce Ismay having ordered a highly selective news blackout. Indeed, a misunderstanding about the *Carpathia*'s destination had led White Star Line officials in New York to despatch a train

"All the News That's Fit to Print."

The New York Times.

THE WEATHER.

VOL. LXI...NO. 19,886.   NEW YORK, TUESDAY, APRIL 16, 1912.—TWENTY-FOUR PAGES.   ONE CENT

TITANIC SINKS FOUR HOURS AFTER HITTING ICEBERG;
866 RESCUED BY CARPATHIA, PROBABLY 1250 PERISH;
ISMAY SAFE, MRS. ASTOR MAYBE, NOTED NAMES MISSING

Col. Astor and Bride,
Isidor Straus and Wife,
and Maj. Butt Aboard.

"RULE OF SEA" FOLLOWED

Women and Children Put Over
in Lifeboats and Are Supposed
to be Safe on Carpathia.

PICKED UP AFTER 8 HOURS

Vincent Astor Calls at White Star
Office for News of His Father
and Leaves Weeping.

FRANKLIN HOPEFUL ALL DAY

Manager of the Line Insisted
Titanic Was Unsinkable Even
After She Had Gone Down.

HEAD OF THE LINE ABOARD

J. Bruce Ismay Making First Trip on
Gigantic Ship That Was to
Surpass All Others.

Biggest Liner Plunges
to the Bottom
at 2:20 A. M.

RESCUERS THERE TOO LATE

Except to Pick Up the Few Hundreds Who Took to the
Lifeboats.

WOMEN AND CHILDREN FIRST

Cunarder Carpathia Rushing to
New York with the
Survivors.

SEA SEARCH FOR OTHERS

The California Stands By on
Chance of Picking Up Other
Boats or Rafts.

OLYMPIC SENDS THE NEWS

Only Ship to Flash Wireless Message to Shore After the
Disaster.

The Lost Titanic Being Towed Out of Belfast Harbor.

CAPT. E. J. SMITH,
Commander of the Titanic.

PARTIAL LIST OF THE SAVED.

Includes Bruce Ismay, Mrs. Widener, Mrs. H. B. Harris, and an Incomplete name, suggesting
Mrs. Astor's.

urgently to Halifax, where they thought the survivors were being taken, to bring them back to New York.

Andrew bought the *Daily Sketch* to read on the train, as its coverage seemed the most comprehensive and up to date. He read of crowds waiting outside the White Star Line offices in Southampton: 'Women with babies in their arms, their cheeks pale and drawn and their eyes red with weeping, have stood for hours reading and re-reading vague messages of the disaster which the company had posted up.' The mayor of Southampton had expressed the view that 'only two per cent' of those saved would be members of the crew.

Andrew took the same rail connections from Dumfries to Liverpool that Jock had taken a week earlier. Liverpool was a city he knew well and from Lime Street he headed briskly towards Church Street, which would lead him to the White Star Line's imposing offices at 30 James Street on the corner of the Strand.

Everywhere Andrew looked, flags were flying at half mast and as he approached the building Andrew also became acutely conscious of the sky darkening, adding to his general feeling of foreboding and gloom. He wondered for a moment if he was going mad or about to faint. Birds were flying in ever-decreasing circles, colliding with each other on their way up or down their spiral. People were standing around in groups, jabbing their fingers at the sky and shouting to one another, some with their fists to their eyes as if holding binoculars, others holding cardboard boxes over their heads. A party of schoolchildren were staring at the sky through pieces of smoked glass. A group of a dozen blind men were staring at the ground listening intently to their escort who was addressing them while pointing upwards. Andrew caught the word 'phenomenon' several times and the blind men nodded knowingly, to acknowledge their understanding of what they were not witnessing.

He told his family later that the scene reminded him of Bedlam or, to be more precise, the Crichton Royal Lunatic Asylum in Dumfries where his father worked as a ward orderly in the final years of his life. It was as if the world were coming to an end and the nearer Hume got to the White Star Line building, the darker the sky became.

In one sense, Andrew Hume's world *was* coming to an end. For the first time he was facing up to the reality that his son had almost certainly died. It was hardly surprising that he had completely forgotten about the event that astronomers had been eagerly awaiting, namely a solar eclipse at 11.17 a.m. on 17 April 1912, the very moment Andrew Hume arrived at his destination. He was not a superstitious man but he rightly saw the darkening sky as a terrible omen. Newspapers next day would describe it as 'the *Titanic* eclipse', a name that would stick and eventually find its way into astronomers' reference books.

Albion House, the Liverpool headquarters of the White Star Line, is to architecture what the *Titanic* was to transatlantic liners: a grandiose monument to the ego of Thomas H. Ismay, founder of the White Star Line. As if launching extravagant steamships was not enough, Thomas Ismay also liked to use bricks and mortar to make an impression. In 1882 the shipping magnate commissioned the London architect Richard Norman Shaw to build him a mansion, enormous even by Victorian standards, called Dawpool at Thurstaston on the Wirral in Cheshire. The house was 'an unhappy mixture of sandstone, ivy and old English revivalist architecture' according to his biographer, Paul Louden-Brown, author of a book on the White Star Line. Dawpool proved difficult to run, 'lacking hot running water and cold with fireplaces that smoked whichever direction the wind blew'. The lack of hot water was one of Ismay's petty meannesses, rather than an engineering oversight: he could not see the need for expensive piping when servants were perfectly able to run up and down stairs with jugs of hot water from the kitchen. Later, the house proved to be unsaleable and after several unsuccessful attempts to demolish it manually, Liverpool Council had to resort to high explosives to reduce it to rubble.

In spite of the problems with his house, Ismay awarded Shaw the contract to build the White Star Line's new headquarters in Liverpool twelve years later. Shaw shamelessly copied the design of red brick and granite that he had used to convert an opera house into what became New Scotland Yard, the former headquarters of the Metropolitan Police, on London's Embankment. Like the shipping line's steamers, Albion House was designed to impress and even today, unoccupied and boarded up as it is, the building remains an imposing landmark in the city, dramatically positioned at the bottom corner of James Street next to the Strand, overlooking the River Mersey.

However grand from the outside, inside its office accommodation was austere, even for directors. Thomas Ismay and his two sons, J. Bruce Ismay and James Ismay, were in adjoining partitioned offices on the ground floor and Mr Imrie, Ismay's partner in the original business, was in a curtained-off alcove in the corner of one of the main offices. Margaret Ismay, who visited her husband Thomas at his office a few weeks after he moved in, did not approve even though there were coal fires in all four directors' offices. 'The offices look very business-like but I miss the cosiness of the old ones,' she wrote in her diary.

By 1912, J. Bruce Ismay was in charge of the business. He had inherited his father's petty meannesses, always taking a tram to the office and imposing his own values on others. One of his fellow directors, Colonel Henry Concanon, who liked to travel to work in the privacy of a dog cart, would get his groom to drop him off round the corner and walk the short distance down James Street so that he could be seen by Ismay to arrive at the office on foot.

When Andrew Hume arrived at the White Star Line building at 30 James Street just before midday, it looked like a temple under siege, the grandness of its architecture at variance with the humanity surrounding it. In the absence of any information from the company, distraught relatives and friends desperate for news of loved ones had decided, like Andrew, to tackle the White Star Line head on. They were 'men and women of all classes of society', as the *Liverpool Post & Mercury* described them in the following day's paper. Some had been sleeping outside the building all night. Many of the women were in tears. Men were shaking their fists and demanding information. Among the crowd was the Revd Latimer Davies, vicar of St James, Toxteth, who had come to seek information about three parishioners who were crew members on the ship. A notice board on an easel had been placed on the pavement near the entrance, presumably to list names of survivors, but there was nothing written on it.

The entrance to the building was up five broad granite

steps through two large wrought-iron gates. A porter's lodge lay to the right, a man in White Star Line uniform positioned to intervene at the first sign of trouble. Inside the large entrance area, two large trestle tables had been hastily erected, one clearly marked 'Passengers', the other 'Crew'. Although strictly 'crew' the *Titanic* musicians had been travelling as passengers on a Second Class ticket. Andrew therefore queued to make enquiries at both desks, neither of them willing to commit to giving him any information about Jock. They did, however, take his name and assured him that they would send a telegram if there was any news when the *Carpathia* arrived in New York.

Today, two oval plaques, erected by the City of Liverpool on either side of the entrance, are the only reminders to passers-by of the building's history. One says, 'Headquarters of the Oceanic Steam Navigation Company (White Star Line). Founded by T. H. Ismay 1869'. The other says, 'Former White Star Building 1896–98, R. Norman Shaw, architect'.

There is no mention of the *Titanic*, which brought shame and infamy to the Ismays and the White Star Line and eventually led to their ruin.

From the White Star building, Andrew walked down the Strand to Brunswick Street, where he turned right and walked up to Castle Street. When he reached number 14 he climbed the spiral wrought-iron staircase through the atrium of the building until he reached the third floor, where an engraved glass panelled door announced the firm of C. W. & F. N. Black, Musical Agents.

Two years earlier, the two brothers, Charles and Frederick Black, had approached all the shipping lines with a proposal that they should be given an exclusive contract to supply and employ musicians for ships' orchestras, relieving the shipping industry of the burden of negotiating individually with musicians whose ability they could not possibly be in a position to judge.

The Blacks promised to give the shipping lines 'a better deal', which they did immediately by cutting the wages of sea-going musicians, from the £6 10s per month they were currently being paid by the ships' owners to £4 per month. At the same time, they withdrew the monthly 'uniform allowance' of 10s per month, making the musicians themselves responsible for their bandsmen's tunics and the brass buttons that had to be changed every time they worked on a different ship, and deducting the cost of their sheet music from their wages. The Amalgamated Musicians Union protested about these enforced terms but their members soon discovered they had little option but to accept them.

Jock, along with the other seven musicians in the *Titanic*'s band, was therefore employed by Blacks and not by the White Star Line. They all travelled on ticket number 250654. Later, this loophole would be exploited by both companies to side step their responsibilities.

Andrew was beginning to regret having come to Liverpool as he had so far learned nothing. But perhaps the Black brothers would be better informed – or more forthcoming – than the White Star Line. And they were. Before taking the train back to Dumfries from Line Street, Andrew had just enough time to send a telegram home to George Street. It said simply:

```
Orchestra sank playing Nearer My God
To Thee.
```

5

Jock and Mary

A thunderbolt at the Rood Fair

At the beginning of the last century, when Jock and Mary were still at school, Dumfries was enjoying something of a renaissance. Education had become both compulsory and free, with rarely more than fifteen to a class. The philanthropist Andrew Carnegie had funded the building of a large and handsome public library, the Ewart. The town's Theatre Royal, Britain's oldest and smallest theatre, where Robert Burns and J. M. Barrie had regularly performed, embraced the new world of cinema by screening silent films. A bridge was built linking the two communities of Dumfries and Maxwelltown for the first time. Although motor cars were seldom seen on the town's cobbled streets, an iron foundry began manufacturing vehicles and a dog-cart builder seized the opportunity to manufacture car bodies. The town's main industry – wool – found profitable new markets overseas.

Opportunities for travel were broadening everyone's horizons. Railway branch lines had been extended, putting the whole of Britain within reach of Dumfries in a day. By sea, coasters laden with Dumfries sandstone or wool provided a quick and easy link to the major ports of Liverpool and Glasgow – and from there to the rest of the world, as Jock would

soon discover. By 1910, the major shipping lines were domi-
nating advertisement pages in the *Dumfries & Galloway
Standard*, offering affordable passages to almost every destination in the world: the United States, Canada, South
America, South Africa, Egypt and Australia.

Yet Dumfries, with wool and clog-making still its main
exports, kept one foot firmly in the past, holding on to its
traditional values and customs. Religion remained a powerful influence on people's lives, with twenty churches serving
eight denominations – Jock worshipped at the Congregational chapel in Waterloo Place where he joined the Sabbath
School. Superstitions, some dating back to the Middle Ages,
continued to hold people in fear – a bird down the chimney
signalling an imminent death in the family. Many children
still ran around in bare feet, although all but the poorest now
had shoes. Centuries-old traditions carried on as before,
particularly the regular fairs held at fixed points in the calen-
dar. These included the 'hiring' fairs held twice a year, at
which farm workers offered themselves for employment,
and the frequent horse and cattle sales, staged weekly on the
broad stretch of land overlooking the River Nith at Whitesands, to which gypsies would journey 100 miles or more to
sell or buy ponies.

The most important event of them all was the Rood Fair,
held on the last Wednesday in September. The Rood Fair
started in the sixteenth century as an agricultural show at
which livestock and produce were sold and exchanged. By
the beginning of the twentieth century it had also become
Dumfries's major social event of the year and been desig-
nated a public holiday. People young and old came from
miles around, everyone dressing up for the occasion. You

could still buy a sheep, a sack of seed potatoes or a bottle of wine shipped from Bordeaux. But there was drinking and dancing, stalls and entertainment. Trading restrictions were lifted for the day and so, too, were other social constraints and inhibitions. Most years, Pinden's Circus would set up their marquee for the whole week, bringing acrobats, jugglers, fortune-tellers and dancing bears. It was always tremendous fun, with stories that had everyone laughing until Christmas. In 1904 a policeman went to investigate a break-in at a grain merchant on Brewery Street. He made a hasty retreat after discovering an elephant called Jumbo with his trunk in a sack of barley.

According to my mother, it was at the Rood Fair in 1909 that Jock's oldest sister, Nellie, introduced Jock to her friend from the glove making factory, Mary Costin, who was eighteen. Jock had recently returned from the maiden voyage of the White Star liner *Megantic*, which had sailed from Liverpool to Montreal and, not surprisingly, he was rather full of himself. He had taken his fiddle with him to the fair and, there and then, played a little jig for Mary. 'And that was it, for both of them,' my great-grandmother, Susan, later told everyone. 'For both of them it was a thunderbolt. They seemed made for each other.'

It says a lot for Mary Costin that she was able to capture young Jock's heart at all, let alone keep his attention for the next two years. He was on a roll at the time, travelling the world on luxury ships, meeting rich and famous people and enjoying a boisterous social life in crew quarters. Emotionally, Jock had already left Dumfries behind him, but at the Rood Fair that day Mary somehow managed to reel him in.

The only picture of my grandmother Mary Costin that has

survived was taken several years later in her mid-twenties, four or five years after his death. She is a good-looking young woman whose appearance is striking, but she has a coolness about her that verges on the intimidating. Maybe this was just what Jock needed to help him keep his feet firmly on the ground. Which makes it even harder to understand why Jock's father Andrew Hume was so implacably opposed to their relationship.

John ('Jock') Law Hume was born on 9 August 1890 at the family home, 5 Nith Place, Dumfries. 'Law' was his mother Grace's maiden name. Jock was Andrew and Grace Hume's second child – Nellie, the first of three daughters, having arrived two years earlier. For all his father's relentless self-promotion as a music teacher and a performer, the Humes were a fairly ordinary family struggling to make ends meet. Andrew was the son of a farm labourer who was now working as an orderly at the Dumfries lunatic asylum; Grace was a former laundress, the daughter of an iron moulder. Today, 5 Nith Place is a kebab takeaway and now, as then, the street is likely to flood when the River Nith bursts its banks. But you would never guess any of these things looking at the studio portrait of Andrew Hume, the dapper dandy with the trim Edwardian moustache, posing with his violin and wearing his tails and white tie.

Jock's two younger sisters, Grace and Catherine (Kate), were born in 1892 and 1897, which suggests that there may have been a miscarriage between the birth of the two girls, the Humes' family planning otherwise falling into the routine of a child every other year. Their last child, Andrew, was clearly an afterthought. He was born in 1901 when Jock was eleven. His mother was unwell even before she became pregnant with him but afterwards she went into a decline, becoming a virtual invalid for the next five years and dying of cancer of the oesophagus in 1906, aged forty.

It would be nice to imagine the Humes as a Scottish von Trapp family making the hills of Dumfries and Galloway come alive with the sound of music. Certainly there was a lot of 'doh re mi' going on in the house: during the day, there was a constant stream of people, young and old, calling at the house for personal tuition in the violin, guitar, banjo or piano. Later, after school, it would be Andrew's own children practising their scales, Kate and Andrew growing up to be talented musicians like their father and their brother Jock. But there was no happy laughter. Andrew Hume was a bully who ruled the family home through an unlovely combination of irritation with his wife and children when he was at home and neglect during his frequent absences on business.

It was particularly difficult for the two older children, Jock and Nellie, who hated their father for not being there and then hated him even more when he came back and made their mother cry. They became the buffers between their father and the rest of the family. The Humes needed a governess with a heart of gold but after Grace's death, instead of Julie Andrews, they got a stereotype wicked stepmother in the form of Alice Mary Alston.

Before and after Jock's death, Andrew Hume took all the credit for his son's considerable skill at playing the violin. What he hadn't taught Jock, he said, he had passed on to his son through his genes. Like so many of Andrew Hume's claims to fame, this was an exaggeration. Jock was a talented violinist and a versatile one but another person played an equally important part in Jock's musical education: John Hendrie, his headmaster at St Michael's School.

John Hendrie had already been headmaster of St Michael's for twenty-five years when Jock joined the school in 1895, by which time St Michael's was known to everyone in Dumfries as 'Hendrie's School', such was his popularity and fame in the town. Hendrie knew how to bring out the best in every pupil and he pushed them to the limits of their ability. He was also an inspiration to the teachers who worked under him. Hendrie's great passion was music and he made it his mission in life that every child at the school would learn an instrument and be encouraged to play it. He formed a choir and organised school parties to give live concerts. He bought one of the first 'His Master's Voice' 78rpm gramophones and took it to school to introduce the children to new composers and new works. Having lobbied the Dumfries School Board successfully for a piano, he was delighted when the young Jock arrived at school with a violin. St Michael's had a choir, now it was halfway to having a string quartet, too. Hendrie obviously liked Jock, whom he later described as 'a merry, bright, laughing boy' whom he remembered 'with pleasure'.

The committee minute book of St Michael's School records a decision made by the Dumfries Burgh School Board on 1 June 1896, the year after Jock started at the school aged five. The appointment of Miss Nellie Lockerbie was recommended 'to provide musical training for the children in her department ... at a salary of £70 a year'. The arrival of a second mentor at school must have been a joy for Jock, who found Mr Hendrie's and Miss Lockerbie's encouragement altogether more inspiring than the irritable disapproval of his stern music-teacher father. By the time Jock left St Michael's aged thirteen, they had helped the young prodigy develop into an accomplished musician. Miss Lockerbie's lessons proved to be such a success that in 1906 Hendrie went back to the school board to request the use of a hall for holding a class he had formed for teaching the violin. His request was approved.

Hendrie was to become a vigorous supporter of the proposal to honour both his old boys, Jock Hume and Thomas Mullin, with a marble plaque at the school as well as a memorial in the park. To this day, children entering and leaving St Michael's have to pass Hendrie's affectionate tribute to the two young men.

Hendrie was headmaster of St Michael's for forty-three years before retiring with his gramophone and record collection to his cottage in Cassalands, Dumfries, where he died aged eighty-eight in 1939. His death was announced to the assembled school at prize-giving next day by the then headmaster, Mr L. Grainger. He told the school: 'You did not know him but your parents and grandparents held him in the greatest respect and the very highest esteem. He made this school famous throughout our countryside . . . he was beloved by the many thousands who passed through his hands, many of whom attained prominent positions.'

During his time at 'Hendrie's School' and throughout his early teens, Jock was a regular member of the Sabbath School at the Waterloo Place Congregational Church, where he joined the Band of Hope, a temperance organisation for working-class children, founded in Leeds in 1847. All members took a pledge of total abstinence and were taught the 'evils of drink'. Music played an important part in Sabbath School activities and there were regular trips to the seaside. For Jock, the music, rather than temperance, was the main attraction and was what the vicar, the Revd James Strachan, remembered him by: 'A cooler young fellow I never knew,' he said. 'He showed his coolness in the way he lifted his violin to his chin when about to play in public . . . I was not at all astonished that he ended his life so bravely.'

Jock could – and should – have gone on from St Michael's to the Dumfries Academy to finish his education. But instead, he left St Michael's, aged thirteen, to work for a local solicitor, James Geddes. It seems an extraordinary decision given his father's middle-class aspirations, but all the Hume children were to leave school at the same age and it seems likely that Andrew Hume simply adopted his own father's 'sink-or-swim' values. He got the children out to work as early as possible so they could start paying their way and contribute to the household expenses.

Another factor which may have come into play in the decision for Jock to leave school so young was his mother's ill health. Grace Hume was already bed-bound following the birth of her fifth child, Andrew, and would be dead before Jock's sixteenth birthday. Her illness must have put a considerable strain on the family finances and it is possible that Jock terminated his education in the family's best financial interests.

If Geddes employed Jock as a favour to his father, he had a pleasant surprise. He found the boy 'an assiduous, intelligent and courteous lad . . . reliable and painstaking in all his work and was of a character that would enable him to carve out a career for himself in any walk of life he was likely to follow. I can only speak of his services with the highest praise.'

Despite winning the approbation of his boss, Jock hated being a pen-pusher confined to an office from dawn until dusk. He quit after a year. 'Like many great men, he found that his bent was not for being confined within the four walls of an office,' Geddes would tactfully relate after Jock's death. Jock had 'achieved a name and a distinction that he would never have had in any other sphere in Dumfries.'

Whatever the reason – whether he went to Geddes willingly or under duress – Jock didn't waste the year. Freed from the nightly obligations of school homework Jock had found he was able to earn extra money in the evenings and at weekends doing what he loved most of all: playing the violin. Like his father, he was a versatile performer who had developed an extensive repertoire, able to switch from 'popular' music, such as ragtime or folk music, to 'salon' music, such as waltzes and popular classical numbers. With his considerable skill with the fiddle came an irresistible boyish charm and a friendly banter.

Before long, Jock was making regular appearances at the Theatre Royal in Shakespeare Street as a 'warm-up' act before curtain-up and during the intervals. He also discovered just how much in demand a young man with a fiddle could be. He started getting invitations to play at dances and at weddings and other events.

***

There are conflicting accounts in the family as to how and why Jock came to spend much of the next six years – including the last days of his life – at sea. Mary Costin's understanding was that Jock wanted to go 'as far away as possible' from Dumfries because the atmosphere at home had become so oppressive.

At fourteen, Jock's relationship with his father was disintegrating. They argued over music, money and Jock's growing need for independence, the disagreements becoming increasingly explosive.

Nellie, Grace and Kate were also at war with their father who, they felt, had treated their mother less than kindly during her long illness. The early appearance on the scene of Alice Alston, whom Andrew Hume would marry fourteen months after Grace's death, was the decisive factor.

A more charitable interpretation of Jock's decision to go to sea is that it was his father's idea – or, at least, an idea that Andrew didn't oppose. This seems more likely as, at Jock's age, it was probably what Andrew would have wished to do himself. Andrew was well networked into the music industry, with connections to agents and impresarios, and would have been able to make the necessary introductions. What is without doubt is that Andrew saw his talented son as a future stream of income for the family and, indeed, was depending on Jock to help pay the mortgage on the new family home in George Street.

By the time Jock died, aged twenty-one, his fiddle had taken him halfway round the world a dozen times. He had sailed to New York and back at least five times and played on liners to South America, Jamaica and Montreal. Just months before his death on the *Titanic*, Jock was sailing around the Mediterranean playing in the orchestra on the Cunard liner *Carmania*. The previous year he had worked on the maiden voyage to New York of the *Titanic*'s sister ship, *Olympic*. Almost as remarkable was Jock's apparently effortless commuting from

Dumfries to the ports of Southampton, Bristol or Liverpool, where most of his voyages began and ended. But this was not unusual: Wallace Hartley, bandleader on the *Titanic*, claimed to have made more than eighty transatlantic crossings in less than three years working for Cunard. Passenger ships were not like today's cruise liners. They were a fast and efficient way – the only way – of travelling between Europe and America, with fast turnaround times after reaching port.

In 1905, the year when Jock first went to sea aged fourteen, there was less for a teenager to lose and everything to gain by being adventurous. And the only passport he needed was his fiddle. Dumfries was still an active port and it was possible to work a free passage on a coaster to Liverpool or Glasgow, both of them less than a day or two away by sea. There were rail links, anyway, from Dumfries to both cities. Most of the shipping lines had offices in Glasgow and Liverpool and all it would have taken to find work was an introduction, an audition – and the courage to be there.

'Jock Hume was a free soul in an era of Victorian/Edwardian suppression,' John Eaton, co-author of the definitive book, *Titanic Triumph and Tragedy,* told me during an exchange of emails about my grandfather. 'Jock has long been a favourite of mine.' On the *Titanic*'s embarkation list Jock's age is given as twenty-eight. For some time I took this to be a clerical error, since there is no doubt that Jock was twenty-one when he boarded the ship. But if he had lied about his age when he first went to sea – saying he was twenty-one when he was still fourteen – his exaggerated age would eventually have become a matter of record, the White Star Line – and the musical agency Blacks – both believing Jock to have been twenty-eight when he boarded the *Titanic*.

It seems likely that Jock started work playing on smaller ships owned by minor shipping companies, slowly working his way up to the flagship liners of the Cunard and White Star lines as his reputation grew. But matching precise dates with destinations and the names of ships that Jock sailed on has proved to be a time-consuming and largely unrewarding task.

My mother remembered as a child seeing her mother with a cardboard box full of Jock's letters and postcards sent from abroad, the cards showing pictures of ports he visited and the ships he sailed with. But none of these survived, my mother's uncle, Menzies Costin, burning them on a bonfire at the back of the house in Buccleuch Street after Mary's death.

Accessing the information through public archives has been fraught with difficulties. In 1966 the Public Record Office in London discarded part of its archive of British shipping records from 1861 to 1913. The decision met with considerable opposition from archivists and maritime historians as the records were considered to be a valuable source of information on the shipping industry in the nineteenth and early twentieth centuries. Eventually some of the records were transferred to the Maritime History Archive at St John's in Nova Scotia, with a number of crew lists and agreements remaining at the National Archive in Britain. Many were lost or mislaid along the way.

However, some records do still exist, and it is possible to put together a picture of Jock's life at sea from manifests that have survived, together with interviews given after his death by fellow musicians and by crew members he worked with. Musicians would sometimes travel as 'crew' and at other times as passengers, for which there were different manifests. On the *Titanic*, for instance, all eight members of the band travelled as passengers. Musicians in ships' orchestras worked much like airline crews today – never quite sure who they would be travelling round the world with until the last minute. Friendships would be formed, suspended, then resumed the next time they met up to play together. Two American musicians, cellist John Carr and bass player Louis Cross, who met Jock for the first time on the *Cedric*, were part of this camaraderie.

In an interview with the *New York Times* after Jock's death Louis Cross described Jock as 'a light hearted, fine tempered young fellow with curly blond hair, a light complexion and a pleasant smile'. He was 'the life of every ship he ever sailed on and was full of fun,' said Cross. According to Cross and Carr, Jock played on the White Star liner *Majestic*, the Anchor Line's *California*, and the White Star liner *Megantic* on its maiden voyage to Montreal. Besides playing in the band of *Titanic*'s sister ship *Olympic* on its maiden voyage to New York in May 1911, he rejoined the ship in September when it had to limp back to Southampton after colliding with the warship, HMS *Hawke*. To be chosen to play on the *Titanic*, the world's biggest and most famous liner on its maiden voyage, was the ultimate accolade for the young musician.

From 1910 most of Jock's engagements were made through the musical agents C. W. and F. N. Black in Liverpool, who had exclusive contracts with all the major shipping lines to supply orchestras on their passenger ships. Although the musicians' pay was fixed at £4 a month the tips were good and the food and accommodation was free.

Few trips took Jock away from Dumfries for more than a

month, including the time it took to travel to and from the port of embarkation. Before the ship sailed there would be rehearsals because most ships' orchestras had never played together before, although many of the musicians knew each other. The longest time Jock spent away from home was four months, during the winter of 1910–1911, not long after he had met Mary. He was engaged to play during the winter season at the Constant Spring Hotel in Jamaica, a three-storey luxury hotel at the foot of the Blue Mountains. The Constant Spring, set in the middle of an exquisitely mani-cured 165-acre estate, was the first hotel in Jamaica to have running water and electric light. It promised its guests a French chef, a concert hall, dancing by moonlight, lavish bedrooms, a hairdressing salon, a huge swimming pool and a nine-hole golf course. It would seem that this booking also came through the Liverpool agency, Blacks, who were engaged by the hotel to recruit musicians for the winter season from Europe. The musicians, including Jock, trav-elled to Jamaica on the *Port Royal*, one of three fast steamers built ten years earlier for the Liverpool shipping company Elder, Dempster & Co. to boost trade and travel between Britain and the Antilles. The shipping company received a £40,000 annual subsidy from the British and Jamaican governments to take tourists out to Jamaica, and return with tropical fruit, mostly bananas. Elder, Dempster & Co. owned an interest in the Constant Spring Hotel, engaging Eugene Smith, a pineapple cultivator from Florida, to grow tropical fruit there.

Jock and the other musicians boarded the *Port Royal* at Bristol and were due to dock in Kingston on Christmas Eve but were delayed by heavy storms in the Caribbean, arriving grey and seasick late on Christmas Day. On the *Port Royal* Jock met cellist John Wesley Woodward for the first time; John would join him on the maiden voyage of the *Olympic* in May the following year. Little more than a year later they would die together on the *Titanic*.

The musicians' arrival was eagerly awaited by the hotel management and the guests. On Christmas Eve 1910 the manager took a prominent advertisement in the *Daily Gleaner* to announce the 'Season Arrangements':

> A first-class Orchestra, consisting of five
> professionals has been engaged in England
> who will play at all dances.
> Select concerts will be given daily from 1 to 3pm
> and every evening from 7.00 to 11 pm.
> The Orchestra is bringing a full programme
> of classical and all the latest dance music.

The orchestra proved to be a huge hit, playing at Cinderella dances, fancy dress balls and golf tournaments as well as giving 'brilliant' classical concerts. 'All who have heard this splendid orchestra declare that it has never been surpassed in this country. Its repertoire is not only extensive but leaves nothing to be desired,' said Lady Olivier, President of the hotel's golf club. John Woodward was a particular success with his cello, an instrument 'seldom heard in Jamaica', and he gave numerous solo performances, all of which were 'warmly applauded'.

Two weeks after the *Titanic* sank, the *Daily Gleaner* published on its front page an affectionate tribute to Jock and to John Woodward, under the heading 'Bandsmen who were known here'. The orchestra, it said, was 'voted the best of its kind that has ever visited Jamaica'. Both musicians were 'popular with the staff of the hotel as well as those who stayed there'. Cellist John Carr and bass player Louis Cross were at the Constant Spring at the same time, and this was their recollection, too. Jock was befriended by an American family wintering at the Constant Spring Hotel. They took a shine to the young Scotsman and asked him to come and visit them next time he came to New York.

It must have been a wonderful experience for the young man. It was the first time Jock had felt warm Caribbean sunshine on his white Scottish back, the first time he had swum in the sea without bristling with goose pimples as he came out of the water. It was also the first time in six years that he had stood still in one place, working with the same musicians. According to Cross, he liked the continuity and enjoyed playing more classical music. He returned home to Dumfries tanned and rested, promising Mary that he would one day take her to Jamaica. Jock had missed her more than he thought he would and, after six years jumping on and off trains and ships, was looking forward to the day he could afford to settle down to a less frenetic life.

There are very few photographs of Jock. The most familiar of them is the studio portrait distributed to the press by the White Star Line immediately after his death. Not the most flattering of pictures, it shows the young Jock looking like a cross between Little Lord Fauntleroy and a startled rabbit. It was most likely a portrait taken in a studio in Dumfries and it is difficult to put a date on it. In July 1912 the *New York Times* published an article about a fundraising event for the families of the *Titanic* musicians with a photograph of 'John' Law

Hume alongside it. Here we see an amused, confident and good-looking young man leaning against a post, a thumb tucked nonchalantly into his belt. He is wearing Bugsy Malone-style gangster spats and a white bib and tucker. Behind him, lying on the grass, is a girl watching him intently. There is no indication of when the photograph was taken, or where, but I believe it was taken at the Constant Spring Hotel some time during his stay there.

The orchestra left Kingston for Southampton on 8 April 1911 on the SS *Oruba*, their fellow passengers including four members of the England Cricket Team returning home after a disappointing tour of the West Indies in which two of their last four matches were rained off. The *Oruba* arrived back at Southampton on 1 May. Telegrams from C. W. & F. N. Black were handed to Jock and to John Woodward as they were disembarking, informing them that they were booked for the maiden voyage of the *Olympic* to New York in May.

Jock spent very little time in Dumfries in the last sixteen months of his life. This may have encouraged Andrew Hume to believe that his son was losing interest in Mary. In fact, the reverse was the case. Like many young men planning to settle down he was working hard to save as much money as possible to find a place of their own to live.

Jock had shared some of these thoughts with Louis Cross, in particular his intention to concentrate eventually on classical music. After Jock's death, Cross talked with affection about his young Scottish friend to a reporter from the *New York Times*. 'He was a young man of exceptional musical ability . . . he could pick up without trouble, difficult compositions which would have taken others long to learn.' Cross added: 'If he had lived I believe he would not long have remained a member of a ship's orchestra. Over in Dumfries I happen to know there's a sweet young girl hoping against hope . . . Jock was to have been married the next time that he made the trip across the ocean.'

If Jock Hume's childhood was a troubled one, Mary Costin's was no less so. Working-class life in Scotland had always been a constant struggle against poverty, sickness and death and the Costins had known more hardship than most. Both parents came from poor families, going back as far as parish records allow into the mid-1700s. Mary's father, William, was the son of a ploughman; her mother Susan, the daughter of a fish dealer, Menzies Kennedy. The couple had six children, two daughters dying in infancy. Ten years into the marriage, William, a van driver, died from a cerebral haemorrhage, leaving Susan with Mary and her three brothers – William, Jock and Menzies – to bring up on her own. A strong and formidable-looking woman, judging from the only photograph of her, Susan Costin had drawn strength and compassion from a lifetime of adversity. She was also extraordinarily kind, welcoming Jock into their lives as if he were her own son.

After the father's death, the family could no longer afford to live in the family home in Bank Street so Susan found a job as an office caretaker for a firm of solicitors and moved to cheaper accommodation in Buccleuch Street. William, the oldest child, left school the following year aged fourteen and went out to work as a fishmonger's assistant to supplement the family income.

As a young woman, Susan Costin had been taken by her stocking-maker grandfather to the mills where he worked.

The family had always managed to survive hard times by weaving at home and Susan had encouraged her daughter Mary to do the same to make a modest income in her spare time while still at school. The wool trade had been Dumfries's main trade since the Middle Ages – a traveller in 1527 described 'Dunfrese' as 'famous in fine claith'. Two hundred years later, another traveller passing through Dumfries reported that 'gloves they make better and cheaper here than in England, sending great quantities thither'. That was ceasing to be the case at the beginning of the twentieth century, until the economics of hosiery production in Dumfries were suddenly revolutionised by the introduction of the Lamb flat-bed knitting machine. Invented in 1863 by the American, Isaac Lamb, the hand-powered machine made possible the rapid production of tube and rib-knitted fabric using cheap, untrained female labour. James McGeorge, the entrepreneurial son of a failed hosiery manufacturer in Dumfries, had heard about the machine and travelled to Ghent to see it in action. McGeorge installed more than 100 of the machines at various production centres in Dumfries and Dalbeattie, 800 workers being employed at the Nithsdale Mills, a large Victorian factory, producing 'woollen gloves, knicker stockings and ties of silk and cotton'. It was here that Mary would work for seven years after leaving school at the age of thirteen.

The 'thunderbolt' that Jock and Mary experienced when they met was clearly based on physical attraction. But they soon discovered they had a lot more in common, despite their different backgrounds. Both had lost a parent at a particularly vulnerable age: Mary, her father; Jock, his mother. Jock had been brought up with sisters and was comfortable in the company of girls. Mary had grown up with brothers and was easy in the company of boys. It was a good base from which to start a relationship and their emotional vulnerabilities undoubtedly drew the two teenagers closer together, providing mutual comfort and reassurance that they had never found elsewhere. Jock's absences at sea, far from getting in the way of their relationship, intensified their feelings for each other, with written declarations of love sandwiched between lingering farewells and passionate reunions.

Mary's mother, Susan, took an immediate liking to Jock when he escorted Mary home after the Rood Fair. She invited him in for tea and he played the fiddle. He also made her laugh. But Susan cautioned her daughter about becoming too involved with the young musician: his long trips away from home, the temptations on board ship with young crew members, the attractions of New York and Jamaica compared to Dumfries . . . all these seemed to Susan to stand in the way of an enduring relationship. But Jock would return from each trip even keener on Mary than he had been when they parted. Postcards and letters from foreign destinations would continue to drop through the letterbox in Buccleuch Street long after his return home. If anything, it was Jock who was jealous of Mary. She was an attractive girl, not without admirers, but after meeting Jock, according to my mother, she never looked at another man.

Courtships in Scotland in those days were generally conducted in secret, at least in the early stages when young couples would only be seen in public together on Fair days.

But Jock had spent enough time away from Dumfries to dispense with Border traditions and Mary seems to have cared little what people thought. Within months of meeting they had become inseparable, at weekends taking a horse bus or a coach to escape to the beautiful coast along the Solway Firth. My mother learned these things only many years later, from an old friend in Dumfries.

Jock's devotion to Mary annoyed and concerned his father, Andrew. He thought his son too young to be thinking of settling down and he believed Jock could 'do better' for himself than Mary – for instance, by finding a girl who might one day bring a small inheritance to the marriage, rather than the financial and emotional burden of a widowed mother. He found Mary's coolness disconcerting; he didn't like the idea of losing his son at the very moment the boy could support himself and start contributing to his own household expenses.

Andrew Hume's mistake, being a bad-tempered man who couldn't control his tongue, was in not keeping these opinions to himself. He forbade Jock from bringing Mary home and made life as difficult as possible for Jock in the hope of keeping him working at sea, away from Mary. But by opposing Jock's relationship with Mary he succeeded only in driving the two of them closer together.

This not-unusual confrontation between father and son had the effect of creating further dissent in the already divided Hume family. For some years a war – a guerrilla war consisting of hit-and-run attacks – had been waged between Andrew's three teenage daughters and their stepmother, Alice. The girls struck in pincer movements. Alice set ambushes. Now Andrew introduced into this domestic theatre of war a new stand-off: an ongoing argument between himself and his son. Jock's oldest sister Nellie had introduced Mary to Jock and continued to encourage the relationship; Kate, his kid sister, worshipped the ground Jock stood on. The girls now ganged up on their father as well as on their stepmother.

It was an intolerable situation for a young man, but much as Jock dreaded coming home to George Street, he had fallen in love with Mary. And it was Mary's mother, a woman with surprisingly modern and enlightened views, who came up with the solution: Jock should come and live with them. The suggestion was not as extraordinary as it may at first seem to be, from our perception of the Edwardian era, at least not in Scotland. Until 1923, a girl over the age of twelve and a boy of fourteen could be legally married in Scotland without their parents' consent. And Gretna Green, the precursor of Las Vegas, was just a few miles down the road from Dumfries. There was an ancient Celtic custom of 'handfasting', which was essentially a form of trial marriage. At a handfasting ceremony, couples would take each other's hands and pledge to live together for a year. If at the end of the year they were both happy with the arrangement, they could live together from then on as a married couple. Children born during this trial period were regarded as legitimate.

Susan told Jock and Mary that they should consider themselves 'handfasted' and that from then on they could share a bed together under her roof. It was a decision that would drive a deep wedge between Jock and his father and make Andrew Hume an implacable enemy of the Costins.

On his return from Jamaica in May 1911 Jock, still only twenty, felt tremendously proud to be chosen to join the band on the new White Star liner *Olympic*, the flagship of the fleet, for its maiden voyage to New York. It was confirmation that Jock had established a reputation both as a musician and as a team player. He returned home to Dumfries on a high and Mary was thrilled to see him again, but less than delighted that he was about to set off for another voyage across the Atlantic.

It must have been around this time that Jock ran into his old school pal, Thomas Mullin, and gave him some advice that was to cost Tom his life. Tom had followed in his father's footsteps and become a pattern weaver in the Rosefield tweed mills. Like his father, he was well liked and a good worker but in his mid-teens Tom's sight had begun to fail and after an unsuccessful operation in Dumfries Infirmary he was told his eyesight would never be good enough to return to work at the mill. It was Jock's idea that he should consider seeking work on passenger ships as a steward where, unlike pattern weaving at the mill, 20/20 vision was not critical to the tasks he would have to carry out. Jock advised Tom to go to Liverpool and Tom was duly taken on by the American Line, to work as a steward on the *St Louis*, which operated a weekly express service between Southampton and New York. Tom took sailor's lodgings in Southampton and made five or six transatlantic crossings between the summer of 1911 and March 1912 as a Third Class saloon steward. It seems likely that Jock and Tom saw each other in Southampton, where Jock also had temporary lodgings. Tom's success in his new job, which brought two promotions, was almost certainly what led to him being offered a position on the *Titanic*, which he and Jock boarded together at Southampton the following April.

Before the *Olympic* sailed on its maiden voyage in May 1911, the White Star Line were to pull off a brilliant public relations coup in May by launching the *Titanic* on the day that *Olympic*, its sister ship, was leaving the Harland & Wolff shipyard in Belfast to prepare for its maiden voyage. More than 100,000 VIPs, journalists and dignitaries who had gathered at the ship-yard for the launch of *Titanic* were able to see these great liners side by side for the first – and only – time. Selected VIPs were taken on board the *Olympic* before it sailed via Liverpool to Southampton. At the helm of the *Olympic* was Captain Edward J. Smith, whose next ship would be the *Titanic*.

The *Olympic* set new benchmarks in speed and luxury, winning acclaim from passengers on both sides of the Atlan-tic; its First Class passenger list was an international *Who's Who* of the rich and famous. When the ship arrived back in Southampton on 4 July there was a message waiting for Jock asking him to make himself available for what would be the *Olympic*'s fourth transatlantic crossing on 20 September.

On 7 September, as Jock was making preparations for his trip south from Dumfries, the Costins received some terri-ble news: Mary's oldest brother, William, who was twenty-three, had been taken ill at the butcher's shop where he now worked and rushed to hospital. He had been complaining of stomach pains for a couple of days and by the time he was admitted to hospital, his appendix had burst. He died the following evening, his wife Maria and his brother John by his side.

Mary was beside herself with grief. She loved William and he had been such a tower of strength when their father had died. Now he was dead, too, leaving a widow and three children under the age of four. For the fourth time in her life Mary found herself in the same cemetery standing at the same grave where her father and two sisters were buried, as William was lowered into the ground. For Susan Costin, burying the third of her six children, it must have been even worse, but there were too many vulnerable people dependent on her to let it show. When they returned to Buccleuch Street, Susan made arrangements for Maria and the children to move in.

After William's death, Jock suggested he abandoned the *Olympic* trip but Mary insisted that he should go and so he left for Southampton a week later. Ten days after his departure he was home again. Within sight of Southampton harbour the *Olympic* had collided with a warship, HMS *Hawke*, tearing a 40ft gash in *Olympic*'s hull and crushing *Hawke*'s bow, almost causing the warship to capsize. While the *Hawke* limped back to Portsmouth, the *Olympic* anchored off the Isle of Wight so that tenders could ferry the passengers and crew to safety. Repairs to the *Olympic* at the Harland & Wolff shipyard would have a knock-on effect on work on the *Titanic* and delay her maiden voyage by several days.

Neither captain was found to be at fault and far from being admonished or relieved of his command, Captain Smith was informed that as repairs to the *Olympic* were going to take many months, he would be given command of the SS *Titanic*. Although there was no loss of life or serious injuries, the *Hawke* incident shook public confidence in passenger liners. Whereas previously they were regarded as safe and practically unsinkable, now they were seen as another of life's risks. Jock's stepmother, Alice, took the accident particularly badly, having had a 'premonition' of a catastrophe in a dream. She begged

Jock not to return to sea. Mary, too, having just buried another member of the family, became hyper-anxious. But Jock took no heed of their pleas or their warnings. He could not afford to. The cancellation of the *Olympic*'s New York trip had left him out of pocket in terms of wages and tips. He could make up some lost ground with a Mediterranean cruise later in the year on the *Carmania* and there was a chance of being offered a place in the orchestra on the *Titanic* the following spring. When he returned, they would have just enough money to get married at Greyfriars Kirk.

Mary's mother Susan, a woman with a big heart and a broad mind, had suspected for some time that her daughter might be pregnant. For more than a year Jock had been staying with them in Buccleuch Street between trips. With so many passionate goodbyes and lustful homecomings, it was no wonder Jock and Mary had become careless. Having condoned then encouraged her daughter's love affair, Susan wished the young couple had waited longer to start a family, but as they were planning to marry when Jock returned from the *Titanic*, she was pleased for them as well as excited by the prospect of another grandchild.

And perhaps it would take a grandchild to bring Andrew Hume to his senses and accept Mary as Jock's wife.

6

Jock's Memorial Service

21 April, Dumfries

We are here to drop a tear on the watery grave of one who for years sat within these walls as a member of the Sabbath school and as a member of our Band of Hope. We knew him as a child, a boy, and a youth. His presence, up to the time of his leaving for the sea, was a familiar one here. We see him again with his violin rendering assistance in the conduct of the service of praise in the Sanctuary. We see on his lips and in his eyes the smile which was a striking characteristic of his familiar countenance. Through our tear-dimmed eyes we see him as he leads his bandsmen in the last of theirs and their vessel's life, in the sweet, holy strains of the music of the well known hymn, 'Nearer My God To Thee'. Thus he died. We weep for him, we weep with his friends.

On cue, sitting in the front pew of Waterloo Place Congregational Church, Jock's sister Kate started to weep. The Revd James Strachan had written and rehearsed his sermon for maximum dramatic effect and Kate's tears were visible reassurance that he had struck just the right note. Strachan had been confident enough to drop off an advance copy of his sermon at the offices of the *Standard* the previous afternoon to ensure that it received maximum coverage in Wednesday's edition. Pausing briefly, as if struggling to control his own emotions, the vicar gripped the front of the pulpit and announced the next hymn, 'Nearer My God To . . .'

Miss Muir the organist had not intended to start playing before the vicar had finished speaking but, like Kate, she had been overcome by the emotion of the moment and having hit the keyboard accidentally, there was no going back. Fortunately, it only took the congregation two lines to catch her up. The vicar had insisted that she played the 'Propior Deo' version of the hymn by Sir Arthur Sullivan and not the Lowell Mason score with which she was more familiar and which, as she pointed out, Jock would have preferred. Jock had often accompanied her on his violin at church musical evenings and carol concerts and they shared similar enthusiasms. But as always, the Revd Strachan stuck to his own agenda.

Next to Kate, at the end of the pew in the front row, Andrew Hume held his hymn book in front of his face, trying to look dignified rather than furious, which is what he felt. Strachan had sprung the memorial service on him when he called at the house to express his sympathy. Andrew thought it far too soon to hold a service, but when Strachan told him that the Revd Slesser was holding a memorial service at Maxwelltown Parish Church for young Thomas Mullin, who had also lost his life when the ship went down, Andrew reluctantly agreed that it should go ahead.

There was another reason why Andrew had tried to persuade the Revd Strachan to call it off: the prospect of a confrontation with Mary Costin. He had arrived early to avoid her, he and Alice sitting protectively either side of Kate and young Andrew, like bookends. Nell and Grace had been living and working away from home for more than a year and had been unwilling to return to Dumfries for the service. Hume's plan was to use Strachan as cover at the end of the service, pretending to wait by the door to receive condolences but making a dash for it at the last moment. With a bit of luck he wouldn't even see Mary, still less speak to her.

He thought for a moment that Mary had not come but in the middle of the first hymn he glanced over his left shoulder and saw her sitting at the back. Mary and her mother Susan had slipped into the church just as the service started, joining Mary's brothers, Jock and Menzies, who had come a few minutes earlier to keep a place for them. Mary had no interest in speaking to Andrew Hume, not since she realised that he knew no more than she did by reading the newspapers. She held him in contempt and if he hated her, then the feeling was entirely mutual. She had come only because she wanted to see Jock's friends, to tell them how sorry she was and to let them see that she was all right.

In spite of the vicar's amateur dramatics, she liked what he said about Jock, particularly the bit about Jock's lips, his eyes and his smile. Those were the things she remembered best, too – and missed. But she had been embarrassed to hear Jock described as *leading* the band. That was another one of his father's lies, which the vicar had inadvertently written into his sermon. Andrew had also told the *Standard* that Jock was the bandleader and played only in First Class, neither of which was true. He had even lied in the death notice – that was a first:

Mr and Mrs Hume and family beg to tender their sincere thanks to all friends for their very kind and sympathetic notes and telegrams on the loss of John Law Hume, leader of the orchestra in the First Class cabin of the unfortunate *Titanic*.

They were silly lies because the national newspapers had already published pictures of Wallace Hartley, who was the leader of the orchestra. Jock would never have pretended to be something he wasn't. What was it about Andrew that made him always fudge the truth?

As the service drew to a close, Miss Muir started to pump wind into her organ, pushing the pedals as hard as if she were riding her bicycle uphill. The last part of the vicar's three-act tragedy was about to begin and she had the starring role, playing the 'Dead March' from *Saul*, by Handel. There would not be a dry eye in the house by the time she finished if she could possibly help it. 'Will you please stand,' the vicar told the congregation. The opening bars triggered another outbreak of sobbing from Kate Hume, who had spent most of the service with a lace handkerchief clamped to her face. When Miss Muir reached the end of the 'Dead March' the Revd Strachan stood facing the congregation to give the blessing.

The Costin party, who were nearest the door, were the first to leave the church, walking briskly back to Buccleuch Street. Susan Costin thought how proud Jock would have been of Mary – dignified, elegant and in control. As they reached the top of Buccleuch Street, Susan said to her daughter: 'When are you going to tell him?'

'Tell who?'

'When are you going to tell Andrew Hume that he's about to become a grandfather.'

7

A Second *Titanic* Hero

29 April, Dumfries

On 24 April the *Dumfries & Galloway Standard* published a prominent letter headed 'A Dumfries Hero'. It was from a colourful character called Robert MacKenna, a celebrated local poet who had 'forsaken the muse' some years earlier to dedicate his life to medicine. Now an equally celebrated dermatologist in Liverpool, he had kept his muse alive as an obsessive writer of letters to newspapers and magazines, in particular the *Standard*, where his greatest fan, Mr John Dickie, was the editor.

The son of a Dumfries vicar, Dr MacKenna was still widely revered and respected in the town and his letter from Liverpool, the city whose name *Titanic* carried on its stern, caught everyone's attention, particularly Mr Dickie who wrote a leader in the same issue commending the letter to his readers.

MacKenna's letter began: 'In the long roll of brave deeds associated with the disaster to the *Titanic*, there is none so sublimely heroic as the conduct of the ship's band.' It continued in the most florid prose for several hundred more words before coming to the point:

```
In that little band of brave men,
Dumfries had a noble representative . . .
I think it only proper that his fellow
townsmen should do something to perpetu-
ate the memory of Mr J. Hume and
commemorate his glorious death. I
venture therefore to suggest that a
committee be formed . . .
```

The following day a committee was formed and on the evening of Monday 29 April a meeting to discuss a *Titanic* memorial was convened at the Town Hall by Provost Thomson; it was attended by every worthy in the town. Mr MacKenna, the originator of the idea, was invited but sent his apologies. Andrew Hume was invited to attend but declined on the grounds that as no one had yet informed him that his son was dead it seemed somewhat premature to be erecting monuments to his memory.

MacKenna's proposals for a monument had been quite modest – a blue plaque on the wall of the Humes' house in George Street. But Provost Thomson opened the meeting by pointing out that not one but two sons of Dumfries had died on the *Titanic*. He proposed that any monument should also include Thomas Mullin, Jock's school friend at St Michael's.

In the general outpouring of grief and praise for the hero-ism of the band, Tom's death had been overlooked by many people, largely because he lived in Maxwelltown – a few hundred yards away on the other side of the river to Dumfries and therefore seen as having nothing whatsoever to do with Dumfries. Provost Thomson said there had been 'a reluctance to trespass upon Maxwelltown's duties' by including Mullin in Dumfries's plans for a memorial. But it was now accepted that Tom was Dumfries born and bred, and that 'the two lads should be classed together'. This suggestion was greeted with loud applause.

Dr MacKenna had failed to mention Tom at all in his letter to the *Standard* but people who knew Tom and his family – they were 'admirable people' – came from far and wide to make sure that he received proper recognition, and not just on a monument. Many affectionate tributes were paid that night to both Jock and Tom, but the meeting in the lower room of the town hall focused for once on Dumfries's other brave young man who had suffered the most terrible misfortunes with great fortitude – only to lose everything on the *Titanic*.

Jock and Tom's former headmaster, John Hendrie, was the first to point out that the family's circumstances were not good. Tom's mother and father had died within a very short time of each other, leaving three younger children who were now being looked after by their grandmother. Both Tom and Jock were 'loving and pleasant in their lives' and he was glad that in their 'sad, deplorable and tragic deaths' they would not be divided.

Bailie Hastie said that Tom had sent £1 home shortly before boarding the *Titanic*. Judge Macaulay added that Tom had been sending money home regularly and recommended that something should be done for the three children and their grandmother. Tom, he said, was 'as heroic as anyone' on the *Titanic*.

Mr S. Charteries said that both Tom and his father had worked for him at Rosefield Mills. His father was an excellent

Jock Hume – portrait released by his family after the *Titanic* sank.

Mary Costin in 1915, after her court victory over Andrew Hume.

Jock Hume (far left) with fellow bandsmen on board the Cunard liner, RMS *Carmania*, which sailed from New York to the Mediterranean, Jock's last trip before the *Titanic*.

The glove mill where Mary worked in Dumfries, famous for its knitwear.

35 Buccleuch Street, Dumfries, home of the Costins, as it is today.

Buccleuch Street circa 1912 – the turreted building (right) is the Sheriff's Court, opposite the Costins' home.

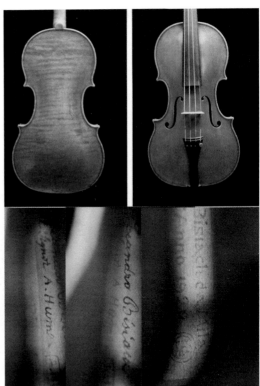

Andrew Hume, Jock's father, the
dapper violinist and conductor.

Andrew's controversial Bisiach violin
with the names of both men.

The Humes' house in George Street, Dumfries, as it is today.

Poster advertising the *Titanic* and her sister ship, *Olympic*.
They were the world's largest steamers, although the
White Star never said they were unsinkable.

Crew are shown how to put on cork life jackets
before the *Titanic* sailed.

The last photograph taken of the *Titanic*, as she left Queenstown,
her last port of call on her maiden voyage to New York.
Many Irish emigrants boarded the ship here.

Col. Jacob Astor and his teenage bride, Madeleine, who was expecting his baby.

The story that shocked the world: the famous photograph of a newsboy
selling papers outside the White Star Line offices in London
the day after the sinking.

The Halifax cable ship *Mackay-Bennett*, chartered by the White Star Line to recover the bodies.

Captain Larnder of the *Mackay-Bennett*.

Seamen from the Halifax cable repair ship *Minia*, which joined the *Mackay-Bennett* in the recovery operation, keep their cutter steady in the swell while their shipmates drag from the sea one of the last *Titanic* bodies to be recovered after the disaster.

'The Heroic Musicians of the Titanic' – a poster produced by the
Amalgamated Musicians' Union to honour the band. Jock is pictured
bottom right. Ten thousand people attended a fund-raising concert
at the Royal Albert Hall conducted by Sir Edward Elgar.

and capable man and young Thomas, who had been a pattern weaver, had given up work only because his sight failed him. He was sure that 'the working classes' would rise to the occasion and heartily support the movement to erect a monument.

Another speaker referred to 'the admirable family life' of the Mullins and the grandmother, Mrs Gunyeon. Tom had gone to sea after coming out of the infirmary, where nothing could be done to help his eyesight, but he had got on very well and promotion was likely.

Provost Thomson moved that a memorial fund be established and 'hoped very much indeed that it would be taken up heartily by the working classes', as 'their threepences and sixpences and shillings would be the best testimonial they could give'.

~ 8 ~

A Bill for Your Dead Son's Uniform

30 April, George Street, Dumfries

Fifteen days had passed since the *Titanic* foundered, yet there was still no definite news of Jock's fate. According to the *Dumfries & Galloway Standard*, the *Mackay-Bennett* had been delayed by storms and would not now arrive back in Halifax until later that day. Having anxiously awaited its return, Andrew was now dreading it: as the ship carried only a cargo of corpses, he reasoned that it could only bring bad news; either Jock's body would be on board, or it would not. Either way Jock was dead.

Of the 2,209 passengers and crew, only a few hundred were known to have survived, most of them rescued by the *Carpathia* in the immediate aftermath of the sinking. They had been taken to New York, where they were now giving interviews to the world's press. The stories they told – of the band bravely playing on as the ship went down – only deepened Andrew's despair. A British teacher and journalist, Lawrence Beesley, who had been on board the *Titanic* and was among the survivors, wrote a dramatic account for the *New York Times*, which was republished at length in the newspapers on 30 April. It began: 'Many brave things were done that night, but none more brave than by those few men playing minute after minute as the ship settled quietly lower and lower in the sea . . .'

Andrew wondered if the fathers of the other bandsmen would feel a warm glow of pride when they read these words. He himself felt only intense irritation with Mr Beesley, whose observations on the death throes of the ship had been made from the safety of a lifeboat two miles away and whose scoop was already making him rich and famous.

Andrew was also sick to death of well-meaning friends and acquaintances telling him how proud he should be of his hero son. Andrew did not want a hero son, even if it did make a good headline. He wanted a son who was alive. Why couldn't people understand that?

Several friends had referred in letters of sympathy to 'Jock's fine example', a ridiculous cliché, thought Andrew, given that Jock's example involved standing on the deck of a sinking ship in the middle of the North Atlantic playing a violin. Just how many people would aspire to that? It gave him no comfort to know that at least 100 people were keeping him and the children 'in their thoughts'. For this reason Andrew had stopped opening letters several days ago, but he scrutinised envelopes looking for one with a Liverpool postmark which might contain information about Jock from the White Star Line.

The first post in George Street was always delivered promptly at 8 a.m. and was one of the few events in Dumfries that you could set your watch by. Andrew's strict adherence to routine dictated that he would be in the dining room at this time, eating breakfast with his wife Alice, his son Andrew and daughter Kate. Each day brought new disappointment as Alice, having heard the clatter of the letter box, brought back to the breakfast table a bundle of ten or twelve letters, none of them from Liverpool. Today there were three hand-written white envelopes with black borders, one hand-written brown envelope immediately recognisable as a circular from the Dumfries Music Society, and a typewritten envelope with a Liverpool postmark.

Andrew snatched the envelope from Alice and tore it open. The letter was not, as he had hoped, from the White Star Line. It was from C. W. & F. N. Black and it said:

```
Dear Sir,

We shall be obliged if you will remit us
the sum of 5s. 4d. which is owing to us
as per enclosed statement. We shall also
be obliged if you will settle the
enclosed uniform account.

Yours faithfully,
C. W. & F. N. Black
```

Andrew read the letter and the accompanying statement three times, each time with growing disbelief. At first he thought it must be a clerical error, or possibly a practical joke in the worst possible taste. Without saying anything, Andrew passed the letter to Alice, who read it and burst into tears.

The statement explained that Jock was to have been paid £4 for the return voyage on the *Titanic*. But as the ship had sunk before even reaching New York, Blacks had terminated his contract from 2.20 a.m. on 15 April – the moment the band could no longer play on. Jock's wages, reduced pro rata, were now insufficient to meet the expenses that Blacks had incurred on his behalf through the outfitters Rayner's. These included the provision of White Star lapel insignias for his bandsman's tunic, sewing White Star buttons on his uniform (one shilling) and Jock's sheet music, which was now floating somewhere in the North Atlantic. The total Andrew was being asked to pay came to 14s 7d, less than £1 but a sum with approximately £40 of buying power in today's currency. There was no accompanying letter of regret, no word of sympathy.

Andrew felt dizzy. He thought for a moment that he was going to faint and quickly sat down to catch his breath. He felt freezing cold and wondered if he might be having a heart attack. He heard Alice say through her tears, 'How could they, Andrew? How could they?'

Suddenly Andrew found himself living in a world where people could send your son to his death and then invoice you for his buttons lying at the bottom of the ocean. He would have his revenge and it didn't matter who would pay for this.

It was bad luck, as well as unfortunate timing, that Mary Costin chose this particular moment to break the news to Andrew Hume that she was expecting Jock's baby. She had judged that 8.45 a.m. would be the best time to arrive, catching him between breakfast and his first lesson of the day at 9 a.m., thus preventing a scene in front of one of his pupils.

However much he had disapproved of her relationship with Jock, she reasoned, he could only be pleased now that Jock had left a son or a daughter, Andrew's first grandchild. It would give his senseless death some meaning. This was the argument that Mary rehearsed in front of the mirror that morning, putting on her best dress and tying her hair back with a comb.

Alice answered the door. When she saw Mary, she said, 'I thought I told you . . .'

'This is important,' said Mary. 'It's about Jock.'

Alice beckoned her in and showed her into the drawing room, where Andrew was standing with his back to the fireplace, where a fire was already lit. She had seen only the back of his head at the memorial service and he looked much older than the last time she had seen him properly, a year ago when he had come to her home, called her a whore in front of her mother and told her to stay away from his son. That was the day before Jock moved in with her for good.

The strain of the last two weeks had taken its toll on him. There were dark lines under his eyes from lack of sleep and the corner of his mouth had slipped as though he had suffered a slight stroke. His hair was unkempt. Alice's hair, piled up high like a governess, gave her a haughty look but she had kind eyes and a gentle mouth. She, too, was very pale. Mary was relieved that she was there. It would have been a more difficult conversation with Andrew on his own.

'I came to tell you that I am expecting his child. I thought you should know.'

Alice burst into tears. Andrew took a menacing step towards Mary, his face flushed and furious. For a moment Mary thought he was going to strike or strangle her. But he just put his face close to hers and hissed: 'Get out of here you little slut, peddling lies about your bastard child. I doubt you know who the father is but it's certainly not my son.'

Alice took her arm, in a kindly way, and led Mary back to the front door. 'I'm sorry,' said Alice. 'You must understand . . .'

Mary was back home in Buccleuch Street less than three minutes later. It had all gone badly wrong but Mary felt curiously calm and wondered if Andrew Hume had any idea what a formidable enemy he had just made.

9

The 'Death Ship' Docks

30 April, Halifax, Nova Scotia

The summit of Citadel Hill in Halifax offers a commanding view of the Nova Scotia coast, a strategic asset that once protected Halifax from its enemies and gave the city its nickname 'Warden of the North'. On a clear day you can see the old Marconi signal station at Camperdown, more than ten miles away. But early on the morning of 30 April 1912 a cold mist hung over the sea and, even with a telescope, the signalman who had been on lookout at Citadel Hill since before dawn was struggling to see the mouth of the harbour. Shortly after 8 a.m. he saw what he had been searching for: two masts, a single funnel, and the blurred but unmistakable outline of the cable ship *Mackay-Bennett*. The signalman hoisted a black flag, the agreed signal, to alert those waiting below. He heard shouted commands and, seconds later, saw five men running to pre-arranged destinations and a horse and carriage taking off at speed.

The cathedral bell was the first to toll, joined one after another by the bells of more than forty churches in Halifax, a deafening chain of grief echoing across the city to mourn the dead who were finally nearing the end of their long voyage. All around the world people who had lost loved ones on the *Titanic* had been waiting for this moment. But the *Mackay-Bennett* would bring no good news for anyone today, not in Halifax – 'the City of Sorrow' – nor in Dumfries, where the Humes and the Costins were waiting anxiously for news, nor anywhere else. The best the bereaved could hope for would be to put a name to a corpse, to plan a place where they could later come to grieve. The worst news would be not knowing – not knowing for days, weeks or even months. But most likely not knowing ever what had happened to the person you loved and whom you would never see again.

On the deck of the *Mackay-Bennett* Captain Larnder could hear the church bells in the distance as the ship passed McNab's Island. For the past three days, as they headed back towards Halifax, Larnder had felt a profound sense of relief that this unpleasant mission would soon be over. He – indeed, all the *Mackay-Bennett*'s crew – had managed to disassociate themselves from the human horror of their work by concentrating on the logistic and physical challenges of their task. Now, surrounded by coffins and corpses, haunted by the sound of the bells in the wind, Larnder faced for the first time the emotional reality of his mission and braced himself for the worst that was still to come. In the distance he could see hundreds, no thousands, of people standing in silence, shoulder to shoulder, the full length of the wharves, their hats removed. Others, further back from the water's edge, were standing on rooftops. Ships in the harbour cut their engines, their flags at half mast as a mark of respect.

This last leg of the *Mackay-Bennett*'s voyage seemed to Larnder to last a lifetime or, rather, 306 lifetimes if you judged it by the number of bodies they had lifted out of the sea. Larnder was in a hurry to get it over with. Last night's storm had stilled, leaving the sea in the harbour glassy smooth, and he ordered the ship to continue ahead at full speed, making a note to that effect in the log. To his annoyance, he saw pilot boat number 2 heading towards them from Herring Cove. The pilot would want to board. He slowed just enough to shout to the pilot, Frank Mackie, that he would not be needed today and carried on towards the harbour. At 8.50 a.m. they passed the Maugher Beach lighthouse on McNabs Island. At 9 a.m., as they approached the quarantine area, the *Mackay-Bennett* was intercepted by the quarantine boat *Monica* and the tugboat *Scotsman*. Now Larnder had no option but to heave to. Dr N. E. Mackay boarded them from the *Monica*, a legal requirement when a ship entered the harbour with a dead body on board. Larnder at once recognised Chief of Police Rudland on board the *Scotsman*. Rudland came on board, accompanied by detectives Kenny and Hanrahan. With them was a representative of the White Star Line, P. V. G. Mitchell. Captain Larnder greeted the men with a firm handshake as they stepped on to the ship, the boarding party visibly shaken to find themselves outnumbered by the dead.

For the first time, those waiting on the shore were able clearly to see the *Mackay-Bennett*. They saw 'her afterdeck piled high with coffins and on her forward deck a hundred unshrouded bodies', the *New York Times* reported next day. Some fainted and fell. Others just turned away in tears.

From here, Larnder would normally have navigated towards the Commercial Cable Company's wharf at 155 Upper Water Street, the *Mackay-Bennett's* usual mooring, but instead he ordered a course towards Flagship Pier, the Canadian Navy's anchorage at Coaling Jetty No. 4. Twenty sailors from the cruiser HMCS *Niobe* were already guarding the gates to keep out intruders, allowing the ship to dock in privacy and unload its cargo of dead away from the scrutiny of crowds and press cameras. Thirty horse-drawn hearses stood in line, the polished glass and lacquer of the carriages and the top hats and morning coats of the undertakers promising at last some dignity for the dead.

At 9.40 a.m. the *Mackay-Bennett* hauled alongside the pier and moored. Suddenly, as if it were a sign from God, the clouds parted and the sun shone brilliantly, turning the leaden water of the harbour into silver. But it seemed to bring no comfort to Captain Larnder who was seen pacing backwards and forwards on the bridge, his hands clasped behind his back, as the crew tied up the *Mackay-Bennett* fore and aft and lowered the gangway. He was not normally a nervous man – quite the contrary – but now it was all over Larnder had become acutely anxious. He had every reason to congratulate himself, having achieved everything that he had set out to do. At considerable risk to his men and his vessel, he had sailed more than 1,500 miles in hazardous conditions through ice fields without a single loss of life. He had recovered more bodies from the wreck of the *Titanic* than anyone could have expected him to. Yet he felt unsettled and full of apprehension and not without cause. At 11.30 a.m. when the last of the bodies had been unloaded from the *Mackay-Bennett*, Captain Larnder 'tall and square of build' invited the press on board. In the dining saloon of the *Mackay-Bennett* he opened the ship's log and, slowly tracing his fingers over the brief entries, recounted the events of the previous ten days. He hadn't, however, anticipated the gathering storm over the large number of bodies that had been buried at sea, nor did he understand the grief and frustration of those whose loved ones had been recovered but who would not have their bodies to take home with them.

'Let me say first of all that I was commissioned to bring aboard all the bodies found floating,' he told the reporters gathered around him. 'But owing to the unanticipated number of bodies found, owing to the bad weather and other conditions, it was impossible to carry out instructions, so some were committed to the deep after a service conducted by Canon Hind.'

Then came the controversial bit:

'No prominent man was recommitted to the deep. It seemed best to embalm as quickly as possible in those cases where large property might be involved. It seemed best to be sure to bring back to land the dead where the death might give rise to such questions as large inheritances and all the litigation.

Most of those who were buried out there were members of the *Titanic*'s crew. The man who lives by the sea ought to be satisfied to be buried at sea. I think it is the best place. For my own part I should be contented to be committed to the deep.'

Larnder's remarks did little to ease the pain or provide comfort to those whose loved ones had been recovered by the *Mackay-Bennett* but not brought back to Halifax. The *New York Times* reported next day that 'the whole colony is stirred by an immense pity that it had to be, and not a few are wondering if it really had to be, a wonder fed by the talk of some of the embalmers ... The large majority [of those buried at sea] were either members of the *Titanic's* crew or steerage passengers.' The publisher of *The Casket*, the official organ of undertakers in North America, condemned in an issue published some months later 'the barbarous use of the ocean's depths as a cemetery'.

What Larnder did not reveal was that it had been his intention to bury many more bodies at sea; even as the *Mackay-Bennett* was approaching Halifax the crew were unstitching canvas body bags and removing iron bars from them.

Later that afternoon, Captain Larnder, having recovered his composure, made his final entries of the voyage in the *Mackay-Bennett's* log:

10 a.m. Commenced discharging bodies, total 201.
1.35 p.m. Police patrol wagon took away personal effects. Cast off and proceeded to CC company wharf. Fast alongside cc wharf.
2.00 p.m. Finished for the day.

The discharging of bodies did not go quite so smoothly as Larnder's log suggests. He might also have added that he had sailed into a storm on dry land.

Even before the *Mackay-Bennett* had embarked on its morbid mission, extensive and efficient arrangements were being made in Halifax to receive the dead. The White Star Line, anticipating an avalanche of bodies, ordered 500 coffins from Ontario and commissioned Snow's to take charge of the processing of the dead. Snow's recruited nine undertakers and forty embalmers from Nova Scotia, New Brunswick and

Prince Edward Island, including two sisters who would embalm any women or children whose bodies were recovered. The Mayflower Curling Rink on Agricola Street was identified as the best facility in the city to serve as a temporary morgue. The ice kept the building chilled and the rink provided more than enough space to lay out the bodies for identification and embalming. Joiners set to work making tables wide enough to take three coffins or bodies side by side. The photography studio of Gauvin & Gentzell was engaged to take photographs of the dead that might later assist in identification, George Gauvin agreeing to take the photographs himself. The White Star Line also negotiated with the city to purchase a large number of burial plots at Fairview Lawn, Mount Olivet and Baron De Hirsch cemeteries.

Everything had been thought of . . . except the needs and feelings of the relatives, loved ones and friends of those who had died. Many of them – those who could afford to, those who lived near enough to come – had travelled to Halifax to await the *Mackay-Bennett*'s arrival. They included *Titanic* survivors, some still suffering from frostbite, who had come by train from New York to identify and claim the bodies of their lost companions. The distressed visitors found a city in mourning, flags at half mast, shop windows draped in black and horse-drawn wagons clattering through the streets loaded with coffins. Their grief was exacerbated by reports of transatlantic liners slicing their way through bodies and wreckage without stopping. Mail ships had been advised to give the area a wide berth but ships continued to report sightings of bodies and wreckage. A party of Scandinavian immigrants en route to Minnesota related an incident 'so heartbreaking and ghastly' that it was brought to the attention of President Taft. 'In several instances,' the immigrants reported, 'bodies were struck by our boat and knocked from the water several feet into the air.'

Lurid newspaper accounts included an interview with a First Class passenger on the Bremen, who reported seeing the body of a woman in her nightdress, clasping a baby to her breast. Close to her was the body of another woman, her arms locked around the dead body of a shaggy dog. Other passengers saw the bodies of three men in a group, all clinging to a chair. Floating by just beyond them were dozens of bodies, wearing lifebelts and clinging desperately together as though in their last struggle for life. The entire surface of the ocean around them formed 'a wreath of deckchairs and other wreckage'.

The phrase 'it is impossible to imagine . . .' is one that recurs time and again in the accounts of people who survived the sinking of the *Titanic* or were involved in the subsequent recovery operation. New York received the survivors and saw many scenes of joy, reunions and relief in the week following the sinking. But the shadow of death fell across Halifax and darkened in the two weeks between the sinking of the *Titanic* and the return of the *Mackay-Bennett*. It is impossible to underestimate the grief that enveloped the 'City of Sorrow'.

While the *Mackay-Bennett* was still at sea, the White Star Line, prolonged and aggravated the agony by withholding information on the identities of the dead whose bodies had been recovered, although the news blackout did not extend to VIPs travelling First Class, such as Jacob Astor. The official excuse was the difficulty in transmitting so many names by Morse code, but the reality was that the White Star Line was reluctant to admit that almost half the bodies that had been identified had already been buried at sea and would not be returning to Halifax. Of the 1,497 who had died only 306 bodies were recovered by the *Mackay-Bennett* and a third of them had been buried at sea.

Within a day of the *Mackay-Bennett* arriving at the scene of the wreck, newspapers in Halifax were drip-feeding information about the number being recovered and speculating as to their identities, with no information coming from the White Star Line itself. Under pressure from the bereaved, most of them American, who had arrived in Halifax in the hope of returning home with the body of a loved one, the Mayor convened a meeting at which a 'mourners' committee' was formed, chaired by the former US Consul-General James Ragsdale.

White Star Line agents responded by opening an 'information bureau' at the Halifax Hotel in Hollis Street three days before the *Mackay-Bennett*'s arrival. The first and only bulletin of the day was a wireless message received from the *Mackay-Bennett*. It read: 'Confirm bodies of Astor and Strauss on board. Due Monday with 189 [sic] bodies.' This was the first admission that more than 100 bodies had been buried at sea. It reduced many relatives who read it to tears and the revelation that the only two bodies identified so far happened to be those of multi-millionaires added anger to their grief. A class system in life had been replaced by a super-class system in death.

The second White Star bulletin of the day provoked even greater outrage:

When bodies are ready for shipment, friends may take them on the same train in the baggage car on payment of the regular first-class fare . . . bodies may also be sent by express on payment of two first-class fares. The offices of the Canadian Express Company are prepared to render every assistance.

Families from Europe who made enquiries about arrangements for transporting the bodies of loved ones back home were told by the White Star Line that 'normal cargo rates would apply'. Sarah Gill, the widow of Second Class passenger John Gill, whose body was recovered by the *Mackay-Bennett*, received a letter from the passenger department of the White Star Line written on 3 May. It said:

> We regret that we do not see our way to bring home the bodies of those recovered free of expense, and in cases where it is desired for this to be done, it can only be carried out provided the body was in a fit state to be returned, and upon receiving a deposit of £20 on account of the expenses.

The White Star Line offered Mrs Gill their 'profound sympathy' for the 'terrible calamity' but regretted that the company could not be held responsible for the results of the 'unfortunate accident'. As it turned out, the White Star Line's hard-hearted response to the widow was quite unnecessary as Mr Gill, a chauffeur to a vicar, had been buried at sea a week earlier. The letter was sold at auction in 2002 for £5,500.

Fortunately the Astor family could afford to make their own arrangements. Colonel Astor's son Vincent, having been alerted by the White Star Line a week earlier that his father's body had been recovered, had already arrived in Halifax in his father's private train, the ironically named *Oceanic*. He was accompanied by the family lawyer, Nicholas Biddle, and the captain of his father's boat, Richard Roberts. The *Oceanic*'s three luxury carriages were shunted to a siding in the former Halifax station in North Street, where they remained with Vincent living on board, until his father's coffin was ready to be transported to New York where it would be interred in the Astor family vault. In an adjoining siding stood another private train, sent by the Grand Trunk Railway to take the body of its president, Charles Melville Hays, to Montreal.

Vincent's first call on arriving in Halifax was to the funeral parlour at 90 Argyle Street of John Snow, father of John R. Snow Jnr the undertaker on the *Mackay-Bennett*. Vincent chose an appropriate casket and floral display to be mounted on the coffin during the rail journey to New York. At a meeting of mourners the next day at the Halifax Hotel, the White Star Line's representative Mr Jones said he had received information that 'certain gentlemen' had tried to bribe undertakers and that the White Star Line 'would not stand for it'. Despite this assurance, the first death certificates to be issued would bear the names of Colonel J. J. Astor and Isidor Strauss, the millionaire retailer and founder of Macy's on Fifth Avenue. Their bodies would also be the first to leave Halifax.

But the American millionaires would not be the first corpses to leave the *Mackay-Bennett*. That honour was accorded to the men lying in the ice – most, if not all, Third Class passengers or crew. They included my grandfather Jock and his pals, the bandmaster Wallace Hartley and

Nobby Clarke. 'They presented such a gruesome sight that it would be most impossible to picture,' wrote a reporter in the *Daily Echo*. Many of them were naked, the rest were in their underclothes, their arms and legs frozen grotesquely so that they looked as if they were gesticulating or kicking at their moment of death. They were carried off the ship on stretchers and loaded on to handcarts, covered with tarpaulins, and transported at speed and with embarrassment to the Mayflower Curling Rink. It is said that the shoulders and hips of some of these dead had to be broken or dislocated to fit them into the narrow coffins.

As the thirty horse-drawn hearses lined up to carry the rest of the bodies to the curling rink, panic broke out among the Astor contingent.

The White Star Line had earlier assured the family of millionaire businessman George D. Widener that Mr Widener had been positively identified in spite of suffering terrible facial injuries and that his body was being brought back to Halifax. But it had subsequently become clear, while the *Mackay-Bennett* was still at sea, that the body was actually that of Widener's manservant Edward Keating, who had in his pocket a letter addressed to his employer, leading to the mistaken identity. Suspicions as to the identity had been aroused by the man's underclothing, which was 'of a poorer texture than Mr Widener would be expected to wear'. A further examination of his clothing revealed the initials EK in his coat, which was also 'of inferior quality'. Now identified for who he really was, a mere humble servant, Keating was promptly sewn up in canvas, weighted with iron bars and tipped overboard. The body of his employer, Widener, was never recovered.

Vincent Astor feared that something similar might have occurred with his own father, whose manservant was also missing. With Astor's body still on board the *Mackay-Bennett*, Captain Roberts was immediately dispatched to the ship to make a positive identification. The lid of Astor's coffin was removed and Roberts peered in. The body was most definitely that of his former employer, he said. 'The features were perfect, the face being only slightly discoloured which would be the result of the action of the icy waters of the Atlantic upon a human body.' Roberts was further reassured after being shown what had been found on the body: the gold-buckled belt that Astor always wore, the diamond cufflinks, 'the $3,000 found in his pockets settling the uncertainty', according to a reporter from the *New York Times*. Roberts was seen 'hurrying through the crowd to the nearest telephone' to inform Astor's son, Vincent. His description of the body of his late employer was a tribute to the embalmer's art of John R. Snow Jnr.

Soon after 11 a.m. the last of the dead had been carried off the *Mackay-Bennett* to the Mayflower Curling Rink, although some reports said that Astor and Strauss were taken directly to Snow's. Relatives who had gathered outside the Mayflower in the hope of discovering whether their loved one was among the dead were told there would be no admission until the following day, as bodies were still being embalmed and prepared for identification.

An interview with John R. Snow Jnr, published in the *Halifax Evening Mail* the next day, caused further distress to relatives. He spoke with gruesome detail of finding the two-year-old boy, of mutilated bodies . . . 'arms and legs shattered, faces and bodies mangled, many still in evening dress, their watches stopped at ten past two'. Twelve women, he said, had been found forty miles from the scene of the wreck. A red skirt had been found tied to an oar in an overturned lifeboat. The manner of the deaths was what upset relatives more than anything else. Snow said: 'There was awful evidence of the fierce struggle for life, hands clutching wildly at clothing, faces distorted with terror . . . ours was a sickening task.'

This image may have been encouraged by the dreadful sight of the bodies consigned to the ice in the hold and the nightmare scenario that greeted those who had to extricate the bodies when the *Mackay-Bennett* returned to Halifax. Snow later denied saying this and the *Mackay-Bennett's* doctor, Thomas Armstrong, gave a wholly different account in the *Morning Chronicle* on Thursday 2 May. 'With the exception of about ten bodies that had received serious injuries their looks were calm and peaceful,' he said. 'In fact so peaceful it was difficult to realise that they were dead.' Subsequent interviews with crew members confirmed Dr Armstrong's account: it may have been a belated attempt to comfort grieving relatives but all the research into death by hypothermia suggests that it is a better way to die than drowning.

By the time the *Mackay-Bennett* had docked, grief was competing with anger and blame as the dominant emotion among 'mourners' in Halifax, as the press had dubbed them, despite the fact they still had no one to mourn. The White Star Line was being held accountable for the causes of the disaster: navigational errors, a flawed watertight doors system and insufficient lifeboats. The order 'women and children first' was also being questioned. We accept today that this is the 'decent' way to behave in such a situation, but we do so partly because of the *Titanic*, where the order determined who lived and who died. But in 1912 the 'women and children first' rule had only one precedent in maritime disasters, many years earlier. Yet no one on board the *Titanic* – crew members or passengers – challenged the command, even though it meant laying down their own life.

Neither the American nor the British public inquiries into the disaster satisfactorily answered the question, 'Who gave the order?' Captain Smith had been heard to shout through his megaphone, 'Be British!' but not much else. Charles Lightoller, the second officer, maintained that Captain Smith had given the order but, if he did, it was by way of an answer to a question that Lightoller himself had posed when ordered by Smith to load the lifeboats, 'Shall we load the women and children first?' to which Smith had replied 'Yes.' On the port side of the *Titanic*, where Lightoller was in charge of lowering the lifeboats, the order was rigorously enforced, but on the starboard side many more men found their way into a lifeboat. It seems to have been Lightoller's enthusiasm to give priority to the women.

Two days after the *Titanic* sank, on 17 April 1912, the *Halifax Daily Echo* published a leader daring to question the command, under the heading, 'Famous Men Chose Death That Penniless Women Might Be Saved'. Colonel Astor, it said, and Charles M. Hays, the President of Grand Trunk Railway, had 'stood aside for the sabot shod illiterate peasant women of Europe', the suggestion being that it should have been the other way around. But by 30 April the *Echo* had changed its tune. Under the heading 'An Honourable Death' the paper said:

The passengers and employees who were left behind must have gone down in the end with the supremely satisfactory feeling that they had done their whole duty and done it nobly. Never have men and women acted better in the world's history under supreme trial than did those of the *Titanic*. Each was for all, and all for each. And they have their reward, not only in what they accomplished for one another, not only in the world's outspoken admiration but above all in the individual comfort which their splendid self restraint, their dignified facing of death, their unwavering thought for others must now bring to surviving relatives and friends.

The *Halifax Evening Mail* warmed to the theme the same day (not realising that the *Titanic* now lay 8,200 feet deep):

The Captains of Industry, the Lords of Money, the Men of Letters, the hard-mouthed seamen, went quietly down to their doom in 1200ft of blue water in order that the women whose lives were in their care might come perchance to a haven of safety. This is our civilisation vindicated.

The theme of 'heroic death' was one taken up by newspapers all over the world. The *Daily Sketch* in London wrote about 'the wonderful scene on the *Titanic* when the band went down at their posts'. At a memorial service in Halifax to honour the dead, Principal Clarence MacKinnon said in his appreciation, 'All we know is that they heard the order "All men step back from the boats", they stepped back and they shall sleep in a hero's grave.' In Dumfries, Jock Hume and Thomas Mullin didn't die, 'they went home, though not to the old burgh by the banks of the Nith but to a happier and better country'.

As for Captain Smith, far from being blamed for steering 1,500 people to their death, he, too, had died 'a simple hero, as a British sea captain should'. The same sentiments would soon sustain the nation through the catastrophe of the First World War, during which a generation of young men laid down their lives for their country.

Jock Hume's body arrived at the Mayflower Curling Rink soon after 11 a.m. He was one of 125 unidentified victims brought back to Halifax and, as such, was not an immediate priority for the embalmers, who set to work on the sixty-five whose names were known. These included Jock's fellow bandsmen Wallace Hartley and Nobby Clarke, both of whom carried identification that could be quickly verified. The embalmers worked right through the night preparing the bodies so that relatives could make formal identifications next morning and claim the bodies or make arrangements for their transportation. Hartley's family asked that Wallace's body be returned home for burial there. Clarke's family requested that he be buried in Halifax in Mount Olivet Roman Catholic cemetery. Of the 190 bodies brought back to Halifax by the *Mackay-Bennett*, fifty-nine were shipped out of Halifax for burial at home, Colonel Astor being the first, departing at 8 a.m. on 1 May in the *Oceanic*, the morning after the *Mackay-Bennett* docked.

Vincent Astor and the Astor lawyer, Mr Biddell, accompanied the coffin, leaving Captain Roberts behind to see if J. J.'s valet Victor Robbins could be identified among the dead.

By the morning of Thursday 2 May, sixty of the dead were still 'keeping the secret of their identity locked up within their rigid forms', the *Daily Echo* reported. Sparing the feelings of its readers, the *Echo* did not add that some of the bodies that had been consigned to the ice were beginning to thaw out and decompose. Many were now considered to be beyond embalming and were placed in coffins in their decomposing state.

George Gauvin and his assistant spent the day photographing the bodies so that the process of identification could continue after burial. The glass negatives were later destroyed by Gauvin & Gentzell, although two or three prints are reported to have survived and have found their way into private collections. Those who have seen them say they are not pleasant viewing. In any event, although there was a need to bury the bodies as soon as possible, there was no hurry to formalise identities as no arrangements had yet been made for headstones and all the dead had numbers to which names could later be added. Simple wooden crosses were cut with the numbers painted onto them. Long trenches had been dug at Fairview, Mount Olivet and Baron De Hirsch cemeteries and burials commenced on Friday 3 May. The only burial on the Saturday was that of the unknown child. Canon Kenneth Hind conducted a special service, which was attended by the seventy-five crew and officers of the *Mackay-Bennett*. Hundreds turned out to see the small casket carried by six men to a horse-drawn hearse which took it to Fairview Lawn Cemetery.

On Monday 4 May thirty-three more unidentified bodies lying at the Mayflower Rink were sent to Fairview for burial. It would appear that Jock was among these but the burial certificate leaves room for uncertainty as, six days later, on 10 May, a further thirty-three bodies were interred at Fairview, some of them having been brought back to Halifax by the *Minia* which recovered seventeen bodies, burying two at sea.

A memorial service for the dead was held at All Saints Cathedral on Sunday 5 May. Principal Clarence MacKinnon paid tribute to the 'unidentified . . . whose graves would be kept forever green'. He said, 'They shall rest quietly in our midst under the murmuring pines and hemlocks but their story shall be told to our children and to our children's children.'

Among the congregation was Captain Larnder and most of his crew. There had been little time for any of them to rest since their return to Halifax on 30 April. The day after unloading their cargo of corpses they had been ordered to prepare for their next voyage. Larnder's log for Wednesday 1 May, headed 'In Port', described that day's activities:

Paid off crew
Checked life belts
Shore gang began coaling ship
Carpenter repaired deck damage
Filling fresh water tanks

When the arrangements for the memorial service became known Larnder asked his employers, the Commercial Cable Company, if the *Mackay-Bennett* could delay sailing so that he and his men could attend the service. Permission was given and early on Monday 6th, the morning after the service, the *Mackay-Bennett* set sail again. Its three tanks, which had served as an ice mortuary, now held huge drums of cable. This time, Larnder's mission was one that would give him pleasure, one that he understood and one for which he had been trained, though no less dangerous. They were to find and repair a break in the world's longest undersea cable, connecting the 3,173 nautical miles between Brest and St Pierre, one of two French islands just off the Burin Peninsula off the south-west coast of Newfoundland. The cable had been laid in 1898 but later extensions took it on to Cape Cod and New York, increasing its importance and value as a fast telegraphic link between Europe and the USA. Larnder would be pleased to know that one hundred years later, the world wide web depended on a similar cable made of fibre optic connecting the two continents.

As they passed George's Island, Larnder started a new page in the log. He headed it: 'Brest–St Pierre' and added for good measure underneath, 'On to Cape Cod then New York'. A storm lay ahead but for the first time in three weeks Captain Frederick Larnder felt in control of his life again.

10

Mutiny on the *Olympic*

4 May, Southampton

As the corpses of seamen were being carried off the *Mackay-Bennett*, fifty-four crew members on the *Titanic's* sister ship, *Olympic*, were appearing in court in Southampton charged with mutiny. The episode has to be one of the most shameful and ill-judged prosecutions ever to come before a British court of law and, if it were not so shocking, it would be pure slapstick, involving as it does a captain called Haddock.

The *Olympic*, under the command of Captain Haddock, had been due to sail from Southampton to New York at noon on 24 April 1912. Like the *Titanic*, the *Olympic* had been built with an insufficient number of lifeboats for the passengers and crew and in the week following the *Titanic* disaster, the White Star Line scrabbled around to find forty more lifeboats before the *Olympic* put to sea. Harland & Wolff, the Belfast firm that had built both liners, were unable to supply wooden lifeboats in time so the White Star Line borrowed forty collapsible boats taken from troopships in Portsmouth harbour and loaded them on board the *Olympic*.

Southampton was still reeling from the death of 500 of its fathers and sons on the *Titanic* and, understandably, the crew of the *Olympic* who had lost family members and friends took more than a passing interest in the condition of the collapsible boats that their lives might depend upon. After examining them they decided the boats were rotten, unseaworthy and, for the most part, unfit for purpose. With only three exceptions, the entire crew of firemen, greasers and trimmers stopped work, collected their kit and left the ship singing, 'We're All Going The Same Way Home', accompanied by a tin whistle band led by a self-appointed conductor.

With passengers already boarding the ship, the situation was not looking good for the White Star Line – and that was before the intervention of their Southampton manager, the unfortunate Mr Curry, who told the men that their refusal to obey orders was 'rank mutiny' and that Captain Haddock could order the police to arrest them for desertion. An impromptu meeting of the strikers was held on the quayside. The secretary of the Seafarers' Union, Mr Cannon, told the men that he did not wish to influence their decision and would be guided by their vote. 'Not a single man voted to rejoin the ship,' wrote a reporter from the New York Times who had watched the situation develop with interest as more than half of the Olympic's passengers were American. Mr Cannon told the Times reporter: 'The men inspected the boats when they were mustered this morning and found many of them in a rotten condition. One man is alleged to have put his hand through the canvas of one boat. All the boats are from six to ten years old, and when the men tried to open them they could not do so.'

The White Star Line began a frantic hunt for substitute firemen and trimmers, having apparently forgotten that it had drowned virtually a whole ship's crew from the town two weeks earlier. Unable to find any living or willing hands in Southampton, it switched its search and managed to recruit

100 men in Portsmouth, bringing 150 more by special train from Liverpool and Sheffield. While the search for blacklegs was going on, the *Olympic* lay at anchor in the Solent, appropriately off Spithead, the scene of a successful Royal Navy mutiny in 1797. By this time, several of the *Olympic*'s 1,400 passengers were considering mutiny themselves, annoyed about going nowhere for two days and increasingly concerned about their own safety. The White Star Line's attempts to amuse them by distributing kites to fly on deck was not a success.

At a meeting of the First Class passengers in the *Olympic*'s smoking room, the Duke of Sutherland decided that the crisis required more leadership than Captain Haddock was providing. Puffing away at a large Cuban cigar, the Duke asked for 'volunteer stokers', who would work in shifts to get the ship to Queenstown where the captain might be able to raise a more amenable Irish crew. Surprisingly, seventeen First Class passengers offered their services, including Ralph A. Sweet who accompanied Sutherland to put their plan to Captain Haddock. 'He thanked us very nicely,' Sweet said later. 'I thought he was going to put us to work right away but he told us that he would not call on our services.'

On the night of 25 April, the substitute firemen and trimmers, having arrived in Southampton, were taken out to the *Olympic* by tugboat. Their arrival did not go down at all well with the fifty-four firemen and stokers remaining on the ship, who objected to the newcomers on the grounds that they were not union members and were unqualified to take the liner across the Atlantic. As soon as the relief crew started up the ladder to board the *Olympic*, they were passed on the way down by the fifty-four seamen, who demanded that the tug took them back to shore.

The Royal Navy now became involved in the dispute. Captain Haddock signalled for assistance by lamp to the cruiser

Cochrane, whose captain, William Goodenough, boarded the tug to warn the men they were guilty of mutiny and liable to heavy punishment. The men still refused to return to the *Olympic*. The tugboat returned with the men on board to Southampton, where it was met by police who arrested them for 'unlawfully disobeying the commands of the master of the ship'.

The White Star Line cancelled *Olympic*'s trip and refunded the passengers' money, some of the passengers 'complaining bitterly of the actions of the sailors declaring they would try to get back the cheques given in aid of the *Titanic* disaster fund', according to White Star Line managers. The company then telegraphed the Postmaster General (the *Olympic* being a Royal Mail ship) as follows:

```
Earnestly hope you will secure for us . . .
the proper punishment of crew's mutinous
behaviour, as unless firmness is shown now
we despair of restoring discipline and
maintain sailings.
```

The 'mutineers' appeared before magistrates at Southampton that morning. At first they were made to stand in two rows facing the magistrates but they were then provided with seats. Mr C. Hiscock 'appeared for the White Star Line'. He explained that the men were charged under the Merchant Shipping Act, which provided that if any seaman was guilty of wilful disobedience he was liable to be imprisoned for a period not exceeding four weeks. The court heard that of the 200 men taken on board to break the strike, only three were able to show they had ever been to sea. The men were remanded until 30 April, when they would appear again before the magistrates and were again remanded. The case received very little coverage, eclipsed as it was by the simultaneous arrival in Britain that day of many of the *Titanic* survivors and the arrival in Halifax of the *Mackay-Bennett* with the dead, including Jock.

On 4 May, the fifty-four seamen were brought back to court, where they pleaded not guilty to mutiny. An ex-Naval officer and quartermaster, George Martell was one of the witnesses for the defence. He said he was 'thoroughly disgusted by the appearance of the men shipped in to take the place of the striking firemen ... They were not the sort of shipmates for me,' he said. They were 'the scallywags of Portsmouth'.

The magistrates decided that the charges were proved but expressed the opinion that it would be 'inexpedient' to imprison or fine the men because of the circumstances which had arisen prior to their refusal to obey orders. The magistrates discharged them all and hoped they would return to duty, which indeed they did on 15 May, much cheered by the sight of forty new Harland & Wolff wooden lifeboats installed on the deck of the *Olympic* in time for its delayed voyage to New York.

'No untoward incident marred the departure of the *Olympic* from Southampton,' the *New York Times* reported the next day. 'Most of the men concerned in the recent dispute rejoined the ship.' The newspaper added that the leading fireman on the *Olympic* as it sailed to New York was a man called Barret, who knew a thing or two about lifeboats having just spent a night in one. One of the few crew members to survive the Titanic, Barret had just returned from New York having arrived there on the *Carpathia* with the other survivors. Before boarding the *Olympic* he was invited to tea by the Wreck Commissioner, who was 'eager to hear his vivid story of the engineers' experience after the collision with the iceberg'.

11

Titanic's Bandmaster Honoured

18 May, Colne, Lancashire

Unlike Jock and Nobby Clarke, who had little to indicate who they were when their bodies were recovered by the *Mackay-Bennett*, Wallace Hartley, the bandmaster, was quickly identified. His violin case was still strapped to his chest; his initials, WHH, were on a gold fountain pen and on a silver matchbox found in his pockets; he carried several letters; and there was a telegram addressed to 'Wallace Hotley, Bandmaster Titanic.'

Although incorrectly listed by the *Mackay-Bennett*'s purser as 'W. Hotley', the mistake was quickly picked up and body number 224 was positively identified as that of Hartley on arrival in Halifax. His family in Colne, Lancashire, were informed by telegram the same day, 1 May, and at once asked for his body to be sent home.

Before the *Mackay-Bennett*'s arrival, White Star Line managers had been maintaining that 'normal cargo rates would apply' if anyone wanted a coffin shipped back to Europe. Whether or not Wallace's family were made to pay we do not know but on the morning of Friday 17 May his coffin arrived in Liverpool on the White Star liner RMS *Arabic*, which also brought home the bodies of two other *Titanic* victims. Wallace's father, Albion, met the liner with a horse-drawn hearse that had travelled the sixty miles from Colne the previous day. There were formalities to be completed before they made the return journey. First, Albion Hartley had the unpleasant task of identifying his son. The American-style coffin allowed part of the lid to be removed and for the face to be seen behind a glass panel; Albion then had to sign the receipt for his son's effects. They included his epaulettes which someone on the *Mackay-Bennett* had thoughtfully removed from his bandsman's uniform before disposing of his clothes.

The return journey would take ten hours, the hearse arriving in Colne in the middle of the night. Hartley's coffin was taken straight to the Bethel Chapel where he had once been a chorister and his father a choirmaster. An inscribed brass plate had been engraved in advance and this was now affixed to the coffin. It said simply:

WALLACE H. HARTLEY
Died April 15th, 1912
Aged 33 years
'Nearer My God To Thee'

All the next morning, mourners filed past the coffin. More than a thousand people came to the service, far more than the chapel could accommodate. But it was the extraordinary scenes afterwards, the outpouring of public grief, that revealed the emotion that the *Titanic*, and in particular the band, had aroused among the ordinary people of Britain. Thirty thousand people, more than the population of the town, lined the streets to pay their respects as the hearse carrying Hartley's coffin made the journey from the chapel to the cemetery at the top of the hill. They came from all around: millworkers, miners, musicians. Four mounted police led the cortège, while thirty other policemen followed on foot. The Colne brass band was joined by several colliery bands from Yorkshire and Lancashire.

Reports and photographs of Hartley's funeral dominated the newspapers for two days. Mary Costin passed the newspaper to her mother after she had finished reading it. 'I know I ought to feel proud,' she told her mother, 'but all I feel is envy that the Hartleys have someone to bury.' She didn't even know that they had found Jock, let alone that he had been buried two weeks earlier.

12

Mary 'Slurs' a Dead Man

28 June, Buccleuch Street, Dumfries

The outpouring of grief that accompanied the sinking of the *Titanic* was immediately followed by the spontaneous desire of ordinary members of the public to help the widows and orphans of those who had died. Many families were facing real hardship, having lost fathers, sons and brothers. Southampton had provided 724 crew members, of whom only 175 returned home to their families.

On both sides of the Atlantic, people responded generously in their hour of need. In Britain, King George V set a sterling example by giving 5,000 guineas; church parish councils, Scout troops and ad hoc collection boxes multiplied this sum many times over as people gave as much as they could afford and more. At Castle Douglas near Dumfries, the Scout troop raised £47, a remarkable sum for boys to raise, equivalent to approximately £2,000 today.

In May, a 500-strong orchestra staged the largest concert ever held at the Royal Albert Hall in aid of the families. Ten thousand people came to see Sir Henry Wood and Edward Elgar conduct an emotional programme. The *Daily Sketch* reported next day:

The supreme moment of the day came when Sir
Henry Wood led the orchestra through the first
eight bars of 'Nearer My God To Thee' and then,
turning to the audience, he conducted the singing to the end. Ten thousand people, whose minds
were filled with thoughts of one of the greatest
sea tragedies ever known, sang the hymn with
deep feeling.

The hymn drew a particularly emotional response from 'two
ladies sitting in a box near the royal party' according to the
Sketch. The last time they had heard 'Nearer My God To Thee'
they had been in a lifeboat while the band played the hymn
on the deck of the *Titanic*.

Several official funds were established in the aftermath of
the tragedy to ensure that donations were distributed fairly
and evenly, the largest being the Lord Mayor of London's fund
and the *Daily Telegraph Titanic* fund. Other collection centres
were set up in Southampton, Glasgow and Liverpool. In time,
these were amalgamated into a single fund called the *Titanic*
Relief Fund, managed from an office in Liverpool.

By the end of June, the *Titanic* Relief Fund had raised
£307,000 – the equivalent of £15 million today – and was
sufficiently well organised to place advertisements in
national and local newspapers inviting applications for
grants from the dependants of those who had died. Mary
Costin wrote to the fund on Friday 28 June, formally lodging
an application for a grant, explaining that she was the fiancée of Jock Law Hume, violinist in the *Titanic*'s band, and was
expecting his child in October. She did so on the advice of
Mr Hendrie, a solicitor in the legal office where her mother

ROYAL ALBERT HALL.

Manager .˙. HILTON CARTER.

FRIDAY, 24th MAY, 1912 (EMPIRE DAY),
at 3 p.m.

The

"Titanic" Band

Memorial Concert

Under the Auspices of

THE ORCHESTRAL ASSOCIATION.

R. FERGUSSON McCONNELL,
10, Newman St., Oxford St., W.

Annotated Programme
. . SIXPENCE. . .

Susan worked as a cleaner and caretaker. After Jock's death in April, Hendrie had told Mary and her mother that he would help in any way he could and that there would be no question of fees. He was pleased to be of assistance.

Since Jock's death, Mary had been overwhelmed by the kindness she had been shown at home and at work. Jock was popular and well known in Dumfries and people had expressed their grief at his loss by going out of their way to be kind to her. Far from being embarrassed by her situation – by the end of June it was quite clear that she was expecting a baby – they seemed genuinely pleased for her. Her mother Susan had made things so much easier with their neighbours by talking at every opportunity about the new grandchild who was on the way, referring to the baby always as 'Jock and Mary's'. No one was left in any doubt that mother and daughter stood side by side in Mary's adversity.

But behind the brave face she put on for the world, Mary was sad, lonely and worried. She was used to Jock not being there – as long as she had known him he had been away at sea for weeks or months at a time – but she found it difficult to come to terms with the idea that he was never coming back. She missed her brother, William, more than ever. And she was worried about money. In October she would have to take time off work to have the baby, with no guarantee that her job at the mill would be waiting for her when she came back.

The *Titanic* Relief Fund's reply to Mary's application came two weeks later, much sooner than she had hoped. But she was not pleased by what she read. The fund would be willing to regard her claim sympathetically, but 'not at the cost of casting a slur on the family of the deceased man'. She should reapply after the birth of the child, providing 'evidence of paternity'. By the time Mary showed the letter to Mr Hendrie in his office, she was in tears. Mr Hendrie was not at all surprised by the fund's reply and tried to reassure her. 'This is just procedure. They are legally obliged to be cautious. After the baby is born we will apply to the court for a paternity order. It is not normally a straightforward process, but in your situation it will be. There is nothing to worry about, I promise you.' Mary was much comforted by what Mr Hendrie told her.

But there was nothing straightforward at all about the fund's response. What neither of them knew was that Andrew Hume himself had also written to the *Titanic* Relief Fund lodging an appeal for a grant as a 'dependant' of the late Jock Law Hume. He added that he had 'conclusive proof' that his son was not the father of the child carried by a Miss Mary Costin of 35 Buccleuch Street, Dumfries.

⟨⟩ 13 ⟨⟩

Andrew Hume

A Fantasy World

All his life, Andrew Hume had been quick to exploit an opportunity and the death of his son Jock would be no exception. He saw the *Titanic* Relief Fund as a welcome windfall, which he had no intention of sharing with Mary or her bastard child. The Fund could make a significant difference to his lifestyle and he was quick to apply for whatever it had to offer while looking around for other low-hanging fruit. And there was plenty of that.

Within weeks of the tragedy, through the Amalgamated Musicians Union of which he was a member, Andrew Hume became aware of various fundraising initiatives in Britain and in the United States to raise money specifically for the families of the musicians who had died. Everyone who went down on the *Titanic* died a hero, but the eight musicians had achieved superhero status by playing on until the ship went down. Musicians, like actors, have always been good at looking after their own, and a series of emotional memorial concerts were held in Britain and in the United States. In New York and Boston they were energetically promoted by some of the wealthy Americans who survived the *Titanic*, all of whom had paid tribute to the band's role in maintaining calm in the hour before the ship went down. They were experienced and influential fundraisers, including Madeleine Astor, who helped organise a concert given by 500 musicians at the Moulin Rouge on Broadway in aid of the *Titanic* band. Her guest of honour at a fundraising lunch for big hitters was Captain Rostron, the captain of the *Carpathia* who had taken the *Titanic* survivors to New York.

None of these socialites knew about the existence of Mary, or that Jock had left behind an unborn child. Consequently, Jock's father, being a musician himself, seemed a natural and deserving recipient of the fundraisers' generosity. Unknown to Mary and most other people, including his family, Andrew Hume banked more than £250 in handouts from charities over the coming months. He also developed a plan that would more than double the money he would receive in compensation for Jock's death.

By 1912, Andrew Hume had established a growing reputation in the music industry throughout Britain as an accomplished all-round musician. He was as proficient with the banjo and guitar as he was with the piano and the violin, as comfortable playing ragtime as Rachmaninov. He performed regularly in concerts and led an orchestra of forty at the newly opened West End Pier in Morecambe, Lancashire, during its opening summer season, spending ten weeks away from home. He taught music, giving private lessons at home as well as taking classes at local schools and academies. He was a conductor, seen with his baton on the bandstand in Dumfries's Dock Park most Sunday afternoons. And he also professed to make violins.

He was a busy man, Andrew Hume. Where music was concerned, it seemed there was nothing he could not do. To his peers in the music world none of this was surprising, as Andrew Hume had an impeccable pedigree. He was said to have studied music under the great Prosper Philippe Sainton, Professor at the Royal Academy of Music; to have mastered the art of violin making as an apprentice in Saxony's famous workshops in Erlbach, Schönbach and Markneukirchen; and to have inherited all this musical talent from his grandfather, the revered and much-loved Scottish composer, poet and folk hero Alexander Hume. Alexander Hume was a cult figure in Scotland, a self-taught composer of natural genius who won widespread acclaim after writing 'The Scottish Emigrant's Farewell' and the much-loved melody to Robert Burns' 'Afton Water'. The son of a wax chandler, Alexander Hume was born in Edinburgh in 1811 and worked as a cabinet-maker all his life, devoting his leisure to singing and writing music and poetry, in all of which he was self-taught. In 1829 he married Ann Lees, with whom he had seven children. The family settled in Glasgow in 1855 where Hume continued to make furniture for a living, while still writing music and poetry and editing *The Lyric Gems of Scotland*. He died a pauper in 1859, 'the temptations of company and conviviality having proved too strong'. Nor was he very diligent about collecting money owed to him. An obituary in the *New York Times* – for his fame had spread far and wide – reported that he did not receive 'even the traditional guinea' for his beautiful setting of 'Afton Water'.

Andrew Hume basked in the reflected glory of his famous grandfather, who gave him artistic credibility and social status. 'The musical talent jumped a generation,' Andrew

Hume would tell people, a dismissive reference to his father, a former farm labourer who became an attendant at the Dumfries lunatic asylum. But Alexander Hume was *not* Andrew Hume's grandfather and Andrew did *not* attend the Royal Academy of Music. He was not a pupil of Prosper Philippe Sainton. Neither did he make all of the violins that bore his name, many of them fine instruments that still fetch good prices at auction today. David Rattray, Instrument Custodian at the Royal Academy of Music, also questions Andrew Hume's claims to have served an apprenticeship in the workshops of Saxony. 'He would have had to be a German speaker,' Rattray told me. 'An apprenticeship would last anything from six to eight years and at the end of it, you would not end up playing the banjo and teaching music in Dumfries.'

These were among the first of many fictions on which Andrew Hume built his life, spinning a web of deceit so complicated that, like many fantasists, he eventually came to believe his own lies. He was a man who was both proud to have escaped his humble beginnings yet ashamed of his background, and who spent his life concealing it or reinventing it.

Although people associate Scotland with bagpipes, it is the sound of the fiddle that has entertained its people for 500 years; the instrument has given pleasure and shaped the country's cultural life more than anything else. Unlike bagpipes, the violin is small, light, highly portable and, in the hands of the right fiddler, will provide singing, dancing and laughter wherever it goes. To this day, a fiddler is never without friends or an invitation to travel.

One of the earliest known makers of stringed instruments in Britain was also called Hume. Richard Hume, an Edinburgh 'viol maker', sold a set of instruments to James V in 1535 for the considerable sum then of £20. He is no relation of our Humes, although no doubt Andrew Hume would have had us believe otherwise. We have to wait another twenty-six years for the next historical reference to fiddles, when Mary Queen of Scots was 'fiddled' into Holyrood Palace by a small company of musicians after landing in Scotland in 1561 to take possession of the crown. 'The melodye,' the Queen said, 'liked her weel' and according to John Knox she requested that the musicians play on 'for some nychts after'. Unfortunately, her Scots subjects, keen to impress their new queen, gave their performances at her chamber window, which was on the ground floor. 'There came under her window', wrote Brentôme, a chronicler of the period, 'five or six hundred citizens of the town who gave her a concert of the vilest Fiddles, wretchedly out of tune . . . what a lullaby for the night.' The next day the Queen 'expressed her pleasure thereat' and moved herself and her large retinue to the far side of the palace.

The violin grew rapidly in popularity over the next hundred years, fuelled by the Scots' enthusiasm for dancing. Many fiddlers with cabinet-making skills discovered it was not difficult to make their own instrument, although a fiddle could be bought for the price of a few rabbits. By the eighteenth century the violin had become an integral part of Scotland's social and cultural life, every community in Scotland having a fiddler and most homes, however poor or rich, owning a fiddle. The skills of playing – and making – violins were passed down through the generations and shared with friends. The fiddle fed Scotland's love of heroes, legends and romance, and there was no occasion at which a violin could not be produced and played – including executions.

Sir Walter Scott recorded the hanging of a notorious Robin Hood character, James Macpherson, in 1700. When Macpherson, as famous for fiddling as he was notorious for robbery, came to 'the fatal tree' where he was to be hanged, he played 'Macpherson's Lament' on his favourite violin, offering his 'cherished instrument' to anyone who would play the tune at his wake. 'None answering,' wrote Scott, 'Macpherson dashed it to pieces over the executioner's head and recklessly flung himself from the ladder.' The remains of his fiddle were thrown into his grave, his cousin Donald retrieving the neck and fragments as a memento.

A Scottish emigrant to New Zealand was more fortunate a century later when he was sentenced to death for sheep stealing. The condemned man, Sandy, was known to be an excellent fiddler and the judges, who were also Scottish, asked if he would be willing to play them a farewell tune. Sandy 'rattled off his favourite strathspeys and reels with unusual vigour' whereupon the judiciary, who had been tapping their feet, 'took to the floor', granting Sandy a reprieve on the grounds that it would be a pity to 'dae awa' with a fiddler of such distinction.

Scotland's 'ploughman poet' Robert Burns embraced the fiddle in much of his writing, penning a poem for his fiddler friend Major Logan, which ended:

Hale be your heart, hale be your fiddle,
Lang may your elbow jink and diddle.

Burns travelled several hundred miles to pay his respects to the most celebrated Scottish fiddler of his generation, Neil Gow, who was born at Inver, Perthshire in 1727, praising Gow's 'kind openheartedness' in his journal. Gow, like many fiddlers, was mostly self-taught. He had an unusually powerful bow arm, which had allowed him to develop a particular upstroke of the bow that 'put new life and mettle into the heels of dancers . . . rousing the spirits of the most inanimate'. Once, when chased by a bull across a field, Gow stopped the bull dead in its tracks by pulling out his violin and playing a couple of sharp upstrokes. For nearly half a century Gow was in constant demand at the grandest dances throughout Scotland.

The mid-eighteenth century brought the dawning of a golden age in cultural life in Scotland, in part due to the popularity of the fiddle, which had triggered an explosion of interest in music generally, with fiddlers writing their own music and playing it on instruments they had made themselves. Centres of violin making sprang up in Edinburgh, Glasgow and Aberdeen, many of the makers being proficient violinists themselves. Schools of music opened across the country and for the first time European performers started taking an interest in Scotland. This soon became a two-way traffic as Scottish violin makers travelled to Europe.

Over the next century, Edinburgh and Glasgow grew in importance as European centres of musical excellence, Edinburgh boasting more than twenty violin workshops, six along the Royal Mile alone. But by the time Andrew Hume was born, in 1864, Dumfriesshire had acquired a reputation for the musical talent of its people. 'Annandale could boast of musicians who had earned celebrity far beyond the borders of the country and whose manipulation of the violin had charmed the highest circles in the land,' wrote Alexander Murdoch, a celebrated Edinburgh violin maker himself, whose entertaining book, *The Fiddle In Scotland*, was published in 1888. According to Murdoch, the most famous of these was a man called Johnstone from Turnmuir near Lockerbie, who was brought up as a ploughman on his father's farm. 'So great was his thirst for excellence that, when at the plough, if some new musical grace struck his imagination he would leave his horses standing in the field, hasten home to his fiddle and perfect the piece before he returned,' wrote Murdoch. Turnmuir, as Johnstone was known, became 'the most noble master of the violin that has at any time appeared in these parts'. He later travelled with his violin around Britain, enjoying great success in Liverpool where he was hailed as 'the Scottish Paganini'. For the young Andrew Hume, who was taught about Turnmuir at school, this local hero's escape from the plough became an inspiration and a hope. From the plough to the podium was not an impossible step to take, as the great Robert Burns, who lived in Dumfries, had first demonstrated, and as Turnmuir himself had also shown. Now Andrew Hume would prove it himself.

Andrew Hume was born on 7 May 1864 in Lochfoot, Lochrutton, near Dumfries, a tiny hamlet surrounded by gentle, rolling hills next to a small loch. He was the fifth of nine children born to John Hume, a farm labourer, and his wife Ellen, née Halliday, daughter of a local farm labourer. Andrew's real grandfather was Robert Hume, also a farm labourer, who lived just a few miles away at Kippford, near Dalbeattie.

For four generations, this area south-west of Dumfries near to the river Urr was the home of the Hume family and, until Andrew broke the mould by becoming a musician, the Humes had always eked out a living by working on the land. Most of the family are buried in the local churchyard, beside the Haugh of Urr kirk, Kirkcudbright.

The family tree starts with a colourful character called Ebenezer Hume, born in 1768. He was also a farm worker albeit a multi-skilled one: in parish records his occupation is described as 'lay church minister, mason, joiner, millwright, carter, spinner, weaver, tailor, water pump maker and farmer'. Lochrutton, where Andrew Hume was born, was as small and poor as a farming community could get in 1864. It is not much different today. The Humes' address was simply 'No 5'. Twenty years of hard times had left everyone with 'yin' – nothing: 'yin to saw, yin to gnaw, and yin to pay the laird with,' as one contemporary writer put it. All the Hume children slept in one bedroom and went to the local school, where the teacher would have taught them the three Rs. Most if not all would have been the children of farm labourers and would have been excused school for days when the turnips were ready for harvesting.

Poor though they were, such communities were made up of God-fearing and literate families, most homes having a well-stocked bookcase with volumes of history and biography passed down through the children. The Humes would almost certainly have walked up the hill every Sunday to Lochrutton Church, a bleak but beautiful church where fifteen gravestones bear the name Halliday, their mother's maiden name. Someone in the community would have been playing or making fiddles, or both.

By 1871, Andrew's father John had abandoned life on the land for a job working at the Dumfries lunatic asylum as an 'attendant'. The census that year finds the family living in Cherrytrees Hamlet, Dumfries, the oldest boy Ebenezer, fourteen, already working as a cropper in the nearby tweed mills. Andrew is seven and John and Ellen's ninth child, Lily, somewhat of an afterthought, is not yet on her way. It is at this point that we lose sight of Andrew Hume for sixteen years. Many of the 1881 Dumfries census records have been lost or destroyed, the Humes' lives vanishing along with the registers. The trail runs cold.

So what happened to Andrew Hume in these missing formative years? It seems likely that at a young age he was introduced to the fiddle and showed a natural talent for playing the violin. It is not too great a leap to believe that this might have taken Andrew to Glasgow, where he became a student of his namesake William Hume, a music teacher and son of the famous Alexander Hume.

William Hume was 'a composer of much merit . . . a man of varied culture and scholarship and an excellent linguist . . . a man of unblemished character and singular attractiveness', according to his obituarist. Like his famous father Alexander, William had started out as a cabinet-maker, worked for a while as a merchant and then become a teacher of music. He also made violins. It is my belief that Andrew Hume became one of his pupils and that William took his namesake under his wing. William, a linguist and trader in violins, made frequent visits to Europe and would have encouraged Andrew to do the same.

Many years later, Andrew's obituary in *The Strad* magazine – the respected and still thriving trade magazine for those who play or trade in stringed instruments – said that Andrew studied violin making in Germany from 1880 to 1888, a period that would have spanned his late teenage years and early twenties. Other references in *The Strad* to Andrew Hume (who is often mistakenly referred to in musical bibliographies as 'Alexander Hume') talk of his summer visits to the violin centres of Saxony and Bohemia where he became 'proficient in the making of violins'. But all this must remain speculation, not least because much of it is based on information provided by Andrew Hume himself – a man, we now know, to whom a lie came more easily than the truth.

All we do know for certain is that in Glasgow on 21 July 1887, aged twenty-three, Andrew married Grace Law, a laundress, describing his own occupation as 'musician'. His father, meanwhile, has temporarily reinvented himself and is described on the wedding certificate as 'apiarist', or beekeeper.

The Laws seem to have come from similarly modest backgrounds as the Humes. Grace's father, John Law, was the son of a blacksmith; her mother, Catherine, had been a domestic servant before her marriage. The Laws had four daughters including Grace, the family apparently having been in the laundry business. In the 1881 census John Law gives his occupation as 'laundry keeper'; Grace, then fifteen, was working as a laundress and her sister Jane, thirteen, is described as a 'laundry message girl'. But by the time of the wedding, Grace's father John Law had died, his last occupation being an iron moulder.

In the summer of 1887, when Andrew Hume arrived back in Dumfries with his bride Grace, Britain was experiencing what later became known as a 'fiddle craze'. For the ambitious young violinist, about to set himself up in business teaching music, the timing could not have been better. The increasingly prosperous middle class had alighted upon the stringed instrument as the new way to self-advancement, sweeping away the taboos that previously discouraged women from playing the violin or cello. 'Every girl you meet in the street nowadays carries a fiddle box,' said a fictional character in a feature in a new magazine called *Strings*, one of six magazines launched around this time to feed this new-found fascination for stringed instruments. The Victorian love affair with the piano was over, at least for the time being.

The fiddle craze was not confined to the middle classes, either. In 1882 the Birmingham and Midland Institute had introduced a 'penny violin class' to encourage working-class people to take up music. Similar schemes sprang up in other parts of the country. Stringed instruments were now desirable and affordable, violins being played 'from among the most exalted in the land to the humblest dweller in the cottage', according to *The Fiddler* magazine, a rival publication to *Strings*. In Scotland, of course, this had always been the case but here, too, the fiddle was enjoying a revival reflecting a growing interest in classical music. New concert halls were opening and Scotland was now producing more violins per capita than any other country in the world.

Andrew Hume was a tall, handsome man with a Victorian authority and persuasive manner that made people like him and encouraged them to trust him. During the next few years, many who had dealings with Andrew Hume – including his wife Grace – would come to regret trusting him as much as they did, but his charm and good looks served him well in establishing himself in business.

The young Humes' first home in Dumfries was a modest rented two-room apartment in a sandstone terraced house in Academy Street, conveniently close to the prestigious Dumfries Academy, where Andrew was to find part-time work as a tutor. Andrew wasted no time in establishing himself as a teacher of music in the town, placing a single-column classified advertisement in the *Dumfries & Galloway Standard* headed: VIOLIN, BANJO AND GUITAR LESSONS. This immediately brought several responses from prospective students young and old, many of them female, as the fiddle craze had already reached Dumfries. Grace brought an all-important seal of trust and respectability to Andrew's new business as no young woman – wife or daughter – would have exposed herself to the potential scandal of spending time alone with a good-looking young stranger in his own home. Not only did Grace open the door to his students, keep his appointments book and take messages, she made sure he had a clean shirt and starched collar every day.

The advertisement also drew a number of enquiries from agents and impresarios with offers of work as a performer. One of these was from the musical director at the Theatre Royal in Shakespeare Street, then as now Britain's oldest working theatre, whose fame far outshone its size. Robert Burns had written prologues for the theatre and J. M. Barrie, who was educated at Dumfries Academy, had patronised it and performed there. Barrie later devoted a whole chapter to it, entitled 'The Smallest Theatre', in his amusing memoir, *The Greenwood Hat*, describing the remarkable feat of putting on four Shakespeare plays in a night, using the same actors. 'I loved that little theatre,' he wrote. 'I had the good fortune to frequent it in what was one of its great years [probably

1877]. I always tried to get the end seat in the front row of the pit, which was also the front row of the house, as there were no stalls.' Andrew would play there regularly for the next fifteen years, as would his son Jock who played solos on stage before curtain-up and during the intervals.

Andrew also secured an appointment to see the head-teacher at the Academy to enquire if there were opportunities for part-time music teaching. There were. And he made himself known to Mr Hannary, the proprietor of the violin shop in the High Street, offering to carry out repairs to customers' violins on his behalf. There was plenty of work there, too.

Andrew Hume had a promising and profitable career ahead of him as a performer as well as a teacher. Still in his mid-twenties he was already a violinist of considerable talent, as well as being a pianist, guitarist and banjo player. Andrew Hume could have been forgiven at this point for a moment's self-congratulation. He had come a long way from the ploughed fields of his forefathers and achieved every-thing through his own hard work and talent. Yet he obviously felt ashamed of his family, in particular his father who was now working as an assistant in the Dumfries lunatic asylum – and escorting small groups of 'safe' patients on monthly visits to the Theatre Royal. Andrew found this excruciatingly embarrassing when he performed there. The Humes were not the family Andrew would have chosen for himself.

It seems that Andrew Hume felt more comfortable being someone else – Alexander Hume's grandson, for instance – just as he felt more comfortable telling lies than the truth. Being known as Alexander Hume's grandson might have brought him credibility but it was a reckless, shameless lie considering that both his parents were alive and living in Dumfries and his eight brothers and sisters also lived in the area. But Andrew's stock-in-trade was reckless lies. Later, as we will see, he repeated the lie on oath in a court of law. We know that he lied to his children, because Jock later told fellow musicians on board ships that he was from 'a famous family' and his great grandfather had written 'The Scottish Emigrant's Farewell'. Did Andrew also lie to Grace, or did she know the truth about him?

The Humes' first child, Nellie, was born in November 1888, a respectable fifteen months after their marriage. Her arrival made it impossible for Andrew to continue to give music lessons from home but as he was now earning enough from lessons and performances to afford a larger apartment they moved to 5 Nith Place. This was a short walk from the Theatre Royal and Jock was born there on 9 August 1890.

It was around this time that Andrew spotted another business opportunity. A College of Violinists had been established in London at the height of the 'fiddle craze' in response to the growing demand for violin lessons, offering students courses with the opportunity of gaining a diploma. To student violinists, the diplomas became an important endorsement of their skill, giving them an advantage when applying for positions. But the college could take only so many students at one time and they had applications from more students than they could satisfy. Andrew recognised that the violin lessons could just as easily be given anywhere in the country – Dumfries, for instance – provided they met the college's high standards and followed the prescribed syllabus for the examination.

Hume wrote to the college, asking to see their syllabus

and requesting an opportunity to meet the board of the college to present his credentials. His suggestion was seized upon and the following week he set off for London. He returned to Dumfries the following day with a significant advantage over his competitors, the six or eight other music teachers in the town who placed classified advertisements in the *Dumfries & Galloway Standard* every week.

Business was booming for Andrew Hume. Bookings were pouring in for tuition and performances. In Dumfries he was asked to conduct concerts in Dock Park on Sunday afternoons, a prestigious proposition. There were new opportunities to appear in summer season musical extravaganzas. The difficulty was fitting in all these opportunities around family life: in August 1892, Grace gave birth to their third child, Grace. Around this time, Andrew received some good news: he was to be included in the prestigious volume *Musical Scotland* – a Who's Who of Scottish musicians from 1400 to the present time. His entry read:

HUME, ANDREW, born Dumfries 7th May 1864. Violinist, bassoonist, banjo player and composer. Pupil of M Sainton. Established in his native city as professor of the above instruments and teacher of music.

Andrew's entry in the directory came immediately after entries for Alexander Hume and his son William, a most convenient juxtaposition, particularly as his own entry was followed by another Hume, Richard, the famous viol maker who sold fiddles to King James in 1530. People would think that the four Humes were related, one big family of famous fiddlers. Andrew also congratulated himself on being able to include in the entry that he had been a pupil of Prosper Sainton, an endorsement of his untruthful claim to have studied at the Royal Academy of Music. Sainton, who had died two years earlier, may indeed have once given Andrew a lesson but it certainly was not at the Royal Academy of Music.

By now, Hume was widely acknowledged in Dumfries to be a 'man of position'. At least, this is how his solicitor described him when on 1 November 1892 Hume was arrested for 'foul-hooking salmon' in the River Nith and escorted home, dripping wet, by two constables. Grace was not pleased. When the case came up in the Dumfries Sheriff's Court two weeks later his solicitor asked the Sheriff to take into consideration his client's 'position in the town' in determining his sentence. It was the first of many appearances Andrew Hume would make in this court over the years and now, as in later arraignments, he lied, telling such whoppers on this occasion that it caused laughter in court. The headline to the long report of the case in the *Dumfries & Galloway Standard* was 'Extraordinary Conflict of Evidence'.

It was, as they say, an open-and-shut case. A fair cop. Andrew and a friend, John Bell, a labourer, went down to the river with rods and lines and baited hooks attached. Superintendent Pool saw Hume fishing in the Nith in a pool at the far end of the island in the centre of the river. This wasn't the first time he had seen him, either, and this time he decided to do something about it. He watched Hume cast his hooks across the stream time and again. He saw him hook a salmon. He observed him haul the salmon on the line to the Dumfries side of the river where he handed his rod to Bell while Hume gaffed the fish. A large crowd had gathered and witnesses corroborated Pool's evidence. The fish, hooked and gaffed, was recovered.

Yet Andrew Hume pleaded not guilty. He wriggled like a fish caught on the end of a line himself, desperate to get off the hook. He said he hadn't done it. He said the superintendent could not have seen them because some clothes that were hanging on railings obscured his view. Then he said he believed they were entitled to be fishing there with baited barbs. Far from taking Hume's 'position in the town' into consideration, the Sheriff fined Hume £3 – three times more than his poacher companion Bell – for 'aggravating the offence' by lying.

Despite these embarrassing revelations, opportunities continued to come Andrew's way. In 1896, amid much razzamatazz, a new pier was opened in Morecambe, Lancashire, a popular seaside destination, second only to Blackpool. Edward de Jong, famous throughout Britain for his 'Popular Concerts', headed the entertainment bill for the summer season and invited Andrew to lead his forty-strong orchestra. De Jong's twice-daily concerts were musical extravaganzas that embraced opera singing, orchestral pieces and other exotic entertainments. These included the Condos, a family of Japanese acrobats, can-can dancers from Paris festooned with ostrich feathers and glittering spangles, and 'Madame Paula'. According to the Morecambe Chronicle, 'Madame Paula, "the queen of alligators, crocodiles and serpents" went through a daring performance with these animals . . . the spice of risk had a powerful effect upon the audience'. The *Dumfries & Galloway Standard* announcement of Andrew's appointment prompted a clutch of letters of congratulations next day.

For Andrew, the summer season away from home on the Lancashire coast provided a welcome break from recalcitrant pupils and from the pressures of family life. It was fun as well as providing valuable publicity and kudos. On his return, Andrew booked a prominent advertisement in the *Standard*, which now said:

> Mr Hume has resumed TEACHING.
> Now the Local Representative for College of
> Violinists. Pupils Prepared for above examination
> in December next.
> Syllabus and Terms on application.

Andrew's reputation was growing. In January 1897, the *Standard* reported: 'Mr A. Hume, the well-known Dumfries violinist, was on Thursday night playing at a grand convert in Cumnock – one of the most musical towns in the west of Scotland – when he completely captivated his audience which was both large and critical. His solos were strictly classical.'

Four years had now passed since the birth of the Humes' youngest child, Grace. Andrew's wife Grace did not enjoy good health – indeed, Andrew took pleasure in telling people that she enjoyed ill health – and she had suffered two early miscarriages. Although the miscarriages had confined Grace to bed for a month at a time and left her severely depressed, they had come as a relief to Andrew, who was finding even three children a distraction from his work. And he did not relish the cost of having to move home again.

But Andrew's summer sortie to Morecambe seems to have rekindled his ardour for Grace, who discovered shortly before Christmas that she was pregnant again. Grace took to her bed for fear of losing another child, while Andrew – furious with his wife as well as with himself – went house-hunting for a larger property. On 28 June 1897 Catherine ('Kate') Hume was born in their new apartment in a long line of terraced houses in Whitesands, overlooking the River Nith. She cried a lot, but not as much or as often, as her father would later unkindly relate, as she sobbed as a teenager.

With four females in the house competing for his attention, Andrew started to bond with the only other male in the house, his son Jock, who was now seven. Nellie, Andrew had decided, was tone deaf. Grace had briefly showed some interest in music but had withdrawn after being smacked hard over the fingers by her father for hitting a wrong key when practising her scales on the piano. But Jock had inherited his father's natural gift for music and was now playing both the piano and the violin. When Andrew wasn't away from home, he gave his son an hour's tuition every day and made him rehearse for an hour on his own before bedtime at 7 p.m.

In spite of the extra space that Whitesands afforded, Andrew hated living there from the moment they moved in and he blamed Grace, even though he had chosen it himself. The pleasant view of the River Nith did not compensate for the damage caused by flooding every time the Nith burst its banks, which it did twice in the first year, entering the house and coming halfway up the stairs. Andrew wished he had paid more attention to the river when considering the property. Nor, when he had walked round the house before signing the lease, had Andrew noticed that his bedroom window overlooked the very place where he had been arrested for poaching. The memory of it still rankled. And, when the wind blew in a certain direction, there was an unpleasant, sickly smell from the half dozen tanneries that were established by the river. But most of all, Andrew felt the street was not appropriate for a person in his position.

The wide open space between the row of terraced houses and the river had made Whitesands a natural place for public gatherings, including the annual Rood Fair. Although the fair took place only once a year, there were many other occasions when the entire population of Dumfries seemed to be camping on Andrew Hume's doorstep. There were livestock sales most months, for instance. Andrew particularly hated these, as the smell of dung and the early-morning mooing of cattle and bleating of sheep reminded him of his childhood on the farm in Lochfoot, a period in his life he preferred to forget. From time to time gypsies would turn up en masse in their caravans to sell ponies, sometimes staying for days at a time. The general disruption of these events, not to mention the constant cackling of geese and the clatter of horses' shoes, made it an unsuitable location for a teacher of music.

One of the original attractions of Whitesands for Andrew had been the proximity of the Coach and Horses, a hostelry much favoured by Burns, giving it a literary reputation. But it had taken a turn for the worse since Burns was last there and was now better known as the haunt of the notorious prostitute Margaret Hog and a magnet for drunks whenever there was a gathering. Sometimes they, too, would spill out of the Coach and Horses on to Andrew's doorstep, shouting profanities up at the window.

Unfortunately, Andrew had committed to a long lease on the house in Whitesands and it was three years before they were able to move back to Nith Place, an altogether much more attractive street at that time, this time to a first-floor apartment at number 9, sandwiched between a butcher's shop and a children's outfitters. It was here that the Hume's fifth and last child, Andrew, was born on 4 November 1901.

Andrew senior would say later that Grace took to her bed for the birth of their son Andrew and seldom got out of it again until her death four and a half years later. He attributed her retreat from family life to 'nerves' and 'women's troubles' and continued with his life as if she no longer existed, employing a nurse to attend to Grace and a nanny to take care of the children so that he was free to accept musical engagements.

Andrew's musical reputation continued to grow. In 1902 he organised an orchestra to play in Dock Park. The *Dumfries & Galloway Standard* reported:

> On Wednesday evening the orchestra organised by Mr Hume, Nith Place, made its first appearance on the bandstand when they submitted a program of high-class music. There was a large attendance of the general public and the efforts of the orchestra were much appreciated . . .
>
> One evening each week will be devoted to getting up a first-class repertoire of music. Additional string players will be heartily welcomed and will receive music to practice at home. The intention is to give a concert during the winter season in aid of local charities.

Meanwhile, Grace's health was deteriorating. Her 'nerves' were almost certainly post-natal depression and her physical weakness would have been the early onset of the disease that killed her after stealing her gentle voice: cancer of the oesophagus. The children spent the next four years watching their mother grow weaker while Andrew, as always, pursued other interests. He was thirty-seven years old, a successful musician, attractive to the opposite sex and married to a woman who was in no position to ask awkward questions. Not for the first time he began to see his five children – the youngest, Andrew, a baby, the oldest, Nellie, a girl of thirteen – as a serious encumbrance to his ambitions. Not for the first time, either, did he start looking around for a woman who could fill the gap left in his life by the ailing Grace.

The solution to both problems came in the convenient form of Alice Mary Alston, a good-looking thirty-seven-year-old woman who ran the ladies and children's outfitters next door – a shop where Grace had always bought the children's clothes – and was therefore known to all the family. Alice, who had never been married and had no children, was the daughter of a wool spinner from Peebles, Thomas Alston. The family had moved to Troqueer, Dumfries, soon after Alice was born.

Alice, feeling sorry for the good-looking musician, offered to look after the children if Andrew ever needed help. Conveniently, she lived a few hundred yards away in Castle Street. It wasn't long before the children were invited to address Alice as 'Aunt Alice', instead of 'Miss Alston'. 'This is so kind of you, Alice,' Grace Hume used to whisper before the cancer took away her voice.

Responsibilities had been piled on Nellie, the oldest of the Hume children, since her younger brother's birth. For almost two years she had been an unpaid nanny to the child whom, surprisingly, she nevertheless liked. Now, aged fourteen, she was an unpaid nurse to her dying mother and unwilling witness to her father's courtship of Alice. She might have borne this with more fortitude had she not been treated like a child by her father, whose criticism and disapproval of her appearance and thoughts were crushing her self-confidence while igniting a desperate desire for freedom. Along with all the children, Nellie was required to be in bed by 7 p.m. and up at 6 a.m. to help with household chores. She was not allowed to bring friends home, nor was she was allowed to see them outside school hours, even during the holidays.

Throughout the children's lives their father had resorted to the belt to punish disobedience or misbehaviour; the belt had been his own father's way of maintaining order and discipline, he told them by way of self-justification. As Nellie reached puberty he seemed to look for opportunities to beat her, she would later say; sometimes these punishments would be administered with a riding crop.

Eventually, Nellie left home and found work as a domestic servant in a local hotel. It was lonely and humiliating but preferable to remaining at home. What hurt her most was that neither her mother nor her father tried to stop her. 'It's probably for the best,' was all her mother said, realising that she was in no position to protect her eldest daughter any longer. 'It's time you earned your own keep, lassie,' said her father. But the 'secret society' – the bond between the older four Hume children, Nellie, Jock, Grace and Kate – held them all together for the time being and a year later, when Nellie went to work in the glove factory, she became friends with Mary Costin whom she introduced to Jock.

For all Andrew Hume's aspirations and pretensions to be a man of culture, his attitude to his children and their education remained that of a working-class Victorian father, frozen in a time when the poor were forced by necessity to get their children out to work as early as possible to start contributing to the family. It was not the norm then for children at St Michael's, Dumfries, to cease full-time education at thirteen: parents were encouraged to leave their children in school until at least fifteen. But, like his sisters, Jock left school aged thirteen, finding a temporary job in a solicitor's office while still living at home, where he continued to receive intensive music lessons from his father who saw his gift for music as a stream of income in the future. There were few constraints on Jock's movements, unlike the curfew imposed on his sisters, and he used his violin to temporarily escape the tense atmosphere at home and earn a few pennies playing in inns and at celebrations in Dumfries, with the occasional appearance at the Theatre Royal.

Grace Hume died on 4 May 1906, Helen Hume, Andrew's mother, succumbing to pneumonia a few months later, soon after Christmas. It must have been difficult for the five Hume children to lose their mother and their grandmother so close together. But it would seem it was not so difficult for their father to lose his wife and mother. Just when Andrew Hume and Alice Alston consummated their affair we will never know, but by the time Grace died Alice had left her parents' home and was living next door in Nith Place. On 19 July 1907, fourteen months after Grace's death, Andrew and Alice married. They were both aged forty-three. A few months later they moved into a substantial sandstone town house at 42 George Street on the corner of Castle Street where, Andrew said, the family 'could make a new start'.

Except they wouldn't. Nellie had already fled the nest; Jock was spending more and more time away from home playing on board passenger ships; and Grace, aged fifteen, was making her own plans to move out, having had a series of blazing rows with her stepmother. That left only the two youngest, Kate and Andrew, at home with their father and new stepmother.

Alice was quick to make her own rules in George Street. This was now her territory, not their mother's. The children, she said, had 'lacked discipline' during their mother's long illness and were out of control. In future they would be in bed by 8 p.m. every night, regardless of age, having spent an hour practising the piano or violin. Rudeness and misbehaviour would be brought to their father's attention, to be punished in the usual way.

From the moment the Humes moved in, 42 George Street was not the happy family home that Andrew Hume had hoped it would be.

14

John Jacob Astor VI

14 August, New York

O n the evening of Tuesday 13 August 1912, newspaper reporters and photographers started to gather outside number 840 Fifth Avenue, New York, better known to their readers as 'the Astor home'. Door-stepping the Astor home was a long-established tradition among New York pressmen and it reaped rich rewards – the comings and goings of the wealthy, the powerful and the beautiful invariably producing a story or a photograph worthy of the front page.

The last time the press had been there in force had been in May, when the body of Colonel J. J. Astor was brought home from Halifax. Hundreds of column inches had been filled by reporters who came no nearer to the family than the sidewalk yet managed to convey to their readers the tragedy that was unfolding in the house. Tonight was a more joyous occasion, but no less competitive: the press had been tipped off that the birth of Astor's posthumous child was 'imminent'. The huge public interest in the event spawned a wholly new press institution, which continues to this day, known as 'the birth watch'. I experienced it myself when editing the *Daily Express* when Diana, Princess of Wales, went into labour. We produced two front pages in advance of an announcement from Buckingham Palace: one saying, 'It's a Boy', the other saying, 'It's a Girl'. We were first off the press with the boy.

The reporters' and photographers' vigil outside the Astor residence continued throughout the night, their patience sustained by hot coffee, hip flasks and the occasional appearance of an Astor servant telling them that it would not be long now, a dollar bill being discreetly exchanged for the information.

By mid morning on Wednesday 14 August, their stake-out was rewarded. The Astor butler 'wearing a broad smile' came to the door and read out a statement issued by Dr Edwin B. Cragin, the physician attending Madeleine Astor. It said: 'Mrs Astor has a son, born at 8.15 o'clock. His name is John Jacob Astor. Mother and son are in good condition.' An hour later Dr Cragin issued another bulletin in which he said: 'The baby weighed seven and three-quarters pounds. There was no other doctor present. The nurses present were Helen Nesbit and Miss McLean.' It was one hundred and twenty-one days since Madeleine had said goodbye to her husband on the deck of the *Titanic* before being helped into lifeboat number 4 by her husband and Colonel Gracie.

Throughout the day more news was passed on to the world's press from the Astor home. The baby was said to be 'strong, well formed and bearing a striking resemblance to his father'. Madeleine's mother and sister had been with her, her father visiting the house shortly after the birth. Servants who had been with the Astor family for years were allowed 'to have a peep' at the baby. The *New York Times* reported next day:

It was said last night at the house that Mrs Astor
and her son were doing splendidly. She has
received many messages of congratulation from
her friends and relatives, among them being a
cablegram from Vincent Astor, who is at present
with his mother, Mrs Ava Willing Astor, on a motor
trip on the European Continent. Shortly after the
receipt of the cablegram an immense box of American Beauty roses came to Mrs Astor from a Fifth
Avenue florist, bearing the name of Vincent Astor.

The huge public interest in the birth of the baby was exceeded
only by fascination and speculation over the provision made
for the child under Colonel Astor's will. Lawyers acting for
the family had let it be known that under the terms of his
will Madeleine would be the beneficiary of a $5 million trust
fund until her death or remarriage. But a clause forbidding a
young widow to remarry on penalty of losing a bequest was
regarded by many lawyers to be unfair and might be
construed as against public policy.

The baby would be made the beneficiary of another trust
fund of $3m 'until attaining majority' – i.e., until the child
was twenty-one. This was the smallest provision made for
anyone in Astor's will. However, trustees and family friends
had made it clear that the trust would probably increase in
value to at least $10m over the period and could even be
worth two or three times this amount. The *New York Times*
was quick to point out that:

The birth of the Astor baby, contrary to some
speculation, is of no financial advantage to its

mother. The will of Col. Astor provides that in the event of a posthumous child dying without issue, its trust fund will revert to the residuary estate, which was willed to William Vincent Astor.

A further complication vexing legal minds was the requirement to appoint guardians to protect beneficiaries who were 'infants'. At the time of Astor's death neither Madeleine, nor his son Vincent, nor his daughter Muriel had 'attained majority' – they were all under the age of twenty-one. The baby thus became the fourth Astor infant in the eyes of the law.

Colonel J. J. Astor could not have made more generous arrangements to provide for the members of his family. But the money would bring them little happiness and, like so many others, Madeleine and her firstborn would live the rest of their lives in the shadow of the *Titanic*.

15

Jock's Worldly Goods

22 August, Dumfries

Some time in June 1912, an album of photographs of the unidentified bodies, taken by George Gauvin in the mortuary at the Mayflower Curling Rink, was sent from Halifax to the White Star Line's offices in Southampton. They included a picture of Jock, photographed on the mortician's table, labelled simply '193'. The content of the album was the stuff of horror films and, to spare the feelings of relatives, it was decided that friends and colleagues of the dead would be asked first if they could positively identify anyone in the ghoulish collection before families were approached. Number 193 was immediately recognised as Jock, who was well known in the White Star Line offices in Canute Road, Southampton. The sight of his pale, lifeless face, a curl of blond hair seemingly falling over his forehead, greatly distressed an officer who had got to know him on the maiden voyage of the *Olympic*.

The positive identification came as no surprise to Andrew Hume, who had identified his son – to his own satisfaction, at least – a month earlier. The White Star Line had written to him setting out their 'belief' that body number 193 was that of Jock Law Hume. Although they had guessed his age wrongly at twenty-eight instead of twenty-one, the description of the body noted by the purser on the deck of the *Mackay-Bennett*, the bandsman's tunic, the inventory of the paltry contents of the young man's pockets . . . all these confirmed to Andrew Hume that this was his son. The violin mute removed any last vestige of uncertainty. Hume wired the White Star Line asking for Jock's effects to be returned to the family as soon as possible but was told this would have to await 'official' confirmation of ownership.

On 16 July Harold Wingate, the White Star Line official in New York responsible for administering the affairs of their late passengers, wrote to Frederick Mathers, the Deputy Provincial Secretary in Halifax.

```
Dear Sir:-
No. 193, Unidentified
Our Southampton Office has advised us
that they have been able to identify No.
193 as John Law Hume, a bandsman of the
"Titanic", from the photograph. We
expected this body to be identified, as
the uniform and effects indicated that
it was that of one of the bandsmen.

The parents of Mr Hume have asked for
the effects, which are of trifling value,
and we hope that you may see your way to
let us have them, which we will greatly
appreciate.
```

WHITE STAR LINE

50 JAMES STREET
LIVERPOOL

CANUTE ROAD
SOUTHAMPTON

1 COCKSPUR ST., S. W.
38 LEADENHALL ST., E. C.
LONDON

9 BROADWAY

TELEGRAPHIC ADDRESS
"ISMAY"

DEPARTMENT

NEW YORK, July 16, 1912.

RECEIVED
JUL 23 1912
Provincial Secretary's
Office.

N. B.—PASSAGES ARE ONLY BOOKED SUBJECT TO ALL THE TERMS
AND CONDITIONS APPEARING ON THE PASSAGE TICKETS.

Fredk. F. Mathers, Esq.,

Deputy Provincial Secretary,

Halifax, Nova Scotia.

Dear Sir:-

No. 193, Unidentified.

Our Southampton Office has advised us that they have been able to identify
No. 193 as John Law Hume, a bandsman of the "Titanic", from the photograph. We
expected this body to be identified, as the uniform and effects indicated that
it was that of one of the bandsmen.

The parents of Mr. Hume have asked for the effects, which are of trifling
value, and we hope that you may see your way to let us have them, which we will
greatly appreciate.

Yours very truly,

For the White Star Line,

TRAVELERS CHECKS ISSUED AVAILABLE ALL OVER THE WORLD

154

Somewhat insensitively, the letter was written on White Star Line writing paper, which had been overprinted with a bleached-out photograph of the *Titanic* steaming ahead, plus a legal caveat: 'N.B. Passages are only booked subject to all the terms and conditions appearing on the passage tickets'.

On 31 July Mathers wrote back to Wingate saying that Jock's possessions were being sent by courier to Wingate in New York for forwarding to the family. 'For expressage purposes,' wrote Mathers, 'I have valued the package at $5.00.' Wingate was required to sign on receipt. The inventory of property was listed as follows:

```
Silver watch
Leather cigarette case
Leather case
Leather pocket marked 'W'
3 half pennies and American cent in
leather bag
Brass button, African Royal Mail
Four studs
Pocket knife
Two lead pencils
Mute
```

On 9 August, Wingate (still using the *Titanic* writing paper) wrote back to Mathers confirming receipt and informing him that the package was being sent to Southampton on the White Star liner, *Oceanic*. Thirteen days later, on 22 August, the package was delivered to the Humes' house at 42 George Street. Andrew Hume was out, giving a music lesson at Dumfries Academy, so Jock's stepmother Alice

PROVINCIAL SECRETARY
NOVA SCOTIA

Inventory of property found on the body alleged to
be that of the late John Law Hume, Number 193.

::::::::::

✓ Silver watch
✓ Leather cigarette case
✓ Leather case
✓ Leather pocket marked "W"
✓ 3 half pennies and American cent in leather bag
✓ Brass button, African Royal Mail
✓ Four studs
✓ Pocket knife
✓ Two lead pencils
✓ Mute

Received from the Provincial Secretary for Nova Scotia
by the White Star Line the above mentioned property which was
taken from the body alleged to be that of the late John Law Hume,
who lost his life in the wreck of the S. S. "Titanic", the same
being all the property of the said John Law Hume that came into
the hands of the Provincial Secretary and for which he is to
account, and which the White Star Line is to deliver to the
person or persons entitled to the custody or possession thereof.

For the White Star Line.

Harold Wingate

signed for it in ink, her signature witnessed by her friend Annie Kellochan, who lived round the corner and was paying her a brief visit. The White Star Line lawyers were taking no chances. By signing the receipt, Alice and Annie were agreeing 'to indemnify and save harmless the White Star Line against the claim of any person on account of the said effects'.

When Alice opened the cardboard box, she had expected to find an envelope containing the few paltry possessions that had been recovered from Jock's pocket. Instead, she found herself holding one of the small 'mortuary bags' stitched hurriedly together on the deck of the *Mackay-Bennett*, this one with the number 193 stencilled on it. It looked like something that had come from a prison or an army store.

When Andrew arrived home shortly before 6 p.m., mortuary bag number 193 was still lying unopened where Alice had put it, on the mahogany table in the drawing room. Andrew cut it open with his pocket knife and tipped out the contents, which spilled across the polished surface.

Jock's pocket watch was rusted beyond repair or restoration, the face washed away, its blackened hands, dislodged from their axis by ten days in the sea, lying askew, just visible through the clouded glass. His leather cigarette case looked like a discarded piece of old cardboard, warped and torn, the pocket knife was corroded, the stubby pencils probably past their useful life even before the ship went down. The wooden violin mute – he would keep that. A nice thing to have, always useful. No point in throwing away the three half pennies, either. He slipped them into his pocket, along with the mute. The African Royal Mail brass button puzzled Andrew as it rolled in the palm of his hand. Where had it

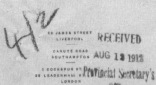

WHITE STAR LINE

9 BROADWAY

RECEIVED
AUG 12 1912
Provincial Secretary's
Office

50 JAMES STREET
LIVERPOOL
CANUTE ROAD
SOUTHAMPTON
1 COCKSPUR ST.
38 LEADENHALL ST.
LONDON

TELEGRAPHIC ADDRESS
"ISMAY"

DEPARTMENT

NEW YORK,   August 9, 1912.

Fred. F. Mathers, Esquire,

    Deputy Provincial Secretary,   "TITANIC."

        Halifax,   Nova Scotia.

N. B.—PASSAGES ARE ONLY BOOKED SUBJECT TO ALL THE TERMS
AND CONDITIONS APPEARING ON THE PASSAGE TICKETS.

Dear Sir:-

        #193, John Law Hume.

We have your favor of July 31, and have to advise that the package of
effects from this passenger arrived in due course, and we are forwarding
them to Southampton by the "Oceanic."

    We thank you for your courtesy in the matter.

        Yours very truly,

          For White Star Line,

           Harold Wingate

TRAVELERS CHECKS ISSUED AVAILABLE ALL OVER THE WORLD

come from? From one of Jock's ships, one of his trips, no doubt. But which one? And why had he kept it? And why only one?

I asked the same questions myself last year and bought one, for £1, from a collector on eBay. It is an important-looking brass button. It has a roped rim inside which run the embossed letters AFRICAN ROYAL MAIL. At the centre is a flag of St George fluttering from a flagpole, a crown at its centre. It invited further inquiry. The African Royal Mail line was owned by Elder, Dempster & Co, running steamships, including the *Scot Union* and the *Calabar*, from Liverpool to the Cameroons via Madeira. There was a weekly service, every Friday, from Southampton to the Cape, also via Madeira. Elder, Dempster & Co also owned the *Port Royal*, on which Jock had sailed to Jamaica. And then, another coincidence: Charles Lightoller, second officer on the *Titanic* (who survived) worked for the African Royal Mail in West Africa for three years. Was the West Africa run another of Jock's 'regulars'? Did Jock and Lightoller know each other from way back?

The following year, through solicitors, Mary asked Andrew Hume if she could have something 'personal' of Jock's to remember him by. She was told there was nothing – and, anyway, she had his child.

16

The Missing Violins

10 September, New York

Andrew Hume had felt humiliated by the bill he had received from C. W. and F. N. Black for Jock's uniform; now the White Star Line had insulted him with their dismissal of Jock's possessions as 'of trifling value'. A further aggravation was the legal advice he had received regarding a claim that was being proposed by some of the other musicians' families against the White Star Line. They were told that a claim against the shipping company was unlikely to succeed because the members of the band were not crew who were accorded some protection under the Workmen's Compensation Act (1906) – they were employed by the Liverpool agency, Blacks. And Blacks could not be legally held to account for an accident at sea.

Meanwhile, stories had begun to appear in newspapers about claims being made against the White Star Line for loss of life and property, further inflaming Hume's sense of injustice. It had been reported that one First Class passenger who survived, American socialite Charlotte Cardeza, was claiming $177,352 for fourteen trunks, forty-three bags, a jewel case and a packing case. Another passenger, Hakan Bjornstrom-Steffanson, son of a Swedish pulp millionaire, had filed a claim for $100,000 for a painting by Blondel, which had gone down with the ship.

These reports undoubtedly sowed the seeds of an idea for a compensation claim against the White Star Line, which Andrew Hume would spend many months pursuing. As insurance frauds go it was as daring as it was imaginative and its success depended on Andrew's expertise in the one subject he knew about: the value of violins.

Erlbach, where the four corners of Turingia, Bavaria, Bohemia and Saxony meet, is known as 'the green heart of Europe'. Here, high in the Alpine forests, grow the best quality maple and spruce that produce the richness of tones that distinguish a great violin from an ordinary instrument; in the valleys below are the workshops of some of the Germany's finest violin makers. It was here that Andrew said he mastered the craft of violin making in his teens. And it was here that he came later, or so he claimed, to purchase supplies of wood, glue and varnish with which to make violins. He almost certainly bought violins 'in the white' – unvarnished and sometimes unassembled instruments, but cut to perfect templates by the master crafts-men of Bohemia. Many violin makers took this short cut, signing the finished product with their own initials.

Hume laid so many false trails about his past that it is difficult to know which one to follow. Quite clearly he acquired during his teens some knowledge of violin making and saw an opportunity for producing or selling quality violins. In Dumfries High Street Mr Hannary was selling violins for less than £1 whereas Andrew Hume knew that wealthy men paid hundreds of pounds for a beautiful instrument. Whether or not forgery was in his mind at this time we cannot know but Hume certainly developed skills which would serve him well later in passing off instruments that weren't always what they seemed, including many that bore his own initials. He studied the designs of Stradivarius, Guarnerius (Paganini's favoured violin), Guadagnini, Amati and Maggini, advancing in letters to the trade press his theories that a smaller instrument frequently had a clearer and more responsive tone than one of larger dimensions. He championed the idea that modern violins could capture the full, soft tone of old violins provided the right varnish and glues were used. He proudly showed his students his stock of seasoned wood acquired during visits to Bohemia.

Around this time, Andrew became a regular correspondent on the letters page of *The Strad*, the respected publication of the violin trade and music profession, writing knowledgeably and at great length about techniques, glues and varnish. His favourite theme was the profession's prejudice against new instruments versus the old, such as those made by the great Italian masters including Antonio Stradivari. 'I beg to differ from the assertion that the art of producing tone equal to the old Italian violins is a lost art,' he wrote.

Hume started to use the letters page ruthlessly to promote his own instruments, which he would later advertise for sale in *The Strad*. But his unerring tendency to be economical with the truth soon got him into trouble with the distinguished violinist and composer John Dunn, author of the definitive *Manual on Violin Playing*. In the February 1910 issue of *The Strad* Andrew Hume wrote:

I recently submitted to Mr John Dunn two violins made of the finest wood procurable . . . his opinion is, 'both your violins are exceedingly fine . . . as compared with my Strad, if there is any difference it could certainly only be detected by an acute and very highly trained ear.'

In the following issue of *The Strad* Mr Dunn took Hume to task for misrepresenting his remarks and quoting him without his permission: 'There was a difference, as compared with the tone of an old violin like my Strad; in the matter of richness and penetrating powers . . . Mr Hume's violins are lacking,' wrote Dunn.

Andrew batted back a reply, with the briefest of apologies, before moving swiftly on to contradict Dunn and praise his own violins again. Hume's letter, published in *The Strad* the following month, reminds one of his defence when caught poaching salmon in the Nith:

I much regret having used Mr Dunn's name and have written him a personal note of apology . . . but I must take exception to one of his sentences: in the matter of richness and penetrating power (of my violins) I have the most incontestable proof that the reverse of this is the case.

He continues his letter with what was to become a familiar whine of indignant self-justification: 'I have been a professional player and teacher for 21 years and the construction of violins and the making of oil varnish has been my pet hobby and occupation . . . not from any pecuniary benefit that might accrue.' Far from having any pecuniary motives, Andrew Hume was already selling violins professionally and, within a year, would be using *The Strad*'s advertisement pages as the shop window for 'his' instruments.

If the White Star Line placed no value on his son's life, Andrew Hume reasoned, perhaps they would be obliged to recognise the worth of his violin that was now a piece of flotsam somewhere out there in the North Atlantic. What if he exaggerated the value of the violin that Jock had taken with him on the ship? There was no one alive who knew that Jock's violin was an instrument that he himself had made. Everything had gone down with the *Titanic*, so there would be no risk of him being caught out on the lie. But how big a lie could it be? A violin by Antonio Stradivari? No, that would be pushing his luck: there were too few of them in existence and they were too valuable. Also, it was unlikely that a twenty-one-year-old bandsman on a ship, however fine a violinist, would have a Strad. How could he have afforded it? Receipts and valuations would be called for. Better to claim for something almost as valuable but less well known. A second-division violin would be a safer bet. One by Nicolo Amati, perhaps? No, too ambitious. And also too expensive. Andrew now cast his mind back to a week he spent in Milan in his late teens when he had held – briefly – a violin by the great eighteenth-century Italian violin maker Giovanni Battista Guadagnini. Yes, a better choice. A Guadagnini could go to the bottom of the ocean and no one would be any the wiser. Andrew had friends whom he could trust to produce some ambiguous documentation. So many members of the family had made them over successive generations and Guadagnini violins always held their value

– £200 would be a modest price to put on the claim for compensation.

Andrew Hume thought about this some more. Who was to say that Jock didn't take with him on the *Titanic* not one but *two* violins? Must not be too greedy. Best not to claim for two Guadagninis. What about Guadagnini's contemporary rival in Naples, Thomaso Eberle? A fine instrument, also expensive, but not in the same class. Worth, say, £125 and even less trouble to obtain receipts and valuations. He would say that he, Andrew, had borrowed them and that Jock had taken them with him on the *Titanic* to choose one as a 'life instrument'. Life instrument had an authentic ring to it, Andrew thought, especially in the hands of a man who would be taking it to his death. It wouldn't bring Jock back but it would go a long way to righting a wrong.

Having made his choices of violin, Andrew Hume hand-wrote a letter to the White Star Line setting out his claim for £625: £325 for the violins, and £300 for the loss of his son's life. Unfortunately no record of this correspondence has survived, the White Star Line destroying most of its files at the time of its merger with Cunard in 1934. But a subsequent letter from Hume, setting out the substance of his claim, has survived in the U.S. National Archives. It is clear from this that Hume's demands for compensation were turned down by the White Star Line and that appeals to its chairman, Bruce Ismay, now safely back in his office in Liverpool, also brought no satisfaction.

In January 1913 Hume turned to the United States to pursue his insurance claim, writing to Alexander Gilchrist Jr., a clerk of the New York District Court who had been appointed special commissioner to deal with claims for compensation resulting from the loss of the SS *Titanic*. The letter is handwritten.

Dear Sir,

I note from a copy of the *Evening World* of January 16th sent by Mr R. Paul, 215 East 122nd Street N.Y. that claims for loss should be presented to you. Herewith I beg to present a claim for $2500 on account of the loss of my Son and two fine violins that he had with him on approval one by G. B. Guadagnini £200 and one by Thomaso Eberle £125.

He was but 21 years of age and had these items on the voyage with him for the purpose of choosing one of them as a life instrument, neither of them was insured unfortunately, and though the Contractors have been sued in the Liverpool Courts for compensation no redress has been obtained. The Mansion House fund have paid £92 declining at the same time any liability, while a personal note to Bruce Ismay of the White Star Line has also failed to obtain any satisfaction.

My Son Jock Law Hume would at this time have been permanently resident here with us and would have been worth at least £100 per annum to us, with this object in view this property was bought 4 years ago jointly by us for £500 on a £400 Bond at 4% £300 of which I am now quite hopelessly faced with alone and as I am now 50 years of age it is most unlikely that I can hope to clear it off without some assistance, the £92 paid being but a small portion. I'll be obliged if you will kindly file this claim and put it forward with the others against the White Star line. Faithfully Yours
A. Hume (Father)

As insurance frauds go, Andrew Hume's claim that Jock took with him on the *Titanic* two fine Italian violins invites disbelief as well as admiration for its audacity. Did Andrew Hume seriously think that anyone would believe that a twenty-one-year-old violin player earning £4 a month would have been given not one but two expensive violins to take with him on the voyage? In November 2006, 'a violin by Giovanni Battista Guadagnini, Milan, 1753' was auctioned in London by Bromptons. The estimate was £150,000 to £200,000; the price realised was £317,250. Eberle violins are similarly prized now, as then, and they would both have been well outside Andrew Hume's price range.

Andrew's regular championing of modern violins on the pages of *The Strad* also makes his claim highly suspicious. Jock is far more likely to have gone to sea with one of his father's violins made 'from the white' and initialled A. H., for by 1912 Hume was trying to make a name for himself as a maker of violins.

But lastly, father and son were hardly speaking, if at all, by the time Jock left Dumfries for Liverpool and Southampton. Jock had been living with Mary Costin for the best part of a year and was planning to marry her against her father's wishes.

The White Star Line declined to pay Andrew Hume one penny, either for the violins or for his son. Commissioner Gilchrist also dismissed his claim. But this did not deter Andrew Hume. He now had another target in his sights: Mary Costin.

EXTRACT OF AN ENTRY IN A REGISTER OF BIRTHS

kept under the Registration of Births, Deaths and Marriages (Scotland) Act 1965

No. (1)	Name and Surname (1)	When and Where Born (2)	Sex (3)	Name, Surname, and Rank or Profession of Father Name, and Maiden Surname of Mother Date and Place of Marriage (4)	Signature and Qualification of Informant, and Residence, if out of the House in which the Birth occurred (5)	When and Where Registered and Signature of Registrar (6)
	Johnann	1912	F		*(Signed)*	1912
	Law	October			M.C. Costin	Novr. 7th
	Hume	eighteenth		Mary Catherine Costin	Mother	At Dumfries
335	COSTIN	11h, A.M.		Glovemaker		*(Signed)*
		35 Buccleuch Street				Sam; Brown.
		Dumfries				Registrar

EXTRACTED from the Register of Births for the .... District .... of ...... Dumfries ....

in the .... County .... of .... Dumfries ....

Given at the General Register Office, New Register House, Edinburgh,

under the Seal of the said Office, this .... 13th .... day of .... September .... 19 ..76.

17

Johnann Law Hume Costin

18 October, Dumfries

My mother, Johnann Law Hume Costin, was born at 11 a.m. on Friday 18 October 1912 at the Costin family home at 35 Buccleuch Street, Dumfries. By all accounts it was a much more straightforward affair than the birth of John Jacob Astor VI at 840 Fifth Avenue, New York, two months earlier. The midwife who helped bring my mother into the world scrubbed up as soon as she was sure that Mary and the baby were all right and left with the customary 15 shillings, which her mother, Susan Costin, gave her on the way out.

Despite the distress and anxiety that Mary had suffered, she was apparently thrilled with the baby, although there was a heated discussion about names. According to my mother, there had been no prior discussion about what the baby would be called. Mary had got it into her head that she was going to have a boy and had determined to call him John Law Hume Costin, the name intended more as a message to the Humes than to the rest of Dumfries, who knew and understood the nature of Jock and Mary's relationship.

The arrival of a girl demanded a rapid rethink. Susan suggested by way of a compromise that the baby should be called Susan Kennedy Law Hume Costin, Susan Kennedy being her own maiden name. But Mary would not be budged, there had to be a 'John' in it and 'Johnann' was the compromise that they agreed. As a girl's Christian name Johnann was not uncommon in Scotland in the nineteenth century, although it was probably a misspelling for Johanna. My mother would later discard it for 'Johanna' and, finally, for 'Jacqueline'.

Mary's mother, Susan Costin, had taken most of what life had thrown at her with dignity and decorum, and very distressing stuff some of it had been, too. In her thirties she had buried two young daughters and her husband. Now in her early fifties, Susan realised that this had been useful training for the assault course of the past year: nursing her dying son, William; losing a son-in-law whom she loved, for that is what Jock was to her; and comforting her grieving, pregnant and unmarried daughter, Mary.

After every one of life's catastrophes, Susan Costin had picked herself up, gathered the survivors of her brood under her warm wings and gone about the business of feeding and looking after them, even if it meant going hungry herself. She never blamed God when things went wrong but always thanked him on the rare occasions they went right. The birth of her new granddaughter, Johnann, was one such occasion and the source of great joy to her.

This might explain why Susan took it upon herself, rather than leaving it to Mary, to break the news to Andrew Hume that he had become a grandfather. She can hardly have expected a warm reception but she probably reasoned – quite wrongly, as things turned out – that the birth of the child might lead to some kind of recognition of what had taken place; an acceptance that things were what they were; some compassion and understanding for what Mary had gone through, too; and something they could build on, for the sake of the child and to honour Jock's memory.

She didn't expect to be told that her daughter was a whore and to have the door slammed in her face.

Susan Costin was not a woman given to displays of emotion. Brought up towards the end of Queen Victoria's reign, she understood the power of the understated: the munificent gaze into the distance to signify amusement, a quizzical knitting of the brow to indicate disapproval. Her children – and her late husband, William – would often gaze anxiously at this strong face to see which way the wind was blowing or to gauge the temperature of the moment.

Susan was a woman who drew strength from adversity, who had a very clear sense of what was right and what was wrong. She had given Andrew Hume the benefit of the doubt for two years but his lack of kindness and respect had made up her mind. Without saying another word to him, she walked down the Yorkstone steps of 42 George Street and carried on walking over the bridge to Maxwelltown until she reached the offices of her employers, Messrs Walker & Sharpe, Writers to the Signet.

18

A Name and a Headstone for Jock

November 1912, Halifax, Nova Scotia

As soon as the White Star Line knew how many bodies had been recovered by the *Mackay-Bennett,* the company purchased a 3,600 sq ft area in Fairview Lawn Cemetery from Halifax council for $846 and engaged a surveyor, F. W. Christie, to design a layout for the 121 plots. Land was also purchased to bury the nineteen *Titanic* Catholic dead in nearby Mount Olivet Cemetery, and in Baron de Hirsch Cemetery where the ten Jewish victims were to be interred.

At Fairview, Christie determined that there should be four rows of graves on a curve which, whether intentional or not, resembles the bow of a ship with a gash down its side. The large number of unidentified victims presented a problem requiring an expedient solution, as the bodies were quickly decomposing. A long trench was cut which would accommodate thirty-seven coffins a few feet apart. It is in this row that my grandfather Jock Hume was buried, a few yards away from the 'unknown child', the youngest recovered victim of the disaster.

The logistics of sourcing the stone and then producing nearly 150 granite headstones in a short space of time was another problem that had to be overcome. The contract for this work was given by the White Star Line to Frederick Bishop of Halifax Marble Works but the lettering was done by Frank Fitzgerald, who did it in such a way that a name could be added to the headstone of a numbered grave at any time in the future.

While Bishops set about this task, numbered wooden crosses served as headstones for the unidentified dead. It seems likely that my grandfather Jock was identified in time for his name to be included on his headstone before Fitzgerald commenced the lettering. By Christmas 1912 all the work was completed and the dead could at last rest in peace. The White Star Line paid for all the burials and set up a trust fund of $7,500 to care for the *Titanic* graves in all three cemeteries. This proved to be insufficient to maintain the areas and for decades there were arguments about grass cutting and tulip planting. In 1944 Halifax City Council assumed responsibility for Fairview Lawn Cemetery.

It is a beautiful and well-maintained cemetery and it is impossible not to be moved by it. People – not only relatives – come here from all over the world to pay their respects to the 121 brave men, women and children here who were betrayed by the arrogance and recklessness of the White Star Line.

I visited my grandfather's grave for the first time in the early nineties and went back there in 2010. Nearly a century on from the disaster, forty of the dead have still not been identified. To the left of Jock lies body number 257, who, according to the archives was a clean-shaven man, aged about thirty-eight, 5ft 7ins tall and weighing 185lbs with 'a very large forehead'. He was wearing a green striped shirt, a boiler suit with a double-breasted jacket on top. 'Possibly an engineer', says the report. To the right of Jock is number 179, 'possibly a fireman' with a small light moustache and weighing 190lbs. His age is estimated at 'about 26' but nothing was found on him to indicate his identity and no one has come forward to claim his body.

There are no flowers on these graves but a few yards to the right is a superior granite monolith marking the grave of the youngest child whose body was recovered, the two-year-old boy whose identity has been debated for a century. When I visited the cemetery in 2010 his grave was festooned with bouquets, teddy bears and a cuddly lamb, in the modern manner of expressing grief. Unlike all the others in the cemetery, the child was not wearing a lifejacket when he was found, having been held tightly in his mother's arms until the sea eventually parted them. The sight of the child floating face upwards 'brought tears to the eyes of hardy sailors' on the *Mackay-Bennett*.

Bruce Ismay's secretary William Harrison is buried here, as is Ismay's assistant Ernest Freeman, number 239. Ismay paid for 'something more substantial' to mark the men's graves, no doubt out of a sense of shame and guilt. Freeman's dedication says: 'He remained at his post of duty, seeking to save other, regardless of his own life and went down with the ship.' One wonders if Ismay, when dictating the words to his replacement secretary, realised the irony of the epitaph he had chosen for Freeman whose 'long and faithful service' was rewarded in this way.

19

Establishing Paternity

2 December, Dumfries Sheriff's Court

It really was extraordinarily bad luck for Andrew Hume that Mary Costin's mother worked for a firm of solicitors. Hume had wrongly assumed the Costins to be a dull-witted, down-at-heel family, lacking in initiative and resources. Mary Costin was an inconvenience and an annoyance but it never occurred to Andrew that she could be a threat to a man in his position. He knew vaguely that Mary worked in a mill where gloves were made – since Jock's death he had turned her occupation into yet another form of insult – but he had never bothered to ask what her mother did, as it was of no interest to him whatsoever.

Had Susan Costin worked for a firm of grain merchants it might all have ended differently. But Messrs Walker & Sharpe had a reputation for looking after their people and that included their caretaker and cleaner, Susan Costin. When Mr Hendrie, who had helped Mary with her application to the *Titanic* Relief Fund, discussed the case with the other partners, they were outraged on her behalf and agreed that the firm should act for Mary on a pro bono basis.

The priority was to make a successful application for paternity, without which the Relief Fund would not consider an award. The legal arguments would centre on the young couple's intentions, the nature of the relationship and Mary's character.

Mr Hendrie wasted no time taking witness statements and collecting relevant evidence, including letters written by Jock. The postcard of the *Titanic* that he sent from Southampton formed part of this evidence. The minister at Greyfriars Kirk confirmed that Jock and Mary worshipped there and had consulted him about their forthcoming marriage plans. Jock's sister Nellie confirmed that she had introduced them and confirmed her late brother's commitment to Mary. She did not tell her father that she had done this. Mary's employer at the mill provided a character reference and offered to give evidence in person if required. Mr Walker himself swore an affidavit saying he had known the family for more than ten years, vouching for their decency and honesty.

Mary spent hours going through Jock's letters trying to find pages that would support her case without causing embarrassment. But the evidence that would count most, Mr Hendrie impressed on Mary, would be her own and her mother's statements and performance in the witness box. He warned her that if Andrew Hume decided to oppose the application, in his capacity as Jock's executor, she would be expected to answer some offensive and challenging questions from the Humes' lawyer.

Speed was of the essence because of Mary's pressing need to provide evidence of paternity to the *Titanic* Relief Fund. Mr Hendrie was given an assurance by the clerk of the court that time would be made for a hearing within three weeks of the application being lodged. Herein lay a dilemma. Mr

Hendrie had discouraged Mary from registering Johnann's birth before the court case because, in cases where the father was dead and the mother unmarried, the registrar was required by law to leave the name of the father blank. Hendrie was hoping to spare Johnann the lifelong stigma of illegitimacy by registering the birth after legally establishing paternity. But he had failed to understand the correct procedure. The law required that Mary's application for paternity had to be accompanied by a birth certificate.

There was no way round the law. On 7 November 1912 Mary registered Johnann's birth, no name being entered on the register for the name of the father. Later that day, Mr Hendrie filed an application at Dumfries Sheriff's Court on behalf of Mary to establish paternity. At the same time, he served notice on Andrew Hume as Jock's executor. The following day Andrew Hume informed the court of his intention to oppose it.

The application for a decree of paternity was heard at Dumfries Sheriff's Court on 2 December 1912. Neither Andrew Hume nor his representatives appeared to contest the application. Neither the pre-trial statements nor the Sheriff's case notes were retained when the files were transferred from Dumfries to the National Archives of Scotland in Edinburgh fifty years ago, so no record of the hearing exists. But the decision of the court is recorded in the archive and the birth register held at the General Register Office for Scotland was amended accordingly at the time. It says:

In an action relating to the paternity of a female child named Johnann Law Hume Costin born at 35 Buccleuch Street, Dumfries on October 18th 1912, at the instance of

Mary Catherine Costin residing at No. 35 Buccleuch Street Dumfries against Andrew Hume, music teacher, Dumfries and others as representatives of the said deceased John Law Hume, the Sheriff Substitute of Dumfries and Galloway upon 2nd December 1912 found that the said child was the illegitimate child of the said Mary Catherine Costin and John Law Hume.

An embalmer prepares a body on the *Minia*, the ship's doctor in attendance.

Horse-drawn hearses meet the *Minia* on its return to Halifax. Photographers were banned from the dock – an officer on the *Minia* took this from the ship's bridge.

FUND FOR FAMILIES OF TITANIC BANDMEN

Relatives of Men Who Played as Ship Went Down Send Thanks to Musicians Here.

W. Theodore Brailey

John Law Hume

Mme. Joseph Regneas of 133 West 180th Street received yesterday the last of a series of letters from relatives of members of the steamship Titanic's band to whom Mme. Regneas sent a fund of $1,000 obtained through a concert which Mme. Regneas and several of her musical friends gave at Mme. Regneas's home in this city on April 27. With the money, the donors sent a message explaining that it was a tribute from musicians in this city to the memory of the men who kept on playing in an effort to calm the passengers on the Titanic as the great liner went down.

The letters received in acknowledgment of the fund expressed the deepest appreciation for the spirit which prompted sending it. Relatives of John Law Hume, known to his associates as "Happy Jock" Hume, and of W. T. Brailey, another of the Titanic's musicians, enclosed with their letters of thanks photographs of these two men, which are reproduced herewith.

Members of Mr. Hume's family have been manufacturers of musical instruments in Scotland for generations. He was educated for concert work but took a place in the Titanic's band for practice. The other members of the band in addition to Mr. Brailey and Mr. Hume were: W. Hattry, the bandmaster; P. C. Taylor, J. W. Woodward, R. Bricoux, James Clark, and George Krius.

The band's courage in playing on deck until the *Titanic* went down was seen in America as important in avoiding panic and thus saving lives. In a report on fundraising events for the band's dependents, the *New York Times* published this picture of 'Happy Jock' Hume (right), probably taken in Jamaica the year before.

A nation mourns: a requiem mass was held in Westminster Cathedral.

The White Star Line building in Liverpool, which was besieged by anxious relatives.

The nation was moved by the plight of the thousands of dependents of those who died – here, boy scouts hold a street collection.

Base of the obelisk in Dock Park, Dumfries in memory of Jock and his school friend Tom Mullin, who died with him on the ship.

The simple granite head stone in Fairview Lawn Cemetery, Halifax, marking Jock's grave, No. 193.

A marble plaque by the school entrance at St Michael's, Dumfries, records the memory of Jock and Tom.

Anti-German war propaganda which fuelled Kate's fantasies.

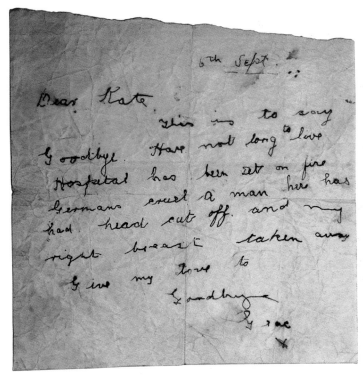

Grace Hume's dramatic 'last letter' describing her mutilation
by the Germans, forged by her sister Kate.

DUMFRIES HOAX CASE.

THE ACCUSED GIRL.

Lord Strathclyde, Scotland's leading Judge who presided over Kate's trial in Edinburgh.

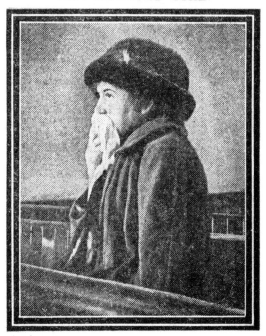

Kate, aged 18, in the dock at her trial.

Thomas Clouston, the psychiatrist who judged her to be sane

The notorious Victorian Calton Jail where Kate was held for two months.

Jock's daughter, 'Johnann' Costin
(the author's mother), aged two.

Vincent Astor, who travelled
from New York to Halifax in the
Astor's private train to bring his
father's body home.

Mary Costin's remarkable
mother, Susan Costin, pictured
here with her granddaughter,
'Johnann' whom she cared for
during the Great War.

Mary Costin with her daughter 'Johnann', the author's mother.

20

The Costins and Humes in Court

11 December, Dumfries

The decree of paternity, confirming that Jock Hume was indeed the father of her child, opened the way for Mary Costin to reapply for assistance from the *Titanic* Relief Fund, which she immediately did. That ought to have been the end of the matter.

Instead, it marked the beginning of a year-long bitter war of attrition between Mary Costin and Andrew Hume. The field of battle was Dumfries Sheriff's Court, directly opposite the Costins' home in Buccleuch Street. And although Mary Costin fired the first shot, it was Andrew Hume who provoked the hostilities by stealing money that had quite clearly been intended for Mary's child, his own granddaughter.

'The *Titanic* Fund Case', as the *Standard* called it, was an extraordinary legal battle. At the end of it all, reputations were ruined and lives broken. It divided the citizens of Dumfries – who followed the story avidly in the *Standard* – this bare-knuckle fight between my grandmother Mary, the unmarried mother, and Hume, the father of the dead bandsman hero.

By Christmas 1912 Mary was feeling relieved to have put

the whole paternity issue behind her. The court order establishing paternity had been forwarded to the *Titanic* Relief Fund by Mr Hendrie and Mary had signed a new application for 'relief'. The matter was now in the hands of the Honorary Secretary of the Liverpool *Titanic* Fund, Mr Percy Fullerton Corkhill, who was responsible for dealing with all applications for grants from Scotland, and from England north of Birmingham.

Mr Corkhill, who was also assistant solicitor to the Corporation of Liverpool as well as private secretary to the Lord Mayor of Liverpool, wrote to Mr Hendrie by return informing him that Mary's claim was 'receiving attention'. Indeed, it received instant attention, as did most things coming across the desk of Mr Corkhill, one of life's natural administrators. The Claims and General Purposes Sub-committee met next day, by which time 'Johnann' had already been allocated a beneficiary number C689 (the 'C' indicating 'crew'). The committee granted a benefit payment of 2s 6d a week (approximately £6 in today's terms) plus an immediate distribution of £67 out of funds for 'aliment' – essentially food, fuel and sustenance, equating to the quite substantial sum of £3,100 in today's terms. The necessary approvals were completed between Christmas and New Year.

So far so good. But unfortunately, instead of being sent to Mary, the cheque for £67 was sent to Andrew Hume by mistake. Hume promptly cashed the cheque at the National Bank of Scotland in Dumfries and pocketed the money, ignoring the accompanying letter from Mr Corkhill, which made it clear that it was a distribution for Mary Costin 'and her child'. Hume then had the audacity to write to Mr Corkhill, on 3 January 1913, acknowledging receipt of the cheque.

Corkhill took the acknowledgement to mean that the money had been passed on to Mary for the child. But it had not. It was around this time that Andrew Hume wrote to Commissioner Gilchrist pressing his false claim for the two violins.

By April, not having heard anything more from the *Titanic* Relief Fund, Mr Hendrie 'caused inquiries to be made' and discovered the administrative error. He wrote to Andrew Hume on 25 April asking him to forward the £67 to Mary Costin, the intended recipient. Hume denied receiving the money. Mr Corkhill also wrote to Hume, who again denied receiving the money despite having acknowledged receipt of the cheque. On 18 June Mr Corkhill wrote again to Hume saying, 'Please understand that the money was intended for the benefit of Miss Costin's child and not in any sense for your own benefit.'

Andrew Hume claimed never to have received this letter so Mr Corkhill wrote a fourth letter, sent by registered post on 23 July, asking for the £67 to be returned. The *Titanic* Relief Fund, he reminded Hume, had been 'raised by public subscription . . . for the aid and relief of the widows, orphans and dependent relatives of the persons who lost their lives by reason of the foundering in the Atlantic Ocean of the steamship *Titanic*'. The committee 'could not, and did not, regard Andrew Hume in any way dependent on the deceased.' Indeed, when the fund had been formally established in July the committee had minuted their decision that 'while each case would be dealt with on its merits and in a generous way, *the fund was not a medium for granting permanent compensation for the loss of future benefits from relatives*'.

Mr Corkhill's letter failed again to get a response, so Mary Costin issued a writ. The case was heard by Sheriff Campion in Dumfries on Friday 8 August, when the brief facts of the case were put forward. Andrew Hume's defence was that he had indeed received the £67 but he had assumed it was for himself and had kept it as he had been in contact with the fund on his own behalf. He then revealed that he had received individual sums of £25, £71 9s. 7d and £140 from the Mansion House and *Daily Telegraph* Funds and a donation for an unspecified amount from the Boston Musicians' *Titanic* Fund earlier in the year, before the child had been born. Mary Costin had not been aware of any of these handouts. The case was adjourned for a month so that the defence had time to prepare their case and so that Mr Corkhill could travel from Liverpool to give evidence.

When the court reconvened, Mr Hendrie informed Sheriff Campion that he had asked his senior partner Mr Bannerman to take over from him as Miss Costin's representative 'because I felt I was an important witness and therefore would not be able to do justice to Miss Costin as her agent'. In his evidence, he led the court through the trail of lies, contradictions and double somersaults that he had encountered in his dealings with Andrew Hume. Mr Bannerman called as witness Mr James Henderson, who said he had previously acted for Mr Hume as agent, or solicitor. Mr Hume had written to the administrators of the *Daily Telegraph Titanic* Fund saying that he had conclusive proof that his son was not the father of Miss Costin's child. When he – Henderson – had asked what the evidence was, Hume had not been able to provide any. He no longer represented Hume.

Mr Corkhill said that Hume had written to him a month after the birth saying, 'I consider that I, as his [Jock's] parent and legal representative ought to have an opportunity of rectifying the alleged evil.' He had made it clear to Hume on several occasions that any grant from the fund would be for the benefit of the child.

This was too much for Andrew Hume's solicitor, Mr I. Edgar, who intervened at this point. He said he found himself in a position that meant he must withdraw from the case. It was only fair that he should do so. He was in his Lordship's hands but begged leave to withdraw. He had taken the case because 'in the notes and papers handed to him there seemed ample justification for a defence'. He had told his client that if it were the case that the sum had been specifically set aside for Miss Costin he could not go on. The Sheriff said he quite understood Mr Edgar's position, indeed it was one he would expect him to take up. After consulting with his client, Mr Edgar said he conceded defeat in the case.

'A Sensational Ending', said the *Dumfries & Galloway Standard*. 'Defender's Agent Withdraws from *Titanic* Fund Case'. But if Mary Costin thought that victory was hers, she had a nasty surprise on 22 October, when Sheriff Campion issued his 'interlocutor' – in Scottish law, his decision, or order, of the court: 'The difficulty I have had all along in the case is whether the pursuer (Mary Costin) is one who has a title to sue this action.' The Sheriff's eccentric legal argument continued as follows: the £67 sent in error to Andrew Hume was a discretionary donation from the *Titanic* Relief Fund. Mary Costin could not have sued the fund for a grant because any distributions were gratuitous – therefore she had no entitlement to sue someone to whom it had been sent in error. This would appear to be a case, he concluded, of *condictio indebiti* – reclaiming wrongful payment – and Mary Costin was therefore not entitled to the money.

Mary appealed. The law lords in Edinburgh considered the case on 3 December 1913 and were unanimous in their verdicts. Lord Justice Clerk said: 'I cannot agree in the judgement at all.' The issue was a simple one. 'A certain sum of money had been sent by A to B to be delivered to her. That is really what it comes to, and that B declines to deliver it. In those circumstances it appears to me that the proper course is to remit the case back to the Sheriff.' Lord Dundas agreed: the Sheriff had 'fallen into error' . . . there was a *non sequitur* about his judgement. Lord Guthrie added: 'The Sheriff has clearly indicated that he has no sympathy with the defender (Andrew Hume's) position . . . the defender was not only bound to know, but actually did know, that he was getting this money for Miss Costin and not for himself at all.' The appeal was allowed and Mary Costin was awarded costs.

Was Andrew Hume bad or just mad? The final act in this legal tragedy – or farce – suggests that he was both. Exactly a year to the day after the court in Dumfries found that Jock was the father of Johnann, Andrew Hume filed a 'Reponing Note'. In Scottish law this is an application to the court to allow someone another chance to defend their case if the Sheriff has already made a decision against them. Hume began an action to have the paternity decision overturned on the grounds that material facts had since come to his attention. His solicitor was again Mr Edgar.

Yet again, Mary Costin found herself crossing the road to the Sheriff's Court in Buccleuch Street. Mary's solicitor Mr Bannerman objected to the application as 'incompetent' and suggested that Andrew Hume was using it as a device to reverse the earlier order that he should repay £67 to Mary Costin. In any event, 'it would be unfair to allow one party to hear the evidence of the other, take a year to think it over and then proceed to hunt up evidence to the contrary'.

Sheriff Campion adjourned the hearing until 12 February 1914, when he issued his 'interlocutor'. He refused the application on the grounds that Andrew Hume had produced no new evidence or any of his promised 'material facts'. His excuses for failing to attend the original paternity hearing a year earlier were unconvincing. It would be 'harsh' to require Mary Costin to reopen the case after twelve months. For Mary, the legal nightmare was finally over. She could now begin to rebuild her life without Jock.

21

Opening Old Wounds

31 May 1913, Dumfries

The court case between Andrew Hume and Mary Costin caused great distress to the Humes' youngest daughter, Kate, now aged almost sixteen. It was bad enough to witness the public humiliation of her father, who was branded a liar and a thief. Kate had seen her father's business as a music teacher fall away and had begun to feel ostracised herself as parents of her school friends discouraged their daughters from going anywhere near the Humes. But perhaps worst of all from Kate's point of view, the court case prolonged her grieving for Jock, whose death had hit her harder than any of the Hume children. He had been her big brother, her protector.

It wasn't just the court case bringing back old memories. A year after Jock's death, it seemed that hardly a month went by without some new tribute to the *Titanic* heroes requiring her attendance. Kate Hume had been particularly dreading the last day of May, 1913. She had been dreading it for a year, ever since the idea of a monument had first been suggested. She had already wept her heart out through two memorial services for Jock in the week following the sinking of the *Titanic* and two months later she had stood in pouring rain during the unveiling of a marble plaque at the entrance to his old school, St Michael's. Now, as she was still struggling to come to terms with her brother's death, there was to be a new outpouring of public grief.

Each one of the three memorial occasions so far had been painful in its own way. The church services had been packed out with older people, few of whom had known Jock, or Tom Mullin. They had paid tribute to 'Dumfries's young heroes' in a way that made it difficult for Kate to relate to these public demonstrations of grief for her brother. The unveiling of the plaque at the school was quite different and had caught her off guard. It was attended almost entirely by children at the school and many of the boys were the same age as Jock in her earliest memories of him – in short trousers, running across the playground to greet her and her mother when they came to collect him. Although few of the pupils attending the ceremony would have known him, many of the boys were in tears, their youth a poignant reminder to Kate of how much of Jock's life had been ahead of him. And Jock's headmaster, Mr Hendrie, a man whose mission in life was the teaching and pastoral guidance of the children in his care, had spoken of Jock and Tom not as heroes but as 'good lads'. It was more than Kate could bear.

But in civic terms, today was to be the 'big one' – the ceremonial unveiling by Provost Thomson of a 16ft granite obelisk in Dock Park, honouring the lives and heroic deaths of Jock and his old school friend Thomas Mullin. Several hundred people were to attend and Kate would sit with her father and stepmother in the front row, alongside the Provost and in full view of everyone in Dumfries. But two people would be conspicuous by their absence: Jock's sisters Nellie, twenty-five, and Grace, twenty-one. Both girls had left home and were working away from Dumfries long before Jock died. Nellie had moved out soon after the death of her mother, disgusted by her father's amorous approaches to Alice. Since Jock's death, Nellie and Grace's trips home to Dumfries had become increasingly infrequent as both girls' relationship with their father and stepmother deteriorated. None of Andrew's daughters got on with Alice, who accused Grace in particular of being rude, lazy and unhelpful. There were explosive rows and by 1913 Nellie had stopped coming home altogether. Their father had written to both girls telling them that he expected them to attend the ceremony. But they were embarrassed by their father's unpredictable behaviour and were determined to avoid any confrontations between their father and Mary Costin, whom they knew would be there with Jock's baby. They sent their apologies.

Andrew Hume had already determined that the youngest member of the family, Andrew, eleven, was too young to be put through another gut-wrenching occasion. That left Kate as her father's buffer against Mary Costin. It would be the first time in months that Mary and Andrew had met outside a courtroom. Kate was dreading it as her father's vendetta against the Costins seemed already to have gone beyond hatred into madness.

The design and construction of the memorial itself had not been without controversy. There had been endless debate about what form it should take and a *Titanic* Memorial Committee had been set up to arrive at a democratic decision. One of the city elders, Mr Hiddleston, thought that two granite tablets bearing the young men's names should be erected in the town hall. Another, Mr Malloch, proposed a granite monument in St Michael's Cemetery as the lads had no graves in Dumfries, both having been buried in Halifax, Nova Scotia.

Mr Mitchell fought for a drinking fountain in St Michael Street. It was Mr Clark, a baker, who had suggested an obelisk in Dock Park, overlooking the River Nith. This won widespread approval and a sub-committee was appointed to agree a design and raise the necessary funds by sending 'subscription sheets' to factories and workshops. A furious row had then ensued over who would design and build the obelisk. A well-known local sculptor, Mr J. W. Dods, made a bid for the contract by joining forces with the building firm, Messrs Stewart of Dumfries. But the draft sketches were deemed to be unsuitable and the proposed costs too high. Other local firms were then asked to tender and they took great exception to being told by the sub-committee that their costs were also too high. It soon became a two-horse race between a local firm of builders, Messrs D. H. & J. Newall from Dalbeattie, and a masonry firm from Trafford Park, Manchester, Messrs Kirkpatrick Bros. Both quoted £100 for the job but Kirkpatrick's tender included the cost of a bronze relief panel with an image of the *Titanic* incorporated into a scroll of music from the hymn, 'Nearer My God To Thee'. As a goodwill gesture they also threw in some railings around the obelisk to protect it. Kirkpatricks were appointed after a heated debate, the vote of 15-9 in favour causing much ill will among local tradesmen, who vowed to boycott the ceremony. The final insult was Kirkpatricks' choice of 'the very best quality of Aberdeen granite' rather than Dumfries's own fine stone.

But all these rivalries and grievances were put aside on the morning of 31 May 1913 as hundreds of townspeople gathered in Dock Park in bright sunshine. Andrew and Alice Hume, with a reluctant Kate in tow, walked the half mile from their home in George Street to the park. Flags flew at half mast from the town hall and Midsteeple. Church bells across Dumfries and Maxwelltown tolled solemnly. On the bandstand the band played 'Nearer My God To Thee'. Two buglers from the 3rd King's Own Scottish Borderers stood to attention either side of the obelisk waiting to sound the 'Last Post'. Sixty Scouts formed a double rank between the bowling pavilion and the memorial; the Provosts of Dumfries and Maxwelltown would walk between them before taking their seats, their chains of office jangling on their chests.

To Kate, it was as if Jock had died all over again, except this time she wasn't numb with shock. More than a year on, she felt her older brother's loss more keenly than ever and her grief fuelled her fury with her father, whom she blamed more than ever for creating the circumstances that led to Jock's death.

The Humes took their seats in the front row just before the Provosts arrived in their civic finery, accompanied by the Revd James Strachan who had also officiated at Jock's memorial service. Revd Strachan led the gathering in prayer and then invited Provost Thomson to officially unveil the memorial. As the curtain was drawn back, Kate was able to read for the first time the inscription on the base of the obelisk. It said:

IN MEMORY OF
JOHN LAW HUME, A MEMBER OF THE BAND,
AND THOMAS MULLIN, STEWARD,
NATIVE OF THESE TOWNS
WHO LOST THEIR LIVES IN THE WRECK OF
THE WHITE STAR LINER 'TITANIC'
WHICH SANK IN MID ATLANTIC ON THE
14TH DAY OF APRIL, 1912
THEY DIED AT THE POST OF DUTY.

The Provost thanked everyone for their 'spontaneous response' to the appeal to erect the monument. 'Upon that gallant ship', he intoned, 'there were 2,206 human beings – the population of a small town – and of those, 1,500 went to a watery grave . . .' The buglers sounded the 'Last Post' and the band played 'O God Of Bethel'.

Provost Nicholson then thanked Provost Thomson for his role in creating a memorial that would be 'a lasting reminder to those who lived in the town . . . and a monument to the greatest disaster in modern times'. Jock's old headmaster Mr Hendrie thanked the Memorial Committee for 'keeping green' the memory of the two young citizens of the burgh. Provost Thomson then sprang to his feet again to propose a vote of thanks to the sculptors and builders for their excellent work. Kate Hume was wondering whether there was anyone left in the world to thank when Provost Thomson leapt up for the third time to thank Captain Wingate of the 3rd King's Own Scottish Borderers for granting the services of the buglers.

'The proceedings terminated with the singing of the National Anthem', the *Dumfries & Galloway Standard* reported, 'and the band thereafter played lively music while the bells pealed forth from the Midsteeple.'

In contrast to the Humes, the entire Costin family turned out for the occasion. Mary came with her mother Susan, her two brothers Jock and Menzies and the eight-month-old Johnann transported in a new Marmet pram, which she had bought using some of the payment from the Relief Fund. They were a proud family and, although not part of the official proceedings, they made their way to the front of the gathering where they were welcomed by friends, including Thomas Mullin's granny, who made a tremendous fuss of the baby.

Unlike Kate, Mary Costin did not go home sobbing or in a state of great distress. She had felt proud that the people of Dumfries thought so well of Jock and Tom that they deserved a memorial, something permanent, a place that people could visit and understand in a hundred years' time. The Costins walked home to Buccleuch Street at a gentle pace, making plenty of time for people to stop and admire the baby: Jock's baby. It gave Mary strength for the next round in the ongoing court battle with Andrew Hume.

22

The Case of the Mutilated Nurse

August 1914

During the summer of 1914, Kate Hume, now an unhappy teenage girl of seventeen, began to consider how she could hurt her father and stepmother. Left alone all day in the offices of Anderson's Electrical Engineers, where she worked as a clerk, Kate had all the time in the world to consider her grievances and to plan her revenge on Andrew and Alice.

The course of events that Kate set in motion would create an international sensation in the early weeks of the First World War. The ensuing court case, which was widely reported, became known as 'The Dumfries Atrocity Hoax'. An account of some of the events appeared in a book published at the time entitled *Falsehood in Wartime* by Arthur Ponsonby, MP for Stirling. He referred to it as 'The Celebrated Case of the Mutilated Nurse'.

The full story of Kate's act of madness has never been fully told. Many of the more interesting details remained undiscovered in pre-trial statements and court notes held in the National Archives of Scotland in Edinburgh. From these and from family accounts, I have pieced together the whole tragic story, which, like everything that involves the Humes and the Costins, has its beginnings in the sinking of the *Titanic*.

In September 1914, Kate had neither seen her parents nor spoken to them for a year – not since her father had thrashed her with a riding crop and her stepmother had struck her with a silver-topped cane. That was the day she left home for good. Although she went to live in lodgings less than a mile away, they had made no attempt to contact her or to find out where she was living.

Kate's complaints had their roots in her mother's death, the sudden introduction into their lives of their step-mother and the death of her beloved brother, Jock. Within each of these traumatic events in her young life there were multiple grievances – or parental offences, as Kate chose to see them.

Kate, a 'flighty, impetuous girl fond of the society of lads' as she was later described by a psychiatrist, was an avid reader of newspapers and detective novels and these fed an already vivid imagination. Like the child heroine of Henry James' *What Maisie Knew*, Kate had seen 'much more than she at first understood'. It had become quite clear to her, now that she had some experience of boys herself, that her father had been having an affair with their stepmother before her mother's death. Far from introducing Alice Alston into their lives as a convenient housekeeper substitute for their mother, as he had claimed, he was marrying his mistress.

Kate had adored Jock and could never forgive her father for the wrong done to her brother. 'Jock' – Kate still couldn't say his name without her eyes filling with tears. Their father had driven Jock away just as surely as she and her sisters had been forced to flee their father's intolerance. The fact that Jock loved the life and the work on board liners did not absolve his father from guilt in his son's death as far as Kate was concerned.

There were other grievances. Her father and stepmother had made no attempt to get in touch with her since she left home. She had been, she thought, a dutiful daughter, accompanying her father on the piano during his musical soirées, receiving no praise or thanks, simply criticism. The thrashing she received had been as humiliating as it was painful, not least because she had been beaten in front of her stepmother. And then there was his lying and cheating, which embarrassed all his children.

Kate's days at Andersons dragged endlessly on. It was no life for a teenager, particularly one as troubled as Kate, and she often sneaked away from the office, sometimes spending an hour or two down by the river if it was a fine day. She found that if she left the door of the office unlocked and a pad and pencil with a half-written sentence on the desk, she could pretend she had just popped out to the post office if her employer Mr Campbell returned unexpectedly. But he rarely did. Most days she just read detective novels or the newspaper. She enjoyed the *Daily Sketch*, which she liked for its strong anti-German line in the war and its dramatic pictures. She had started reading it two years earlier when Jock had died as she found its coverage of the *Titanic* the most dramatic of all the newspapers. Now the war had become a subject of fascination for her, particularly the reports of atrocities. One story had gripped Kate's imagination. A group of 'Heinous Huns', as the *Sketch* described them, were reported to have burned down a village in Belgium after raping and mutilating the women by cutting off their breasts with their bayonets. Kate cut out the article and put it under some invoices in her desk drawer. This would be her inspiration for the punishment she would mete out to her father and stepmother.

Her original plan had been to burn down their house in George Street but she had quickly dismissed this idea on the grounds that innocent people, such as her young brother Andrew, might be killed or injured. She had then warmed to the idea of destroying her father's precious violins and his cello. This would certainly cause him a great deal of grief and expense. She thought about chopping them up with an axe, burning them or stealing them and dumping them in the River Nith, where they would be discovered but not in time to be saved or repaired. But Kate dismissed this last idea, too, as it wouldn't satisfy her desire for revenge on her stepmother.

She wondered briefly about sending an anonymous letter to the authorities about their father's claim that Jock had taken two expensive violins with him on the *Titanic*. Everyone in the family, Mary Costin included, knew that Jock had set off with one violin, the one he always used, and it certainly wasn't a valuable eighteenth-century Guadagnini. But Kate doubted if they would take the word of a teenage girl against her father. And it wouldn't bring Alice into the net, except indirectly, so she dismissed this option, too.

The only time Kate, or any of the children for that matter, had seen their father and stepmother seriously distressed was when they heard the news about Jock. Her mother's death seemed to come as a relief to them both and neither, as far as Kate knew, had shed a tear. But when the *Titanic* went down, her father had been out of his mind with grief and even Alice had wept. When Alice pulled out a lace handkerchief from her sleeve to dry a tear on her alabaster-white cheek, Kate's sister Grace had unkindly remarked later that it was like watching rainwater run down a marble statue.

This gave Kate the idea for the form that her vengeance on her father and stepmother would take. She would make them think that one of her other siblings had died. Like Jock's death, it would have to be a heroic death. The war provided the perfect setting. Grace was in Huddersfield training to be a nurse. Her father and stepmother hadn't been in touch with her for more than a year, and had no idea where she was. Kate would contrive a letter that would lead them to believe that Grace had become the latest victim of the villainous 'Bosch'; there were plenty of such stories in the *Daily Sketch*. Her father and stepmother would be grief-stricken, just as they had been by Jock's death, horrified at the manner of her murder and consumed by guilt at having indirectly led to it by driving her away from home.

She didn't – at least not at this moment – consider what they would think, say or do when they discovered that Grace was alive and well. Neither did she consider what other people might think. Taking a blank sheet of paper from one of the twenty compartments in Mr Campbell's roll-top desk, Kate started to put her plan into action. She would write a letter to herself, purporting to come from someone – another brave nurse – who was with Grace at the Front when she died. 'Nurse Mullard' had a nice ring to it. And she would give Grace a heroic death, like Jock's. Using Mr Campbell's best pen and sitting at his desk, she began to write:

Vilvorde, near Brussels

To Miss Hume,

I have been asked by your sister, Nurse Grace Hume, to
hand the enclosed letter to you. My name is Nurse Mullard,
and I was with your sister when she died. Our camp hospital at Vilvorde was burned to the ground and out of 1,517
men and 23 nurses only 19 nurses were saved, but 149 men
managed to get clear away. I expect to pass through
Dumfries about the 15th September, but am writing this in
case I should not see you. Your sister gave me your address,
so, as I know Dumfries well, I shall send it to your office, if I
do not see you.

As there is a shortage of nurses in Inverness, 15 of us are
to be sent there. Grace requested me to tell you that her last
thoughts were of Andrew and you, and that you were not
to worry over her as she would be going to meet "her Jock".
These were her words.

She endured great agony in her last hour. One of the
soldiers (our men) caught two German soldiers in the act of
cutting off her left breast, her right one having been already
cut off. They were killed instantly by our soldier.

Grace managed to scrawl this enclosed note before I
found her. We can all say that your sister was a heroine. She
was a "loose nurse" – that is, she was out on the fields
looking for wounded soldiers – and on one occasion when
bringing in a wounded soldier a German attacked her. She
threw the soldier's gun at him and shot him with her rifle.
Of course, all nurses here are armed.

I have just received word this moment to pack for

Scotland, so will try and get this handed to you as there is no post from here, and we are making the best of a broken down wagon truck for a shelter. Will give you fuller details when I see you. We are all quite safe here now, as there have been reinforcements.

I am, yours sincerely,
J. M. MULLARD
Nurse, Royal Irish Troop
(am not allowed to say which special troop)

Kate wrote the letter out three times before she was satisfied with it, eliminating spelling and grammatical mistakes while trying to write it in a hand that did not look like her own. In this she was not successful. However, she was pleased with the letter, which she thought had an authentic air about it provided no one asked who Nurse Mullard was. Then, using her left hand in order to disguise her own handwriting, she set about writing a note supposedly from Grace in her dying moments. This would deliver the looked-for revenge to her neglectful and unkind father and stepmother. Dated 6 September, it said:

Dear Kate
This is to say Goodbye. Have not long to live. Hospital has been set on fire. Germans cruel. A man here has had head cut off. And my right breast taken away.
Give my love to . . .
Goodbye,
Grac X

When Kate had finished forging the letters she crumpled the note from Grace so that it looked authentic – as if it had been taken, as she said later, 'from Grace's dying grasp'. She also frayed the edges to give it a war-torn effect. Then, putting both letters in one of the envelopes from Mr Campbell's roll-top desk, she went home to her lodgings shortly before noon. Her landlady, Mrs McMinn, surprised to see Kate home so early, asked if she was all right. Kate said at first that she had a headache but then almost immediately burst into tears, flinging her arms round Mrs McMinn, and telling her that her sister Grace was dead. She showed her the letters 'brought to her office that morning by an unexpected visitor'.

Mrs McMinn, a kindly soul, found some smelling salts and made Kate a cup of tea. An hour later, Kate said she felt well enough to go back to work and, an hour later, Mr Campbell arrived. Kate gave a repeat performance for Mr Campbell's benefit, showing him the letters and assuring him that she had told her parents the terrible news. Mr Campbell's hug of consolation was slightly longer and closer than she would have liked.

By the following morning – Saturday – Grace Hume's murder and mutilation was the talk of Dumfries, having spread like wildfire. It seems that everyone knew except Andrew and Alice Hume. It had come to the attention of the Chief of Police, who decided that no action was called for, the crime having been committed outside the immediate environs of the Dumfries and Galloway district. Mr William Dickie, the editor of the *Dumfries & Galloway Standard*, had also heard about it but, as it was the weekend and his newspaper would not be published again until next Wednesday,

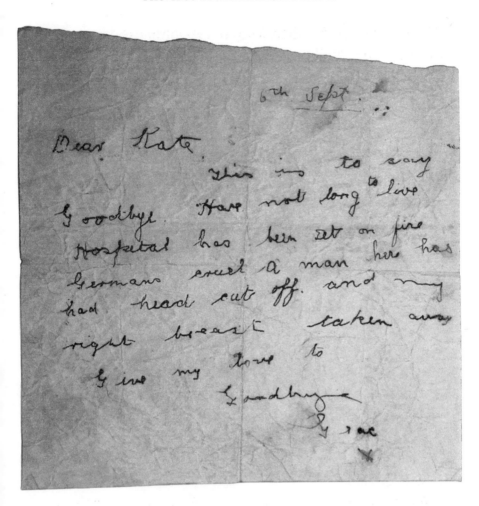

he spent the afternoon editing the minutes of the previous week's meeting of the Dumfries and Galloway Natural History and Antiquarian Society.

Kate, meanwhile, remained at home with her roommate and old school friend, Robina and Robina's parents. Having hatched such an elaborate and imaginative plot, she still had no strategy for delivering the news of Grace's death to her father and stepmother. Then she remembered that Robina was friends with Edward Whitehead, a twenty-two-year-old cub reporter on the newspaper. It was only Saturday so there would be plenty of time for him to place it for the Wednesday edition.

Young Whitehead was about to land what he thought might be one of the greatest scoops in newspaper history.

23

Grace Hume 'Murdered'

16 September 1914

A few days before the *Dumfries & Galloway Standard* published their report of Grace's murder, it fell to Mrs Robertson, a plasterer's wife from Dockhead and well-known local gossip and busybody, to break the news to Andrew and Alice Hume that their daughter had been murdered and mutilated. A loud knocking on the door of 42 George Street, followed one minute later by a persistent jangling of the bell, pre-empted the announcement.

Alice Hume, alone in the house, on the top floor looking for a hat to wear at a wedding the following Saturday, was not pleased to be summoned downstairs again. The arthritis in her knees had made the ascent painful and a rapid descent to open the front door would take a double toll. She wondered if she should bother at all. But curiosity got the better of her and, grasping the mahogany handrail of the handsome Georgian staircase, she made the descent sideways, one painful step at a time, to the ground floor. When she opened the front door, she was particularly annoyed to see Mrs Robertson standing there. She disliked people who called without an invitation and, anyway, Alice could not conceive of any situation that might lead her to invite Mrs Robertson into her home. They were at best on nodding terms, attending the same congregation at St Michael's Episcopal Church, and they had sat next to each other at one of those interminable Burns Night dinners; that was the extent of their acquaintance. But as Mrs Robertson was holding a lace handkerchief to her face and had obviously been crying, Alice felt obliged to let her in.

'Oh, my dear, what is the matter?' said Alice, trying to sound and look concerned. 'Please come in, Mrs Robertson.' Alice closed the door behind her uninvited guest, determined to contain her in the hall where Mrs Robertson would be forced to stand, rather than invite her into the drawing room where Alice would be expected to serve tea and biscuits.

'It's about your stepdaughter, Grace,' said Mrs Robertson. 'Everyone is talking about her, I just wanted to say . . .'

'Talking about what, exactly?' said Alice, now sounding distinctly irritated.

'About the dreadful business in Belgium.'

'What dreadful business, may I ask?'

'You mean you haven't heard?' asked Mrs Robertson, trying to look aghast but secretly thrilled that she was breaking such important news. Her hands shot back up to her face in mock horror. 'Grace has been mutilated and murdered by the Germans.'

'Grace? Mutilated? Murdered?' For a brief moment Alice considered how often she herself had wished to murder Grace. Indeed, there were occasions when she had felt like murdering all three of her stepdaughters, in particular Kate, although they had yet to provoke her so much that she had contemplated mutilation.

'I thought you knew, otherwise I would never have called,' said Mrs Robertson, who enjoyed nothing more in life than announcing bad news to those who had yet to hear it. 'A nurse – Nurse Mullard was her name, I think – has told your stepdaughter Kate all about it and given her a letter from Grace. Apparently Grace was a heroine, attending wounded soldiers at the Front in Belgium, when the Germans attacked. Before killing her, they cut off her . . .' Mrs Robertson started sobbing convulsively.

'Please don't distress yourself any more,' said Alice, maintaining her own composure while skilfully turning Mrs Robertson around and guiding her back to the front door. 'When my husband returns we will speak to Kate as a matter of urgency and get to the bottom of this matter. Good day, Mrs Robertson, and thank you very much indeed for bringing it to our attention.'

Alice sat on the chaise longue in the drawing room and watched Mrs Robertson walking away from the house. When Mrs Robertson was out of sight, Alice considered calmly what she had just heard. She realised that she had no immediate way of getting in touch with Kate to ask her what had happened, as they had no idea where she was living. She was glad she hadn't revealed that to Mrs Robertson, who swapped gossip like children swapped marbles. Alice recalled the last time she had seen Kate. She would never forget Kate's defiant face as she had swept out, slamming the front door. At least her father had given her a good hiding before she left and for once he hadn't blamed her – Alice – for driving his daughters away.

As for Grace, they had neither seen nor spoken to Grace for more than a year, although until now, anyway, they thought they knew where she lived. Bradford, wasn't it? Or perhaps it was Huddersfield. She really couldn't remember.

Alice must have considered the effect that this new catastrophe would have on their lives, whatever the truth of it. The family had suffered enough already with Jock's death and a year of courtroom battles with Mary Costin. It hadn't been easy being a stepmother to Andrew's five children before Jock died, but there was no doubt that his death had magnified the difficulties, in particular her relationship with her stepdaughters.

But was it true? In one sense, Alice probably wished it were. Grace and Kate hunted in a pack and it would at least halve her stepdaughter problem if one of them was dead. But Alice was suspicious. For a start, Kate was a pathological liar like her father. Even Alice had been forced to accept this uncomfortable truth about her husband. And Grace had never struck her as either a heroine or a victim. She was a timid girl with no nursing qualifications and no initiative. The idea of her being in the front line in the war in Belgium seemed improbable to Alice, to say the least. She often wondered how she had travelled unassisted all the way from Dumfries to wherever it was she went. But Alice could hardly present the news this way to Grace's father when he returned home. She would try to sound more sympathetic.

The ticking of the grandfather clock seemed to get louder and slower as Alice counted the minutes until Andrew arrived home shortly before 4 p.m. He still had his key in the door when Alice blurted out, word for word, what she had been told by Mrs Robertson. To Alice's relief, Andrew also found the story improbable, agreeing that they had to speak to Kate as a matter of urgency. But where was she? Andrew and Alice went to bed on Saturday night still not knowing what had happened to Grace. It seems extraordinary that the whole of Sunday passed without any contact between Kate and her parents. The Humes went to church as normal and in the afternoon Andrew wrote a polite letter to the War Office in London, asking if they could furnish him with information that would confirm or contradict the report of his daughter's death.

On Sunday night, Kate gave the letters to Robina and asked her to pass them on to her reporter friend Edward. Realising he had a scoop, the young Edward immediately took the letters to his editor, Mr Dickie, who decided to lead Wednesday's edition of the newspaper with the sensational story. Even as the *Standard* was preparing the story, Andrew and Alice Hume were still none the wiser. No one from the newspaper had been to see them and no reply had yet been received from the War Office. Andrew and Alice seemed peculiarly unconcerned about the fate of Grace and it is extraordinary that they apparently made no attempts to contact Kate. On the Monday, Andrew went, as he did every Monday, to the nearby Wallace Hall Academy where he taught the violin. On the Tuesday he took an early train to Annan to conduct a lunchtime concert.

Alice was waiting anxiously for him at the barrier on his return. Andrew's niece, who had seen Kate the previous day, had persuaded Kate to allow her to make a pencil copy of the letters and Andrew's sister, Mrs Irving, had brought the transcript round to George Street. What Andrew read alarmed him and he went immediately from Dumfries station to the *Standard*'s offices and asked to see the editor. He demanded that Dickie postpone publication, at least until after he had received a reply from the War Office. The editor declined on the grounds that he believed the story and that it was in the national interest, at a time of war, to publish it. What he didn't tell Andrew Hume was that Grace Hume's scribbled dying note had already been sent for engraving. He also failed to tell him that in his top left desk drawer he had the original letter from 'Nurse Mullard', a letter that Andrew Hume had never seen. If the editor had shown him even a page of it, Andrew would immediately have recognised the writing as Kate's. But Dickie was not about to allow Andrew Hume to spoil a good story.

Although Dickie had worked for the *Standard* for forty-four years, he had been editor of the newspaper for only five months, since the unexpected death of his predecessor, Thomas Watson. Dickie had joined the *Standard* aged fifteen, serving his apprenticeship as a compositor before becoming a member of the reporting staff some years later. A series of promotions over the years, mostly prompted by the death or retirement of a colleague, had eventually led to his appointment as deputy editor, a position he considered the pinnacle of his career. He was, in truth, one of life's natural deputies. But Mr Watson's death had changed all that and handed him an opportunity he had never dreamed of having.

William Dickie's hero was the man who had edited the *Standard* for forty-two years, William McDowall, on whom he had modelled his life and, so far as it was possible, even his appearance – both men having full beards and moustaches. McDowall had been appointed editor aged thirty-one in 1846, three years after the *Standard* was founded 'to promote the views of the Evangelical majority in the Church' and to support the causes of liberalism and social reform.

Apart from a brief spell in 1854, when he left to edit a newspaper in Sunderland, McDowall held the position until his death in 1888.

Dickie walked doggedly in the footsteps of McDowall, under whom he served for sixteen years. Whatever McDowall had done, Dickie would do it, too. McDowall was a founding member of the Dumfries and Galloway Natural History and Antiquarian Society; Dickie later became its vice-president. McDowall wrote the definitive *History of Dumfries*; Dickie wrote a similar booklet called *Dumfries and Round About*. McDowall was the driving force behind the movement to build a statue to Robert Burns in the High Street; Dickie became president of Dumfries Burns Club. McDowall lived in Maxwelltown; the Dickies bought a house in a neighbouring street. McDowall made a point of always walking to work so that he could pass the time of day with his readers; so did Dickie. Both men shared an enthusiasm for carboniferous fossils. Even their manner of dying would be the same, both men 'dying in harness' as the *Standard* described it. But there was one important difference between the two men: McDowall would never have allowed Kate Hume's story to get into print.

In the annals of journalistic blunders there can be few greater cock-ups than the *Dumfries & Galloway Standard & Advertiser's* world exclusive about the murder and mutilation of Grace Hume. Nor can there be many stories that have been proved to be so completely wrong so soon after publication.

Like all newspaper editors who destroy their careers and become the laughing stock of their colleagues through a momentary misjudgement, Dickie wanted the story to be true, abandoning years of experience and caution in pursuit of a moment of personal and professional glory. The story ought to have rung all the usual warning bells. No one on the *Standard*'s staff had spoken to Kate Hume. Nurses in war are *not* armed. The girl's father, who was clearly not grieving, sat opposite him urging him to wait for confirmation from the War Office before rushing into print. At least one trusted colleague in the office had read a galley proof while drawing air through his teeth, shaking his head and saying, 'I don't like the look of this, Mr Dickie. Something about it isn't quite right.' But Dickie wasn't listening.

Britain had declared war on Germany less than two months earlier and anti-German feelings were running high. The battles of the Marne and Mons had already been fought and a growing list of casualties had been appearing in newspapers, including the *Standard*. Wounded soldiers serving with the King's Own Scottish Borderers were being invalided home and Gordon Highlanders had been taken prisoner. A major sea battle was under way in Heligoland. The people of Dumfries had responded generously to an appeal by the *Standard* for blankets to be sent to the Front. Here, exclusive to the *Standard*, was a heartbreaking account of Scotland's bravest in the front line of the Great War: a young girl from Dumfries, no less.

Dickie put the story at the top of page two, the place reserved for the lead article, and he wrote the headline himself. He advised his production manager to expect extra demand and to increase the print run accordingly. On the morning of Wednesday 16 September, queues formed outside newsagents' shops in Dumfries to buy the *Standard*.

It has to be said that, if it had been true, it would have been a very good story.

TERRIBLE DEATH OF A DUMFRIES NURSE
ATROCITIES BY GERMAN SOLDIERS

The story ran the length of the page and reproduced in full the letter written by 'Nurse Mullard' and the note scribbled by Grace in her dying moments.

> Information has been received in Dumfries of brutalities perpetrated by German soldiers on Nurse Grace Hume, a young woman belonging to the town, who was engaged in Red Cross work in Belgium. Nurse Hume, who was twenty-three years of age, was on the nursing staff of a Huddersfield hospital, and about three weeks ago she volunteered for service at the Front, and proceeded to Belgium. She had already given admirable services on the field, performing deeds of genuine heroism, when on Sunday 6th September, the field hospital at Vilvorde, near Brussels, to which she was attached, was set on fire by German soldiers, and numerous atrocities perpetrated on the wounded and the nursing staff.
>
> Nurse Hume is a daughter of Mr A Hume, music teacher, Dumfries, and in a letter which has been received by her sister, Miss Kate Hume, Dumfries, who is living apart from her father and step-mother, a nurse who formed one of the hospital staff describes the circumstances under which Nurse Hume met her

death. The letter was written by Nurse Mullard, who, on her way from Belgium to Inverness, on Friday last broke her journey at Dumfries, and conveyed to Miss Hume the news of her sister's terrible death. She had written the account of Nurse Hume's death, intending to have it forwarded to her sister, but on account of her being ordered home from Belgium for duty at Inverness, she was enabled to hand the letter personally to Miss Hume, and also to give her some fuller details.

It appears that Nurse Hume was the victim of horrible cruelty at the hands of German soldiers, and died in great agony after being terribly mutilated. When the hospital had been set on fire by the Germans, they started to wreak vengeance on the wounded soldiers and the nurses who were in attendance on them, and the letter describes how one of the Allies' soldiers caught two German soldiers in the act of cutting off Nurse Hume's left breast, her right one having been already cut off. The Germans were instantly killed.

Nurse Mullard, in her letter, also gives an example of the bravery displayed by Nurse Hume in her work, and in conversation with Miss Hume she gave a fuller account of her heroic action on the field, when she saved a wounded soldier from a barbarous attack by a German. While bringing in a wounded soldier she was attacked by the German, who was disguised in the uniform of one of the allied troops. He made to fire at the wounded soldier, when the nurse with great bravery threw a gun at him, thus deflecting his aim. Before he had time to recover she shot him dead.

Shortly before she died Nurse Hume, although

suffering great pain as the result of the horrible treatment she had received, was able to write a note on a
scrap of paper, which she handed to Nurse Mullard,
with the request that it should be forwarded to her
sister in Dumfries.

The story was immediately picked up by the wire services
and published in later editions of some national newspapers,
including the *Yorkshire Post*. The atmosphere at the *Standard*'s
office was electric, the newsroom bursting with pride. The
Standard's young reporter, Edward Whitehead, spent the day
basking in everyone's approval and accepting congratulations on his world scoop. The paper's subeditor Robert
Laidlaw found a quiet corner where he couldn't be overheard
and filed the story to several newspapers and agency wire
services, hoping to make a pound or two from this enter-
prising piece of freelancing. Mr Dickie, rarely seen outside
his office, took to the editorial floor, telling anyone who
cared to listen, including the company secretary Mr Hunter,
that the qualities of good judgement, decisiveness and courage were what set editors apart from ordinary journalists.

In the afternoon, Laidlaw, the story now being too important for the young Whitehead, went to interview Kate for a
follow-up story for Saturday's paper (the *Standard* appeared
twice a week, on Wednesdays and Saturdays). Kate gave him
just what he needed – details of Nurse Mullard's visit and a
description: 'A woman of about thirty-eight years of age,
rather tall, thin; she has a very sweet, soft face; brown eyes,
fair brown wavy hair; she wore a navy blue costume and
carried a small handbag.' Laidlaw made a verbatim note of
this in shorthand in his notebook.

Around the same time, 200 miles away in Huddersfield, Grace Hume was walking past a newsagent's shop when she saw a billboard for the *Yorkshire Post* which said:

```
GERMANS MURDER SCOTTISH NURSE.
```

Out of curiosity she went in and bought the paper, wondering if it was anyone she knew. At first she couldn't believe what she read. Then she wondered if Nurse Mullard had somehow got someone else's name mixed up with her own. Realising the distress the erroneous report of her death must have caused her father, she went at once to the nearest telegraph office and sent a telegram to her father. It was brief and to the point:

```
REPORTS UNTRUE. SAFE IN HUDDERSFIELD.
GRACE.
```

She then wrote a postcard to her sister Kate. It was rather witty, although it is unlikely she intended it to be:

'Just received news of my own murder in Belgium. Can you give me name and address of person calling herself Mullard. Write by return. Important, Grace.'

The telegram was delivered to 42 George Street shortly before 7 p.m. that evening. When Andrew Hume read it he was neither surprised nor relieved, as he had never for a moment thought that Grace was dead. Once the full facts had been revealed to him, he had taken the rather uncharitable view that Grace had neither the competence to qualify as a nurse nor the courage or initiative to go to Belgium. Alice had taken an even more aggressive view of the whole drama as it had unfolded, telling friends that if indeed her step-daughter had been murdered and mutilated, which she doubted, 'it was the death she deserved to die'.

Andrew then telephoned Mr Dickie, who was horrified to hear that Grace was alive and well, while trying to sound quite the opposite. 'What wonderful news, Mr Hume,' he lied. He promised Andrew an immediate inquiry to get to the bottom of 'Nurse Mullard's hoax', as he described it, and in the meantime he would put a notice in the window of the *Standard*'s offices and publish a prominent story in Saturday's edition correcting the story. He sent Mr Laidlaw to George Street to collect the telegram with instructions to put it into the *Standard*'s window under a notice saying, 'Nurse Hume Alive and Well'.

All newspapermen take some enjoyment from their colleagues' misfortunes but it is difficult not to feel sorry for Mr Dickie. How badly he had been let down by his staff, he must have thought. How he wished he had listened to his colleagues misgivings instead of setting aside all caution in the hope of a scoop. He must have wondered how he would explain this reversal to the *Standard*'s most avid reader, his wife, when he returned home. Before tomorrow he would have to decide how he would also explain it to Mr Hunter, the company secretary.

Grace Hume's revelation that she was alive and well in Huddersfield came just hours too late to stop the following day's newspapers repeating the story and even embellishing on it. Editors fell like hungry wolves on a story that confirmed everyone's worst fears and prejudices about the Germans. The *Yorkshire Post* wrote about 'monsters in human form' and 'the blond brute avid of lust and prey'. In London, the *Pall Mall Gazette*, the *Westminster Gazette*, the *Globe* and the *Evening Standard* published the story. It was picked up in newspapers abroad. Several newspapers, including *The Times*, ran leaders condemning the shocking barbarity of the villainous Bosch, holding up Grace's murder as vindication of Britain's decision to go to war. Reporters were despatched to Dumfries on the overnight train to interview the grieving father and stepmother. Members of Parliament tabled questions in the House. The story attracted huge public interest, developing a political dimension which kept the debate alive even when the story was exposed next day as a hoax. The Germans accused Britain's secret service of planting the story to whip up anti-German sentiment. *The Times* countered by suggesting that the story had been put about by German agents 'in order to discredit all atrocity stories', the assumption being that 'Nurse Mullard' was a German agent who forged the letters and handed them to Grace's unsuspecting sister.

On Saturday the *Standard* published its correction, carefully pitched by Mr Dickie to save his neck.

A CRUEL HOAX
NURSE HUME ALIVE AND WELL

The story of the Dumfries nurse named Grace Hume having been brutally murdered at Vilvorde by German soldiers has proved to be a malicious invention. The letters given to the press by Miss Kate Hume and published on Wednesday are forgeries and the Scottish Office are instituting an inquiry as to their origin.

The *Standard* report, which ran to over a thousand words, made it sound as if its own wide-ranging investigation had exposed the truth of the matter and reunited Grace with her father and stepmother.

> We regret that the publication of the forged letters should have been the means of harrowing the feelings of our readers. But it is satisfactory to know that the appearance in 'The Standard' was the occasion of the immediate exposure of the imposture and of putting her family in communication with the young woman within a few hours and thus relieving anxiety regarding her fate which they had endured for days.

For good measure, the *Standard* even threw in an apology to the German army: 'It is satisfactory to know that the character of the German soldiery has been saved from this foul stain.'

As the innocent party in the hoax, Grace Hume must have felt compromised, for she wrote to her father that day from her lodgings at 62 Trinity Street, Huddersfield, to assure him that she had nothing to do with it:

> Dear Father,
> I am sorry you have been made miserable over the false report. I knew nothing about it until yesterday when I saw placards in the town . . . it is an absolute mystery to me. I neither know, nor yet have I heard of such a person as Nurse Mullard, neither have I been out of Hudd since war was declared . . .
> I am very sorry that you should be put to any trouble and

inconvenience at all but I hope you will understand that it is as much a worry and a trouble to me as well. The person who concocted the tale undoubtedly knows all about us . . .
Yours,
Grace

For the first time, the authorities started to take an interest in the affair. This was not good news for Kate, who had never wanted the story to go any further than George Street. The War Office had already been alerted by Andrew's letter asking for news about his daughter, and the Scottish Office, concerned about the murder and mutilation of one of its citizens abroad, fired off a dozen letters. The Foreign Office was asked to make enquiries about the mysterious Nurse Mullard in Belgium. The Lord Advocate in Edinburgh asked the Procurator Fiscal in Dumfries for a full report. The Procurator Fiscal instructed Dumfries police to make enquiries – the Chief Constable of Dumfries, Mr William Black, heading the investigation himself. Nothing less than a prosecution followed by a public trial would satisfy the authorities: they wanted someone's head on a plate.

The full force and fury of the state and the law now turned on Kate Hume, an unhappy seventeen-year-old girl who had staged a silly hoax in order to hurt her parents. The police investigation quickly established that Nurse Mullard was not a German agent but a fiction of Kate's fertile imagination. When interviewed, Kate admitted forging the letters and, asked why she had done it, replied, 'To hurt my father and stepmother.' It should have ended then and there. But no one had thought to advise the police, before they commenced their investigation, on what crime Kate was supposed to have committed. She had certainly caused everyone a lot of trouble and she had forged two letters, but she had not done it for personal gain – her only motive was to annoy her parents. As one of the investigating officers observed, if that was a crime, then Scotland's prisons would be full of teenagers, including his own daughters.

The Chief Constable, having now interviewed Kate himself, consulted the Procurator Fiscal because he felt that, unless 'felonious intention' could be proved, Kate had not been guilty of any crime. The Procurator Fiscal then consulted the Lord Advocate who had no doubt at all what Kate should be charged with. Kate's actions were a clear contravention of Section 21 of the Defence of the Realm Regulations 1914, an emergency Act that had been introduced a month earlier to protect Britain at war. Anyone charged with an offence under the Act would face a military trial by court martial. The maximum sentence was death by hanging or firing squad.

The Defence of the Realm Act (DORA) gave wide-ranging powers to the government for the duration of the First World War. It included bans on flying kites, lighting bonfires, buying binoculars and, even more bizarrely, feeding bread to wild animals. Its principal objective was to keep morale at home high and to prevent people from passing on information that might assist the enemy. In their wisdom, the various authorities believed that Kate had indeed assisted the enemy and she was duly charged at the end of September and held in police custody. The police, in accordance with the provisions of the Act, then contacted the military authorities at Hamilton where, it was proposed, she would be imprisoned pending her court martial. The police would provide the necessary evidence for her trial.

The military authorities at Hamilton – busy training soldiers for war and at the same time rounding up drunkards and deserters – didn't at all like the idea of keeping a seventeen-year-old girl in their cells, court-martialling her and then possibly standing her blindfolded against a wall and shooting her. They started looking at the small print of DORA's regulations and decided that the regulations only applied in areas which were 'Proclaimed Areas' within the meaning of the Regulations, and that Dumfries did not constitute a proclaimed area, whereas Vilvoorde did. Kate had never been to Vilvoorde and neither had her sister Grace. Hamilton made the strongest of polite protests to the Lord Advocate, asking him to review the decision.

The Lord Advocate asked a distinguished King's Counsel, Mr J. Duncan Millar, Liberal MP for North East Lanarkshire, for a second opinion. Mr Millar agreed, in a private memorandum, that a charge under DORA might be difficult to sustain and that a safer course was to press charges of forgery in a criminal court. As a result, the charge against Kate was amended to 'concocting and fabricating' letters and forging signatures 'with the intent of alarming and annoying the lieges, and in particular your father Andrew Hume and your stepmother Alice Mary Hume, both residing at 42 George Street, Dumfries'. Kate was remanded in custody to Edinburgh prison.

Soon afterwards, the Lord Advocate received another opinion – a rather more unwelcome one but also given in private – this time from the Solicitor General, Sir Thomas Brash Morison. He wrote expressing his concerns about charging Kate with anything: 'A difficulty might arise at the trial from the preposterous nature of the story . . . I have doubts whether anyone at all seriously believed it (the hoax).'

Meanwhile, in spite of Kate's confession, the police went about their business of gathering evidence for the prosecution. Handwriting experts were called in to compare Kate's handwriting with that of 'Nurse Mullard' and forensic examination of plain sheets of paper found in Kate's office revealed that they had a similar composition and texture to the paper that 'Nurse Mullard' had used to write to Kate. In all, twenty-two witnesses were interviewed, including her father and stepmother who were to give evidence for the prosecution. However, there was one major obstacle that still had to be overcome. The police had great difficulty in establishing beyond any reasonable doubt that Nurse Mullard did not exist, and this was a fundamental pillar of the prosecution case. While the War Office was fairly certain that there was no one called Nurse Hume on the casualty lists, they had no way of knowing if there was, or wasn't, anyone called Nurse Mullard helping at the Front. Indeed, they had little idea of what was going in Vilvoorde, having had difficulty at first even in ascertaining where it was. The Crown Agent for Scotland started applying pressure in Whitehall to answer the question, provoking a flurry of letters between the Foreign Office and the War Office. On 6 November, even as thousands of troops were taking up their positions in trenches and as Vilvoorde was being shelled by the Germans, Ralph Paget, Assistant Under-Secretary of State for Foreign Affairs, found time to write to the Secretary to the Army Council as follows:

```
Sir:-
I am directed by Secretary Sir E. Grey
to acknowledge the receipt of your
letter of the 1st instant enclosing a
copy of a letter from the Crown Agent
```

```
for Scotland, enquiring whether a nurse
of the name of J. M. Mullard was
employed in a camp hospital at Vilvoorde
on September 7th last.
   I am to express Sir E. Grey's regret
that he has at his disposal no means of
obtaining the information desired by the
Crown Agent.
I am,
Sir,
your most obedient,
Humble Servant
Ralph Paget
```

In the end, the Red Cross came to the rescue. After a month-long investigation in Belgium and a thorough search of filing cabinets in London, Frank Hastings, Secretary of the British Red Cross Society, wrote to the War Office:

```
I am instructed to state that no person
of the name of Nurse Mullard has ever
been engaged by this Society in connec-
tion with its War work and indeed it may
be added that no person bearing this
name has ever been employed in any
capacity by this Society.
```

Kate's trial was set for 27 and 28 December before Scotland's most senior judge, Lord Strathclyde, Lord President of the Court of Session, in the High Court of Justiciary in Edinburgh. The Lord Advocate, Mr Robert Munro KC, MP would lead the prosecution.

Telephone No.
REGENT 6151 (seven lines).
Telegraphic Address
"Assistance Charles London."

BRITISH RED CROSS SOCIETY.

Incorporated by Royal Charter. 1908.

Any further communication on this
subject should be addressed to
THE SECRETARY,
and the following number quoted

A16.

83, PALL MALL,
LONDON, S.W.

4th November, 1914.

Sir,

In answer to your letter dated the 1st instant No: 0154/3740 (M.O.5), I am instructed to state that no person of the name of Nurse Mullard has ever been engaged by this Society in connection with its War work; and indeed it may be added that no person bearing this name has ever been employed in any capacity by this Society.

I am, Sir,

Your obedient Servant,

Frank Hastings

Secretary.

The Secretary,

War Office,

WHITEHALL, S. W.

24

The Trial of Kate Hume

27 December 1914

John Wilson KC, Kate's defence counsel, was not a man to be easily shocked. During his years at the Bar in Scotland he had witnessed several hangings, had prosecuted or defended more than 100 hardened criminals and had experienced first-hand the punitive hardships of the Victorian prison system while visiting inmates. As a member of the General Board of Lunacy he had visited numerous lunatic asylums where the living conditions were atrocious. Yet nothing had quite prepared him for his first meeting with Kate Hume in her cell at Calton Jail in Edinburgh on Boxing Day 1914. Since her arrest in September, Kate had spent more than three months in prison awaiting trial. The intense cold of a Scottish winter and the unsanitary conditions had taken a terrible toll on her health and to the experienced barrister she looked more like a sick woman of forty than a girl of seventeen. She was pale and gaunt and her cheeks and eyes were hollow, leaving only the briefest trace of her pretty face. Her once-curly hair was dirty and knotted. The long fingers that had played the piano so beautifully were covered with callouses and her fingernails were broken from slopping out and scrubbing. She had a bruise on her cheek where a fellow prisoner in the women's wing had struck her with a broom-stick. Condensation ran down the walls of her bare cell, where the temperature fell below freezing at night.

Built in the early nineteenth century to the design of a grand castle, Calton Jail's delicate castellation concealed the cruelty and suffering that went on behind its walls. One inmate at the time described Calton as 'the poorhouse of all prisons, with the cold chill of a grim fortress'. For fifty years it had been the scene of public executions, a crowd of 20,000 turning up in June 1864 when a carter named George Bryce was hanged for murdering a nursemaid. Thereafter, executions continued inside the jail: Patrick Higgins, a labourer from Linlithgow who murdered his two sons by throwing them into a quarry, was hanged there just a year before Kate passed through the gates.

Wilson's arrival at the jail was delayed by a long line of prisoners in leg irons and manacles being marched along Princes Street through Gorgie to Saughton, where they would work all day on the new prison, the authorities recognising at last that Calton belonged to another age.

Wilson had not wanted to take this brief. The prosecution's case was so seriously flawed that it was quite shocking, in Wilson's view, that it had been allowed to go to trial. But it had become clear that the authorities wanted to make an example of Kate Hume and his career might suffer if he refused the brief or challenged the Lord Advocate's legal arguments. And yet, as he entered her cell, he felt immediately outraged on Kate's behalf. He promptly sent his clerk out to buy some soup, and a warm blanket for Kate to wrap round herself.

The defence team had made several applications to the court to release Kate on bail on compassionate and health grounds but they had all been unsuccessful. For some reason the prison governor had taken against Kate, writing in a private note to the court: 'The prisoner has shewn tendencies of a criminal nature which require to be checked and controlled.' However, he recommended that Kate should be sent to Borstal if found guilty, which could be taken as an admission that he recognised Calton was no place for a teenager to be held.

Neither Kate's father nor her stepmother had been to visit her during her thirteen weeks in prison, nor had they written to the authorities making representations on her behalf. The only letter from Andrew Hume among the court papers is an inquiry, dated 11 November 1914, about how long he would be needed at the trial and a request for reimbursement of his expenses. Addressed to The Master of the Court, Parliament House, it says:

> I . . . will be obliged if you will kindly inform me as to
> defraying of fare and other expenses, also the probable
> period for which I shall be required together with Mrs
> Hume, in order that I may have my work here arranged for.

It seems extraordinary that Hume was not only willing to give evidence against his own daughter but was not even intending to stay for the full length of her two-day trial.

Wilson was glad that he had immediately rejected the defence solicitor's suggestion that Kate should plead insanity and that they should ask for a reduced sentence accordingly. Her crime, if indeed it was one, might have been the desperate act of a person temporarily deranged, but Wilson had read nothing in any of the statements to suggest that Kate was mad. Wilson had served on the General Board of Commissioners in Lunacy for Scotland and drafted their 54th Annual Report; he knew only too well that madness had become a convenient way for husbands and fathers to dispose of wives and daughters who, for whatever reason, had become an embarrassment. The male-dominated courts were inclined to do the same. In Scotland there were 19,034 insane people officially known to the General Board of Lunacy, 'not including those insane persons maintained at home', an increase of 398 over the previous year. Wilson realised that insanity was a life sentence from which Kate would never escape. He knew that this was also the view of Sir Thomas Clouston MD, who had been called in by the prosecution because of his 'large experience of mental and nervous diseases that occur during the adolescent period of human life'. He examined Kate on Christmas Eve with Dr George Robertson, superintendent at the Morningside lunatic asylum. Both men wrote their reports on Christmas Day 1914. Clouston found Kate to be 'a girl of nervous temperament, with an hysterical tendency and wanting in self control'. But both he and Robertson attributed her actions to her unhappy home life. Her mother had died after a long illness when she was eight, her brother when she was fifteen. Clouston wrote:

She seems to have of late been punished, sometimes severely, even within the past two years. She says her father horse-whipped her last year and her step-mother thrashed her with a stick, leaving a mark on her eye . . . she says she got 'no sympathy' at home.

Her favourite brother was lost in the *Titanic* and that made the first strong impression on her mind in her life. She used to dream about him. There was a lawsuit about his affairs too, which went on for long and kept up her distress. Two tablets were put up to his memory, at the unveiling of which she was present and was much upset.

The two next events that deeply affected her were her leaving home for the first time, after a quarrel, and the present war . . . she has been growing fast of late years, having gained half an inch in height since she has been in prison, and is now five feet, seven inches.

Dr Robertson agreed: 'She has had an unhappy home life. Her mother is dead and she has not got on with her step-mother. I could not certify her to be of unsound mind.'

Wilson, who had got to know Clouston on the General Board for Lunacy, had discussed the case with him. Kate's breaking point seemed to be the argument with her step-mother about helping around the house and keeping her own room tidier. As the children's challenges to Andrew Hume's authority grew, so did the severity and frequency of his punishments. But this was the first time he had used a whip on her and the first time he had beaten her in the presence of her stepmother. Kate had been determined not to cry. When her father released her she stood up without looking at him, straightened her skirt and, holding her head high, walked towards the door of the morning room where Alice was standing. Words were exchanged between stepdaughter and stepmother. Alice, who had just returned from a walk and was carrying a silver-topped cane, struck out at Kate, bruising her cheek and cutting her just above the eye. Kate had run up the stairs to her bedroom, thrown some things into a suitcase and left. She had no plan in mind, except never to return home. She walked to Irish Street, about ten minutes away, where Mrs McKinn, the mother of her old school friend Robina, kept a boarding house. 'You can stay here as long as you like, my dear,' said Mrs McKinn who knew about Kate's difficulties at home.

Kate had 'spoken bitterly' of the assault the next day to PC Robert Beattie, a familiar and friendly presence on St Andrew Street where Kate worked, but he told her that the police didn't like to get involved in family matters. Beattie would give evidence at Kate's trial to that effect, substantiating her allegations of brutal treatment by her father and stepmother.

Kate's story was further reinforced by a pre-trial report by the Procurator Fiscal in Dumfries who had interviewed her sister Grace, who told him of her own unhappy experiences with her father and stepmother when she had come home for a two-week holiday earlier in the year, in July. 'Her stepmother complained of her lazy and careless habits and the inconvenience thereby caused in the household arrangements. As a result, Grace left her father's house and took lodgings in town for the next ten days. Her father and mother have had no correspondence with her since.'

It was Kate's extraordinary good fortune that John Wilson was assigned to her case. As a defence counsel he had a track record of success due to his 'marked ability, forcefulness and courage' in presenting a case to the jury. His 'wide knowledge of law and his great capacity for work' had also won respect and admiration among his colleagues at the Bar, according to the *Scotsman*. But perhaps more important in preparing the defence case for Kate was his essential 'goodness of heart', remarked upon in an appreciation by his friend and colleague Lord Sands, the Lord Justice General, which was published nearly twenty years later after his death. 'He would take endless trouble to help anyone who happened to be in a difficulty. I knew of many acts of personal kindness on his part when he went out of his way to help a lame dog,' wrote Lord Sands.

On Boxing Day 1914, the defence case for Kate Hume was already taking shape in Wilson's legal mind. He accepted that it was highly likely that Kate would be found guilty but he was determined to present her to the jury in a way that would make them sympathetic to her. She might be the prisoner in the dock, but Wilson would switch the spotlight onto her father and step-mother through his cross-examination. By the end of the trial the jury would come to think that Andrew and Alice Hume should have been the ones on trial for their unkindness.

Two days later, at 8 a.m. on 28 December, the teenager was taken from her cell in handcuffs and driven in a horse-drawn prison van to the High Court in Edinburgh, where, flanked by two police officers, she stood in the dock as the charges were read out before an all-male jury. The public gallery was packed with spectators and the atmosphere tense. She pleaded not guilty. The trial would last two days.

Kate, who wore a blue overcoat and a fur-trimmed velour hat, sat with her head bowed. A photograph published in the *Scotsman* showed her with a handkerchief pressed to her nose. She cut 'a pathetic figure', according to the *Dumfries & Galloway Standard*'s reporter. Having been taken in by the hoax, Mr Dickie had a few scores to settle. The *Standard*'s five-page report, published on the following Wednesday, was written and presented in a way intended to cause the maximum embar-rassment to the Hume family. It also served to distract readers from the growing number of Scottish casualties in the war.

More than twenty witnesses gave evidence, Kate's father and stepmother giving evidence for the prosecution. First to take the stand was Kate's father, Andrew. He confirmed the prosecution's account of events. Kate's defence counsel, John Wilson, then stood up to strip away the deceit and conceit. These exchanges are taken from newspaper reports of Kate's trial:

John Wilson, QC: 'Mr Hume, as regards Kate's own mother, that was your first wife, you said she had been an invalid for several years?

Andrew Hume: 'Yes, about eight years. She was in bed most of the time.'

'For some years before her death did you notice periods of marked depression on your wife's part?'

'I did, sir, very much. I don't know what caused it.'

'About two or three years ago was there a very sad blow to the family in the death of one of the members?'

'Yes, sir, that was my son John.'

'He died well. He was one of the men who went down on the *Titanic*?'

'He was, sir.'

'And attention was called to the loss of your son particularly by the fact that he was the leader, I think, of the band?'

'Yes, sir.'

[This was Andrew Hume's first lie: Jock had not been the leader of the band].

'And the band went down playing the hymn, "Nearer my God to Thee"?'

'Yes.' Andrew Hume became very emotional at this point, his voice breaking up. 'There were five of the family altogether, and Kate, the accused, is now seventeen. John was just over twenty-one when he was drowned.'

'It is the case that Kate and he were bound up in each other?'

'Very much so.'

'And did she take the death of her brother very badly?'

'Yes.'

'Looking back upon the last two years, has she ever been the same girl since?'

'She has not, sir. I remarked that from time to time.'

'You are a musician yourself?'

'Yes.'

Now the QC led Andrew Hume into repeating on oath and elaborating upon, the lie about his grandfather. Did Wilson know the truth, I wonder, that Andrew's father was not Alexander Hume but a farm labourer called Robert Hume?

'Is it the case that for some generations the family has shown marked musical talent?'

'They have, sir, except my father.'

'So the talent missed your father, but your grandfather was the author of several of the best known Scotch tunes like "Afton Water". He wrote music to that?'

'Yes, the new edition.'

'And "The Emigrant's Farewell"?'

'Yes'

'And am I wrong in saying also some of the psalm tunes?'

'Quite a few of them.'

'And others?'

'Yes.'

'With regard to your own family, is there one of them who has the promise of musical talent as bright as your grandfather's?'

'Yes, two of them. Kate herself is one, and her younger brother.'

'Has Kate shown marked musical talent already?'

'Very much so.'

Having extracted from Kate's father an admission that his daughter was a talented young musician, Wilson used his cross-examination of Alice Hume to paint a picture of Kate as an abused child.

Alice Hume: 'I am fifty years of age, and I am the wife of and reside with Andrew Hume, the last witness, in Dumfries. I was married in 1907. I found it rather difficult to get on with the stepchildren who were in the house. Kate was rather headstrong. Our relations became strained a little bit within the last year.'

John Wilson QC: 'Did she approve or resent interference on your part?'

'Oh, well, sometimes she rather resented it, of course.'

'And she left your house in August of this year

and went into lodgings? Why? As you understood at the time?'

This was a trap laid by Wilson to undermine Alice Hume's credibility as he knew the judge and jury would shortly hear from Clouston about the beatings.

'Well, I think perhaps she wanted more liberty. She attended to her duties fairly well while she was living in my house. What led up to the differences between us was that sometimes, of course, she perhaps did not do things exactly in the way I wanted them, and I had to check her sometimes for being a bit careless, just like other young girls.'

'What I want to get at, Mrs Hume, is what led up to the strong step of your daughter leaving the house?'

'Well, I think the real reason was that she wanted more liberty to get out.'

The next stage of Wilson's defence strategy was to demonstrate that Kate's elaborate hoax would have had no effect whatsoever had it not been for the irresponsibility of the *Dumfries & Galloway Standard* in publishing them. The editor, Mr Dickie, took the stand.

'I understand that you got these two letters from your reporter, Mr Dickie?'

'Yes, from Mr Whitehead on Monday 14th September.'

'What did you do with them when you got them?'

234

'I had a copy made of number 1 for our own use, and got a clerk in the publishing office to send the original to be lithographed. I did that on the Monday, and I got the block on the Tuesday afternoon before Mr Hume called.'

'So you had so far committed yourself?'

'Yes. The irrevocable decision to publish was not arrived at until after Mr Hume had been there. We have to cut out columns frequently after that time.'

'But you had your editorial written?'

'As a matter of fact I was beginning to write a note on the subject when Mr Hume came in.'

'So it must have been painful for you not to publish it?'

'On the contrary it would have been a great relief if we had seen any reason to doubt the truth of the story and to withhold it from publication.'

'What appeared in your paper was a sensational bit of news?'

'It was a sensational occurrence being reported.'

'And therefore good copy in common phrase?'

'Certainly, but I did not consider it from the commercial stand-point, and had no occasion to do so.'

'But you admit that the object of the father's call on the Tuesday night was to get you to refrain from publishing these letters in the following day's paper?'

'That was the purpose, but about the motive I have my own views.'

'What do you mean?'

'What his motive was in wishing it withheld.'

'But whatever his motive was, his purpose was to get you to withhold publication?'

'Yes, but I am not satisfied that he told me the truth when he said he had written to the War Office and wished publication delayed.'

'Do you not now think it would have been reasonable, and prudent possibly, instead of going upon what your reporter said as to the consent of a young girl of seventeen, to have agreed to her father's desire that you should delay the publication?'

'No. I was not impressed by the father's desire at all.'

'In short, you were hostile to the father?'

'No, I was not in the least hostile, but he did not give me any reason for delaying it, and I had his assurance that the letter was genuine. I did not say that he had seen the letter. I say that he said to me he had seen it. He told me he had seen the letter, and he was convinced the handwriting was Grace's.'

'When did he say he had seen it?'

'He did not say either when or where.'

'You had had it since the Monday yourself?'

'Yes.'

'So he could not have seen it since the Monday?'

'No.'

'Then when could he have seen it?'

'Well, according to the girl's statement it was

received on the Thursday, and there were Friday, Saturday and Sunday for him to see it.'

'How was he to see it? You said they were on such relations that you would not even take the letter to him?'

'If I had had any doubt about it I would probably have taken it to him, but I had not any. I had no personal knowledge of their relations. It was public property that this girl was living away from her father's house, and we know there had been litigation. It was not a personal matter. We know there was a state of antagonism between the girl and her father.'

'How do you suggest he saw that letter if there was a state of antagonism which you say existed?'

'The antagonism may be there, but even if a girl has an ill-will to her father and receives an account of a terrible tragedy concerning a member of the family, it is surely conceivable that she would overcome the feeling of resentment and go to her father and say that a letter had been received, or that she should send it by some friend, which I was told had been done.'

When the time came for Kate to give evidence, Wilson was keen for her to be questioned away from the dock, in the witness box where all the other witnesses had given evidence. The judge consented. Wilson knew how to appeal to a jury and played the *Titanic* card straight away. He knew that it would win their sympathy.

'Looking back upon your life, Miss Hume, one of the hardest blows was the death of your brother John?'

'Yes.'

'You were awfully fond of him?'

'Yes.'

'In consequence of his tragic death you suffered very badly?'

'Yes, sir.'

'As regards your leaving home, you thought, rightly or wrongly, that your stepmother was too careful about your getting out?'

'Sometimes.'

'One of your hardships, I think, was being sent early to bed?'

'Not particularly.' (This was a reference to evidence given earlier in the trial that her father had required Kate to be in bed by 8 p.m every night.)

'In any case you wanted a little more freedom?'

'Yes. In consequence I went to Mrs McMinn's. I had known her daughter at school.'

'Is it the case that before you left your father's house you at times felt yourself greatly depressed?'

'Long before I left my father's house. I had headaches and could not sleep, and gave way to crying when left alone. I often went to bed crying. After I went to Mrs McMinn's week after week passed without getting a letter from Grace.'

Now Wilson played the war card.

'At Mrs McMinn's you read everything you could get bearing on the war?'

'Not everything. I read about the Germans being so cruel, and everybody was talking about it; and I thought at that time, seeing that my sister Grace was not writing, that she had really gone to the front. I wrote to her and tried to get a reply, but could get none. My father and stepmother did not come near me, as I did not go to them.'

Even before the judge, Lord Strathclyde, began his summing up, Wilson knew that he had won his client's freedom, whatever the jury's verdict. He had presented her as she was: a girl who had suffered two huge emotional blows, first the death of her mother, then the death of her brother. Her father and stepmother had been exposed as more than unkind, brutal even. In legal terms it all came down to a 'degree of guilt' and Wilson's skilful revelation of Mr Dickie's haste in rushing to press suddenly left Kate looking much less guilty. The jury had been won over. The judge encouraged them to take a compassionate view:

'If you came to the conclusion that the defendant was in a slightly emotional and hysterical condition at the time, that would not affect the guilt, but it would affect seriously the degree of it, and that might probably lead to no punishment being imposed at all. Here, gentlemen, emerges the stage of the case at which you are able to render me very material service.'

The jury retired to consider their verdict at ten minutes to three, and returned fifteen minutes later. The foreman of the jury said:

'My Lord, we, the jury, unanimously find the accused guilty of writing the letters as charged, but at the time she did not realise she was committing a crime. We earnestly recommend her to the leniency of the Court.'

Lord Strathclyde said:

'I am not quite clear what you desire. Do you mean you find the prisoner guilty of the crime and recommend her to leniency? Is that your intention?'

'That is so,' replied the foreman. Mr Wilson rose to his feet:

'I take it, my lord, that the verdict is one of not guilty.' Lord Strathclyde replied, 'The jury have explained. The clerk will read the verdict.'

A hush fell over the court as the clerk then read out the jury's verdict:

'The jury unanimously find the plaintiff guilty as charged, and earnestly recommend her to the leniency of the Court.'

At this, the judge declared,

> 'Kate Hume, I am very willing to accede to the earnest recommendations of the jury. They have given most careful attention to your case, and in consideration of the fact that you have already been upwards of three months in prison, having regard to your previous good character and your youth I consider it expedient – and this is the order of the court – that you be released now.'

There was a roar of approval from the public gallery. Kate burst into tears. She left the court accompanied by a woman warder, her solicitor and Mr Wilson. Her father and step-mother were not in court to hear the jury's verdict.

25

The Fall and Rise of Andrew Hume

29 December 1914

A wave of public sympathy greeted Kate Hume's release from prison but Andrew Hume was not in court in Edinburgh to see his daughter freed, neither was he there to steer her through the cheering crowds in the street outside. Andrew had gone to ground with Alice at home in Dumfries, where he now faced personal, professional and financial ruin. His year-long court battle with Mary Costin had exposed him as a liar and a thief who stole from his own granddaughter. Now his own daughter had heaped further shame on him by denouncing him as a tyrannical father who horsewhipped his children.

There had always been something not quite right about Andrew Hume. He was charming, but just when you thought you had engaged his attention he left you feeling he had seen someone more interesting over your shoulder. Although apparently well-off, he would keep tradesmen waiting weeks for payment, disputing bills for months after they had become due. He had a reputation for giving his solemn word then going back on it. He was good-looking, but unashamedly vain, making minor adjustments to his moustache, his hair or his cravat after catching sight of his reflection in shop windows. And while affecting to be a musician with a sensitive soul, the façade often fell to reveal a mean streak and a bad temper.

Friends and neighbours who had comforted Andrew after the death of his wife Grace felt cheated when they discovered he had taken up with his next-door neighbour Alice Alston with such indecent haste. After Jock's death, they felt deceived again, having given comfort and support to a man whose actions would have distressed and angered his late son. Andrew's persecution of Mary Costin further confirmed everyone's suspicions that he was not all that he pretended to be.

The adverse publicity had a dramatic effect on Andrew Hume's business as a music teacher, his main source of income. One by one, with every new revelation, his pupils had drifted away. At first, people made polite excuses for cancelling their music lessons. Soon they didn't bother to explain why: they just didn't turn up. Mothers did not want to leave their daughters alone with a man who whipped his own daughters; husbands were disinclined to leave their wives alone with a man so clearly lacking in moral fibre. The Dumfries Academy, sensitive to the feelings of governors and parents alike, informed Andrew that they would no longer be requiring his part-time services. The Provost cancelled a meeting that had been arranged to agree a programme of summer public concerts in Dock Park, due to be conducted by Andrew.

Before Kate's trial, Andrew had become aware of the social awkwardness his presence was causing, but the coverage of the trial in the local and national press turned him into a pariah overnight. It wasn't just that friends and neighbours were crossing the street to avoid him – when he walked into a shop, people he had known all his life were abandoning purchases in mid-transaction and walking out. Andrew Hume was a ruined man – in Dumfries, anyway. Short of cash, he started selling off his stock of violins and making plans for the future. In July 1913 he had taken two months off in the middle of his court skirmishes with Mary Costin to travel to Bohemia. He revealed his trip in a letter to *The Strad* magazine then as now 'the essential magazine that gets you closer to the best players, the finest instruments, and the most famous makers every month.' The letter was about the effect of different varnishes on the tonal quality of a violin but, as always, Hume couldn't resist a throwaway brag:

'The July issue of *The Strad* reached me in Bohemia where I have been on a journey to procure suitable wood for violin making,' wrote Hume. 'The *proper* kind is, to my mind, very hard to get and also comes expensive.'

The most likely reason for Hume's trip was to buy violins 'in the white'. Most of these instruments, crafted from the finest wood by some of the world's best violin makers, would have come with their front, back and sides pre-assembled and glued. The profit on reselling them would come from Andrew's considerable skill in varnishing them. Other instruments would come pre-cut but unassembled, requiring gluing and shaping as well as varnishing. Andrew Hume was very good at doing this, recreating classic violin designs, ageing them, and adding his own initials

His favoured medium for advertising his finished products was *The Strad*. His frequent letters to the editor and the classified advertisements that he placed in almost every issue, provide a fascinating insight into the next twenty years of Andrew's professional life and are, indeed, the only proper record of it. They reveal his highs and his lows, his successes and his failures, his lies and his deceits. An advertisement that appeared in *The Strad* shortly before Christmas 1913, for instance, reveals as much about the irrepressible Andrew as it does about the violins he was selling:

GREAT VIOLIN BARGAINS
A few of my earlier make at £5. 5s. each have
been sold as per advt in October *Strad*.
One purchaser writes: "Violin safely to hand! I
have seen and tried a great many violins during
the past twenty years as a professional player and
this is assuredly the very best toned instrument I
ever drew a bow across. I enclose a further cheque
for another of the same. Tone, wood, varnish, etc.,
are equally magnificent and with this one I envy
nobody their 'Strads'." Be in time while they last
as they cannot stay long here.
A. HUME, 42 George Street, Dumfries.

It would seem that Andrew and Alice were making plans to leave Dumfries even before Kate's trial, as Andrew carried on selling his stock throughout 1914, having apparently given up teaching and playing. After Kate's arrest in September, Andrew dropped the price of his violins to £5 and also advertised for sale '30,000 sets of Orchestral Music, with or without piano, from 2d per set. Also 2,000 sets for Military Band (State wants)'.

At around this time, Andrew Hume set in motion a carefully orchestrated plan to reinvent himself as a master maker of violins. Part of this process was a long interview that he gave to *The Strad*, and which appeared in their April 1915 issue under the [appropriate] heading: 'Fiddles by Living Makers: Alexander Hume'. It is a flattering account of 'Alexander' Hume's life and work in Dumfries, the years he spent learning his craft in the workshops of Erlbach, Schönbach and Marneukirchen, his ability to replicate an Amati violin and his skill as a bow maker. But the significance of the article only becomes clear in the following month's issue of *The Strad*, which published a short correction stating that the interview with Alexander Hume was in fact an interview with *Andrew* Hume. This time the author, Towry Piper, was no junior reporter on the *Dumfries & Galloway Standard*. Piper was a fifty-six-year-old former solicitor and one-time pupil of Carl Jung who had joined the staff of *The Strad* some years earlier to pursue his passion for violins. Piper was at the time writing a book that was published the following year, *Violin Tone and Violin Makers*, and had taken the trouble to travel from London to Dumfries to find out more about Andrew, whom he described a 'brither Scot'. Referring to Andrew Hume as 'Alexander' was no slip of the pen. It is clear that Andrew deliberately misled Piper about his name because, just as Andrew had once pretended Alexander Hume was his grandfather, he was now laying another false trail by adopting the name Alexander for himself. The *Strad* article was the sowing the seeds for a future fraud.

Around the time that the *Strad* article appeared, the Humes – Andrew, Alice and young Andrew – left Dumfries for good and the house in George Street was repossessed. For a while during my research I lost track of them completely. Neither the Ewart Library in Dumfries nor the archives of the *Dumfries & Galloway Standard* could offer a clue as to the whereabouts of this once-celebrated family. A blog on an ancestry website suggested that he had fled to America to start a new life but I could find no trace of him on shipping lists of emigrants. Another ancestry site suggested that he had died of a broken heart but I could find no record of his death, at least not in Scotland. The trail had gone cold when suddenly Andrew Hume reappeared in *The Strad* magazine, still trying to offload the 30,000 sets of orchestral music. He was in Peterborough.

VIOLINS, VIOLAS, CELLOS, &c.
Also Large Lot of ORCHESTRAL MUSIC
The professionals' ideal Instruments may now be
had at most reasonable prices:
cash or exchange, as may be agreed upon.
A good stock on hand, ancient and modern, cheap.
Prompt and Expert attention to all orders.
A. HUME,
Professional Player and Maker,
39 Granville Street, Peterborough.

Why Peterborough? Why Andrew and Alice chose to go there rather than London, where they eventually ended up, remains a mystery. Granville Street is a pleasant street of terraced houses near King's School, which is probably why Andrew chose it as the base for his business, just as he chose a house near the Academy when he moved to Dumfries. Andrew and Alice – still with Jock's young brother Andrew Jnr, now four-teen, in tow – rented a house less a mile away at 9 Parliament Street. It was from here, on 12 April 1916, that Andrew Hume wrote again to the Public Trustee of the *Titanic* Relief Fund.

re Titanic Case No. 689
The Public Trustee
Sir

In view of the grossly inhumane treatment dispensed in the above case, partly due to the action of an unscrupulous agent who in order to save himself has now absconded, and which, in the period that has elapsed since the disaster has resulted in the complete breakdown of my wife's health, my youngest daughter also having been placed under restraint for one year through acute mental hysteria. My house is now being compulsorily sold up by my late agents, my social and business life having been also ruined, I am compelled to seek employment elsewhere as a musician.

I respectfully request that you now institute a searching enquiry into this matter as it is utterly impossible for me to reconcile myself to the position which now exists.
I am at this address endeavouring to get a new home together
Faithfully yours,
A Hume,
Parent of late J. L. Hume.

Hume makes no mention in the letter of his attempts to claim compensation from the White Star Line for the two valuable violins he alleged Jock took with him on the *Titanic*. There is no record of a reply from the Public Trustee. The tone and content of Andrew's letter suggests that he was desperate, almost to the point of being suicidal. Yet, as he was soon to demonstrate, he was very far from being down and out. Andrew was already well on the way to reinventing himself.

The Humes stayed in Peterborough until the end of the First World War, Andrew making violins, finishing them, and buying and selling them. They then moved briefly to Bedford before settling in London, where he set up shop at 167 Brixton Road. From here he advertised in *The Strad*:

> a few fine old Italian violins and best modern maker's specimens for sale, cheap. Also good bows, violas, etc. Highest-class repairs and refitting executed to order.

Brixton did not suit the Humes and within a few months he took a lease on a more central property in Great Portland Street on the other side of Oxford Street from Soho, where most of the quality shops selling musical instruments were, and still are, to be found. Here, away from the scandals, the tragedies and the memories of Dumfries, Andrew Hume regained his old confidence and Andrew Jnr, now aged nineteen, launched himself in his own career as a musician, forming a quartet called Andy and the Boys.

In 1920 Hume acquired a fine violin by the Milanese violin maker Leandro Bisiach. It seems to have been made for Hume as Bisiach has signed the instrument and seems to have added Andrew Hume's name to the label inside it. How Hume came by it, or was able to afford it, is one of those mysteries that provide endless debate in the elegant and subtle world of violins. After Hume's death it found its way to the collection of the famous violinist Howard Davis, leader for 35 years of the Alberni Quartet and a teacher at the

Royal Academy of Music. For a period, it was Davis's own preferred instrument. After Davis's death in 1984 it was sold for £6,000 and is still in use today in the hands of a gifted violinist with the Welsh National Opera.

Around this time, Hume also seems to have acquired a Guadagnini. It featured in one of Andrew's first advertisements for his new business at 34 Great Portland Street near Oxford Circus, where he and Alice lived above the shop. It appeared in *The Strad* in 1921:

FINE VIOLINS THIS MONTH BY
PRESSENDA, 1830; ROCCA, 1855;
L. GUADAGNINI, CERUTI
Also best Moderns, Bows, Strings, etc
Old instruments bought or exchanged
If your old instrument is not giving you
its usual satisfaction
send it on for rebarring or readjustment to:-
HUME, 34 Great Portland Street, W.1

By the following year, Andrew Hume was taking a large advertisement the full width of the page in *The Strad*. He was now describing himself as a 'Violin Expert, Maker & Repairer'. The instruments offered for sale included 'One baby Grand Piano as supplied to the Court of Italy', a Stradivari from the 'Heroz Coburg-Gotha collection' [sic] and 'a few of my own specials'.

A. Hume – significantly, he never used his Christian name, Andrew – became a prodigious correspondent on *The Strad*'s letters pages, contributing to debates about varnish and glues, and shamelessly exploiting any opportunity to promote his own instruments and expertise. In 1921 he wrote:

Since the June issue of your esteemed paper I have had a great many visitors to examine the specimens I have on hand at present, all parties making practically the same remark, viz., that they have never seen any varnish so perfect and beautiful, the wood and workmanship being equally so.

Hume also entered music competitions, sharing a twenty-guinea prize donated by the philanthropist Walter Wilson Cobbett in a competition organised by the Royal College of Music and winning a gold medal at the British Empire Wembley Exhibition of 1924–25. The Wembley exhibition seems to have been a turning point in Andrew's new life. It was opened by King George V, who made the first ever broadcast by a British monarch and further marked the occasion by sending a telegram to himself around the world and back (via every far-flung outpost of the British Empire, of course); it took one minute and twenty seconds. Sir Edward Elgar brought 'a choir of 10,000 voices' to the opening ceremony. Andrew seized the opportunity offered by the huge public interest in the exhibition and took a stand – number v.917 in the 'Palace of Industry' – personally welcoming visitors. His advertisement in the April 1924 issue of The Strad made what was to be an irresistible offer to readers:

Empire Exhibition Wembley
Stand v.917 Palace of Industries [sic]
Should your violin NOT be giving you all the
pleasure you desire when in use, take or send it to
the above stand from 11am till 4pm any day and

have my personal comment upon it. The following
is one of many recently expressed opinions on the
results of this course:

Dear Sir, My lucky star was in the ascendant
when I brought my fiddle to you. You are a magi-
cian. The tonal improvement in it since can only
be described as magical, the former 'rawness' has
vanished and left a pure and clear singing tone
behind. If the cost to me had been many times
what it was, I would still be your debtor.
With many thanks, Yours truly, J.G.A.

Having relaunched his career through the exhibition,
Andrew spent the next two years using the exhibition to
promote himself relentlessly in a series of advertisements in
The Strad.

The Hume Violin, Viola, Cello
Highest Award, London, 1918 and
B.E. Exhibition 1924–25
Pronounced by Messrs Strockoff, Thibaud
to be quite unsurpassable on all points.
A recent purchaser writes:
There is a charm, delicacy and refinement about it,
as well as power and a wonderful reserve that is
very rare, the more I play upon it the better I like
it and I am enjoying my music more now than in
the past. I simply can't let it alone.

Andrew's pioneering use of celebrity endorsements – Leo
Strockoff and Jacques Thibaud were two of the greatest

virtuoso violinists of their generation – would not stop there. From his stand at the exhibition Andrew was selling a gadget for anchoring cellos firmly to the floor. This 'perfect cello and bass fixer' cost 4s 6d and came with an endorsement from Pablo Casals: 'Very simple and most efficient. Sincere congratulations – Pablo Casals.'

Given Andrew's track record for deceit, it seems highly unlikely that Strockoff, Thibaud or Casals had said what Andrew claimed. However, modesty and caution were not among Hume's characteristics and now he was back in his stride, boasting and selling:

> I have ten recipes of Old Italian Varnishes of dates 1550, 1564 and 1745. I made the varnish used on this speci-men (violin) in 1907. I consider it to be the very purest and finest preservative to be seen today . . .
> I have also a number of FINE OLD MASTER VIOLINS, VIOLAS and CELLOS for disposal.

It had taken Andrew Hume ten years to rebuild his life from the wreckage he had left behind in Dumfries. Once again he was a man of position, with a prosperous business and a great gift – this time for making and restoring violins, rather than playing them. Yet despite the veneer of success and the confidence he exuded, scandal and suspicions continued to follow him, centring around instruments that Hume referred to modestly as 'one of my own specials'. They carried the initials A. H. but no one – including Andrew Hume himself – knew whether the 'A' stood for Alexander or Andrew. He signed all letters 'A. Hume' and called his business 'A. Hume'.

Andrew's great skill in obtaining and applying old Italian varnishes lay behind many of the doubts surrounding instruments he made or sold. He had a reputation in the trade for selling violins that were not always what he claimed they were. Mistakes were sometimes found in certificates of authenticity. There were disputes over provenance. 'Let's just say that people in the trade had learned to be very careful when they were offered an instrument by Andrew Hume,' says David Rattray, the distinguished Custodian of Instruments at the Royal Academy of Music and author of several books on the violin:

Early in March 1934 Andrew Hume sold his last instrument, a violin by Giovanni Guadagnini which he had advertised for sale in that month's *The Strad*, a similar instrument to the one that Jock had supposedly taken with him on the *Titanic*. On 24 March Andrew collapsed after suffering a cerebral haemorrhage in his workshop in Great Portland Street. He was taken to the Charing Cross Hospital, where he died next day. He was sixty-nine. After the funeral, which none of his children attended, Alice returned to Scotland, but not to Dumfries. She died in Edinburgh on 11 April 1939, aged seventy-four.

The Strad had already gone to press and the month after Andrew's death it published his last classified advertisement:

> Specially Fine Violins. No cracks. Chappuy, £8; Mezzin, £6; Degani, Bausch and others. Silver plated quick change to A flat Trumpet, low pitch and unused. A and B flat Clarionets,

Albert and Boehm.
A. Hume, 34 Gt Portland Street, W.1.

It was not his only epitaph. The following month, *The Strad* published a short obituary, which began:

> We regret to record the recent death of Mr A.
> Hume, the well-known maker and repairer of
> Great Portland Street, London . . . whose instru-
> ments gained an award at the Wembley Exhibition
> of 1924–25.

The Strad did not say whether they were recording the death of Andrew Hume or Alexander Hume.

On 5 October 2009 a violin labelled 'Alexander Hume London Anno 1930' and further labelled 'Copy Antonius Stradivarius, Cremona' was sold at auction by Brompton's the London auctioneers for £1,200. The initials A.H. were engraved on it. The violin was probably one of the last instruments Andrew Hume made. If it was not exactly as described in the catalogue, it is most certainly a collector's item.

26

The Life and Death of Johnann Costin

1912–1996

My mother said that from the moment she was born she was made to feel different from other children, and that this feeling continued throughout her life. One can understand why. Her father had died a hero's death; she carried the stigma of illegitimacy in spite of the court confirmation of her paternity; and she became a 'charity's child' through the support of the *Titanic* Relief Fund. She was painfully aware, from a very early age, of people pointing her out in the street in Dumfries. 'That's the Costin girl,' they would say. Or sometimes, 'There's Jock Hume's bairn.'

For this reason, her mother Mary Costin always made sure Johnann was beautifully dressed, her clothes washed and pressed, her hair brushed and combed. For the first year of her life she was wheeled around Dumfries in a two-tone Marmet pram, the very best there was apart from a Silver Cross. Mary made a fuss of her daughter, in private and in public. Yet the proud mother was also a hard-working single parent, continuing to work at the glove factory to make ends meet. My mother can remember her coming home at night and making starch from potatoes to keep their clothes smart.

All this is reflected in the portrait of the young Johnann

taken when she was about two years old: the string of pearls round her neck, the carefully tied silk bow, the hands clasped together – a picture of sweetness and innocence. The next photograph of her, taken with her mother two years later, shows her in a smock with her new boots carefully tied. Again, there is a bow in her hair. But the face now is anxious, uncertain, slightly fearful even.

While Mary continued to work, Johnann was looked after by her grandmother, Susan, at the family home at 35 Buccleuch Street, attending the George Street primary school round the corner. Johnann adored her grandmother and Susan loved her. The arrival of a new granddaughter must have gone some way towards making up for the loss of her oldest son, William, in 1911.

It was not an unusual arrangement then, or now, for a grandmother to assume the role of mother in her daughter's absence. But it seems that between 1912 and 1915 there was a gradual transfer of responsibilities from mother to grandmother, at the end of which Susan became the parent, at least in Johnann's eyes. 'I was brought up by Grandmother,' my mother always said. If it wasn't true in the early years, it certainly became true later.

The outbreak of the First World War had an immediate and dramatic impact on the Costins, as it did on most families. Both Mary's brothers, John and Menzies, signed up, Menzies joining the 2nd Argyll and Sutherland Highlanders. Mary, too, joined the war effort. She left her job at the glove factory and went to work at the Arrol-Johnson works at Heathhall, just outside Dumfries. Arrol-Johnson had been founded in 1894 to make steam trams but had moved into motor-car manufacture at the beginning of the twentieth century. With a war on, it switched its production to manufacturing aero engines and artillery shells and took on more than 1,000 extra employees. Mary worked there until the end of the war.

At some time during the war Mary met a soldier home on leave, Walter Thomson, the son of a gamekeeper. Walter was two years her junior. A month after the end of the war, on 12 December 1918, Walter and Mary, who was now twenty-seven, married in Dumfries. Walter's address is recorded on the register as 'c/o BEF France' (British Expeditionary Force), indicating that he was still a serving soldier, although he gave his occupation as 'chauffeur'.

My mother, who would then have been six years old, had no recollection of the wedding taking place; perhaps she did not attend. In any case, it seems that she had no place in her mother's life from then on. Early in 1919 Mary and Walter took a small apartment in nearby St Andrew Street, leaving Johnann with her grandmother. Later that year, Mary gave birth to their first child, Walter, and in September 1921 she had a second son, Kennedy. It is hard to understand why Mary abandoned her daughter, especially after she had fought so many battles over her, but she did. My mother saw nothing of her half-brothers and very little of her mother. It seems a heartless thing for Mary to have done, but it is always possible that she had intended one day to merge her two families. We will never know the truth, though, because on 6 November 1922 Mary died from tuberculosis. She was thirty-two.

If it was a tragedy for Johnann, orphaned at the age of ten, it must have been painful, too, for Mary's mother Susan, who was burying the fourth of her six children. At the same time she was nursing her older son, John, who had returned wounded from the war, shell-shocked and with severe breathing difficulties as a result of having been gassed. John-ann continued to live with her grandmother, but not for long: fourteen months later, on 10 January 1924, her beloved granny Susan died of pernicious anaemia, aged sixty-two. Johnann was just twelve years old.

My mother's version of what happened next was quite clear, although the details were never elaborated upon. Her uncle Menzies and his wife became her guardians; she lived on the Isle of Skye for some time; there were suggestions that Menzies abused her; at fifteen she ran away to London to escape him and worked in a hat shop in Sloane Street. It was a part of her life that she preferred to draw a veil over and one had to respect that. But in 1935, when she was twenty-three, Johnann, now 'Jackie' Costin, met my father John Ward, a reporter on the *London Evening News*. They married two years later at Kew Church. Her name appears on the certificate as 'Jacqueline Law Hume Costin', her occupation as 'sales assistant'. She gave birth to my sister, Cherry, the following year and then to me, during the war in 1942. In 1944 my father, who was in the RAF, became seriously ill with a brain tumour and died the following year; my mother became the third generation of Costin women to bring up a young family on her own.

Like her mother and grandmother, she understood that the first priority was to get a job. She was taken on by two rising stars of the British film industry, Herbert Wilcox and Anna Neagle, to manage their publicity, and worked in the film business until she was in her mid-fifties, when she made a career switch into the tourist industry. She carried on working well into her seventies and died aged eighty-three, never having remarried. She never spoke an ill word about her mother. In spite of her catastrophic start in life, Johnann was a wonderful mother to my sister and me, so she must have experienced good mothering herself, from both her mother and grandmother. 'What happened to me was nobody's fault,' she once said. 'It was all determined by the *Titanic*.'

27

Our Heart Will Glow With Pride

2010

Early in 2010, when this book was still nothing more than a family ancestry project, I contacted Jock's old school, St Michael's, in an attempt to confirm some dates and find out if any records existed of his time there. In this I was unsuccessful, the records having long since been lost or destroyed. But I was lucky in my timing because some months later I was contacted by the head teacher, Mrs Sommerville, who invited me to attend a parents' evening in April when the children would be unveiling what she called a '*Titanic* project' they had been working on for some time. 'I think you will enjoy it,' she said, 'and the children will be interested to meet the grandson of Jock Hume.'

It was a delightful and moving occasion, full of optimism, energy and creativity. A huge, colourful mural of the *Titanic*, painted to scale, extended the full length of one wall of the classroom. A smaller scale model of the ship, built by the children, stood in front of it. Every inch of the walls was covered by *Titanic* memorabilia created by the children: passenger lists, menus, White Star Line posters, all carefully researched. The children involved in the project, and their teachers, came dressed in period costumes, either as passengers or members of the ship's crew. Mrs Sommerville herself gave a very good impersonation of a First Class passenger and one boy played the part of Harold Bride, the young Marconi wireless operator who survived. The enthusiastic curator of the Dalbeattie Museum, Tommy Henderson, provided a wide range of period props – a Morse code key, a *Titanic* lifebelt and copies of original newspapers reporting the disaster.

I didn't know then about Jock's headmaster, Mr Hendrie, who had played such an important part in the school's formative years, involving, challenging, stretching and inspiring the school children in his care, but clearly his presence is still felt there. To enter the school you have to walk past the marble plaque to the left of the door commemorating his two old boys, Jock and Tom, who died on the *Titanic*. Passing it could be a mournful experience, but above it is the uplifting exhortation, 'Our School Aim is to . . . Reach For the Stars,' above a painting of two outstretched hands reaching up towards a blue, star-filled sky.

I left the party with a spring in my step. The evening had been a celebration of success and of achievement, a recognition of the courage of two former pupils who went to sea, an encouragement for young people to aspire to brave things, not to be deterred by the fear of catastrophe.

I was reminded of the evening some months later, leafing through 1912 issues of the *Dumfries & Galloway Standard & Advertiser* and coming across *The Last Hymn* – an anonymous appreciation of Jock published the week after the *Titanic* sank. I quoted the first paragraph of the letter in the epigraph to this book but it is worth reading in its entirety because, like that *Titanic* evening at St Michael's, its message is such an optimistic one. I wondered whether Mr Hendrie himself had written it.

'No one was a greater favourite at school than 'Johnny', as he was always called. Indeed everyone who knew the happy faced lad will have felt a lump in their throat when they read that poor Johnny had, 'like the Wanderer,' gone through the darkness to his rest. Yet, withal, pride masters our grief, for the lad died a hero, his beloved violin clasped to his breast, playing in that last requiem for the passing soul of others and for his own.

Johnny loved his violin, and we, who have heard him play, loved both. We expected the lad to do great things with his violin, and we have not been disappointed. In the old days we have heard him, in the old Shakespeare Street Theatre, playing till the curtain should rise on many a mimic tragedy. We thought he would fiddle himself into fame, and he has done so, but in a grander and more heroic way than ever we dreamed of. Again, and for the last time, he played the curtain up on a tragedy, not the mimic one of the stage, but on a grim, awful tragedy of real life and death.

Johnny has gone and his violin is silenced forever; yet, while memory keeps its seat, that sad, sweet, solemn strain of the last hymn he helped to play shall be wafted to us across the intervening ocean of time. Our eyes may become misty at the sound of the ghostly strain, and we will grow sad to think so bright, cheery, and clever a young man has gone, but, anon, our hearts will glow with pride when we remember the grand heroic order of his going.'

⨀~ Epilogue ~⨀

Madeleine Astor inherited the income from a $5 million trust fund set up by her husband, Colonel J. J. Astor, and was given lifelong use of the Astor residence in Manhattan as long as she did not remarry. In June 1916 Madeleine married her childhood friend and banker, William Dick, part owner and a director of the *Brooklyn Times*. She moved out of the Astor residence but held on to a large part of her inheritance. She had two children with Dick but they divorced in 1933. Four months later she married a twenty-six-year-old Italian boxer, Enzo Fiermonte, but they divorced five years later. She died aged forty-six.

John Jacob Astor VI Colonel Astor's posthumous *Titanic* son inherited $3 million on his birth in 1912 and a further $5 million on his twenty-first birthday. He had a troubled life, marrying four times. He died in Miami Beach, Florida in 1992, aged seventy-nine.

Kate Hume never fully recovered from Jock's death or the many catastrophes that engulfed the Hume family afterwards, including her imprisonment and trial. Her father would later say that she had to be 'put under restraint' for acute mental hysteria. After her release from jail, Kate went into domestic service and in 1919 she married a railway engine driver,

Thomas Terbit, with whom she had four children. In 1927 she had a son whom she christened John Law Hume Terbit. The boy died in 1946, aged eighteen, from cerebrospinal meningitis. Kate died the following year. She was fifty.

John Wilson, Kate's defence counsel, went on to become one of the best-loved and most prominent counsels at the Scottish Bar. In 1917 he was appointed Sheriff of Perthshire and, ex-officio, a member of HM Prison Board for Scotland, a position he used to press for reforms in the prison system. As a Law Lord he took the title Lord Ashmore, after his home in Perthshire. He died in 1932.

William Dickie survived the 'mutilated nurse' scandal, continuing as editor of the *Dumfries & Galloway Standard*. But he suffered a series of personal tragedies that undoubtedly accelerated his death at the age of sixty-two, less than five years later. His elder son, Lieutenant William Dickie of the KOSB, was killed at Beaumont Hamel on the first day of the Somme, 1 July 1916. His commanding officer wrote to Mr and Mrs Dickie: 'Although wounded, he continued to lead his platoon until shot dead. All ranks mourn the loss of a gallant officer and wish me to convey their deepest sympathy.' At his memorial service in Dumfries, fellow officers who served with the young Oxford graduate in Gallipoli and on the Somme spoke of his courage under fire and great personal kindness to his wounded soldiers.

Dickie 'never recovered' from William's death and when his wife Jane died after a short illness the following year, Dickie went into a steep decline, dying on 12 August 1919. The obituary in his own newspaper, where he had worked for forty-eight years, said: 'With characteristic devotion to duty, even though his strength was greatly impaired, he continued to edit the paper . . . and it may be said that he literally died in harness.'

Andrew Hume Jnr formed a band called Andy and the Boys, who enjoyed moderate success for a while. He married, divorced, remarried and disappeared to Australia in the fifties without leaving a forwarding address.

Nellie Hume and **Grace Hume** both left Dumfries and never returned after the scandal of Kate's trial and their father's court cases. I have been unable to find out what happened to them.

The *Mackay-Bennett* continued to repair undersea cables throughout the First World War. She was finally retired in May 1922, and her last voyage was to Plymouth, England, to be used for storage. During the Second World War she was sunk during a bombing raid but later refloated. She was scrapped in 1963.

Captain Frederick Larnder joined the Royal Navy during the First World War and saw active service. His son, also called Frederick, served on HMS *Canada* as an able seaman and was killed at the end of the war.

Tom Mullins continued to be pursued by bad luck beyond the grave. Recovered by the SS *Minia*, he was identified by his steward's badge, No. 32, and buried in Fairview Lawn Cemetery, Halifax. His brother and two sisters received financial assistance from the Titanic Relief Fund. Mullin's badge, along with his watch, steward's pocket-book and a postcard, were returned to his family. In 2003 a relative, believing they were bringing the family continuing bad luck, put them into an auction in Dumfries where a retired policeman bought them for £102. The following year the badge was bought by an unnamed collector at auction for £28,000. Similar sums were offered for his watch, which is also believed to be in the hands of a collector.

Bibliography

Reference Books:

Anthony, Richard. *Herds and Hinds – Farm Labour in Lowland Scotland 1900-1939*.

Baptie, David. *Musical Scotland, Past and Present: Being A Dictionary Of Scottish Musicians, From About 1400 Till The Present Time (1894)*. Paisley: J & R Parlane, 1894.

Barrie, J. M. *The Greenwood Hat*. London: Peter Davies Limited, 1937.

Barczewski, Stephanie. *Titanic: A Night Remembered*. London: Hambledon and London (no date).

Beavis, Debbie. *Who Died on the Titanic?* Ian Allen Publishing, 2002.

Beed, Blair. *Titanic Victims in Halifax Graveyards*. Nova Scotia: Dtours Visitors and Convention Service, 2001.

Beesley, Lawrence. *The Loss Of The SS Titanic*. USA: 7 C's Press, Inc., 1973.

Booth, Dorothy Hyslop. *Echoes from the Border Hills*.

Brown, Richard. *Voyage Of The Iceberg – The Story of the Iceberg that Sank the Titanic*. Toronto: James Lorimer & Company, 1983.

Bryceson, Dave. *The Titanic Disaster – As reported in the British National Press April-July 1912*. Yeovil: Haynes Publishing, 1997.

Bullock, Shan F. *'A Titanic Hero' – Thomas Andrews, Shipbuilder.* USA: 7 C's Press, Inc., 1973.

Carroll, David. *Scotland in Old Photographs – Dumfries*

Carroll, Yvonne. *A Hymn for Eternity – The Story of Wallace Hartley, Titanic Bandmaster.* Stroud: Tempus Publishing Limited, 2002.

Cussler, Clive. *Raise The Titanic!* London: Michael Joseph Limited, 1977.

Davie, Michael. *The Titanic – The Full Story Of A Tragedy.* London: The Bodley Head Ltd, 1986.

Donnachie, Ian. *Scottish Textile Industry.*

Donnachie, Ian L. and Innes MacLeod. *Old Galloway.*

Eaton, John P. and Haas, Charles A. *Titanic – Triumph and Tragedy.* Yeovil: Patrick Stephens Limited, 1998.

Everett, Marshall. *Story of the Wreck of the Titanic.* L. H. Walter, 1912.

Gracie, Colonel Archibald. *The Truth About The Titanic.* USA: 7 C's Press, Inc., 1973.

Houston, George. *The Third Statistical Account of Scotland – The County of Dumfries.*

Hume, Yvonne. *RMS Titanic – Dinner is Served.* Catrine: Stenlake Publishing Limited, 2010.

Jeffers, Alan and Gordon, Rob. *Titanic Halifax – A Guide To Sites.* Nova Scotia: Nimbus Publishing Limited, 1998.

Lockwood, David. *Dumfries Story – a tribute to William McDowall.*

Lord, Walter. *A Night To Remember.* Middlesex: Penguin Books Ltd, 1976.

MacLeod, Innes. *Where the Whaups are Crying – a Dumfries and Galloway Anthology.*

Mackay, J. A. *Pictorial History of Dumfries.* Darvel: Alloway Publishing Ltd, 1990.

Maxtone-Graham, John. *Titanic Survivor – The Newly Discovered Memoirs Of Violet Jessop Who Survived both the Titanic and Britannic Disasters.* New York: Sheridan House Ltd, 1997.

Murdoch, Alexander G. *The Fiddle in Scotland.* Simpkin, Marshall & Co, 1888

Myers, L. T. *The Sinking Of The Titanic.* Nova Scotia: Nimbus Publishing Limited, 1998.

Robertson, Morgan. *The Doomed Unsinkable Ship. The Wreck of The Titan.* USA: 7 C's Press, Inc., 1974.

Rattray, David. *Masterpieces of Italian Violin Making 1620-1850.* London: The Royal Academy of Music, 1991.

Rattray, David. *Violin Making in Scotland 1750-1950.* Oxford: British Violin Making Association, 2006.

Ruffman, Alan. *Titanic Remembered – The Unsinkable Ship and Halifax.* Nova Scotia: Formac Publishing Company Limited, 2005.

Scarth, Alan. *Titanic and Liverpool.* Liverpool: Liverpool University Press and National Museums Liverpool, 2009.

Smith, Robin. *The Making of Scotland.*

Storrier, Susan. *Scottish Life & Society – A Compendium of Scottish Ethnology,* Vol 6, Tuckwell Press Limited.

Towler, David S. *Lighthouses of Atlantic Canada.* Nova Scotia: Excel Publishing, 2005.

Wade, Wyn Craig. *The Titanic – End Of A Dream.* London: George Weidenfield & Nicolson Limited, 1980.

Other Reference Material:

Daily Sketch
The Courier, Liverpool
The Daily Echo, Evening Mail, Morning Chronical, Halifax

Bibliography

The Daily Gleaner, Jamaica
The Dumfries & Galloway Standard & Advertiser
The Diary of Frederick Hamilton, National Maritime Museum, Greenwich
The New York Times
The Titanic Commutator (multiple editions over several years), published by the Titanic Historical Society

Websites:

The Strad magazine online archive, http://www.orpheusmusicshop.com/category-105.html
Encyclopaedia Titanica, http://www.encyclopedia-titanica.org/
Nova Scotia Archives and Records Management, http://gov.ns.ca/nsarm/virtual/titanic/
Titanic Historical Society, http://www.titanichistoricalsociety.org/index.asp
Titanic Inquiry Project, http://www.titanicinquiry.org/
New York Times Archive, http://www.nytimes.com/
The Atlantic Cable website, http://www.atlantic-cable.com/
Maritime Museum of the Atlantic, http://museum.gov.ns.ca/mmanew/en/home/default.aspx
The US National Archives and Records Administration, http://www.archives.gov/
Scotland's People, http://www.scotlandspeople.gov.uk/

∽◦ Acknowledgements ◦∽

I owe a great debt of thanks to my friends Mark and Colette Douglas Home who not only encouraged me to write this book but introduced me to their agent, Maggie Pearlstine, who made it happen. My publisher at Hodder & Stoughton, Rupert Lancaster, then nursed me through it, helping me make the giant leap from tabloid journalist to author. My thanks, too, to Camilla Dowse and Kate Miles at Hodder: Camilla researching and sourcing most of the images in this book and Kate bringing the whole project together in a very short period of time.

Many people have kindly given me many hours of their time assisting me with research. David Rattray, Keeper of Instruments at the Royal Academy of Music, provided an important insight into the wonderful world of stringed instruments, in particular the fiddle, which was central to understanding the mind and life of Andrew Hume. Alan Ruffman, author of the definitive book on the aftermath, *Titanic Remembered – The Unsinkable Ship And Halifax*, shared his encyclopaedic knowledge with me. Garry Shutlak, Senior Reference Archivist at the Nova Scotia Archives, who would win *Mastermind* on the subject of the *Titanic*, also steered me in the right direction in the Halifax archives and corrected multiple misconceptions. Lynne Marie Richard at the marvellous Maritime Museum in Halifax was kind enough to let me read the *Mackay-Bennett* log in the middle of a busy morning when she was setting up a new exhibition. Ed Kamuda, who founded and runs the Titanic Historical Society with his wife Karen and sister Barbara, welcomed my wife and me to their museum in Indian Orchard, Massachusetts. Brian Ticehurst, a former newspaper press operative in Southampton, who has made a lifetime study of the *Titanic* Relief Fund's distributions, generously opened his voluminous files to me.

Tommy Henderson, creator and curator of the delightful Dalbeattie Museum, took me back in time to Dumfries & Galloway's early days.

Motorbooks in Cecil Court, Covent Garden, assisted me putting the Humes on the right trains from Dumfries to Liverpool. Isla Robertson researched Dumfries and Galloway history and did much background sleuthing on my behalf in archives in Dumfries, Edinburgh and Glasgow.

Erica Johnson, archivist, and all the other staff at the Ewart Library in Dumfries, worked like terriers in sniffing out missing pieces of my family history. Erica, who specialises in ancestry research, could teach Miss Marple and Hercule Poirot a thing or three. My thanks and appreciation go, too, to the patience of staff at the libraries and museums where I spent many productive and interesting hours in 2010. These include the Merseyside Maritime Museum, the Liverpool Library, the National Archive of Scotland, and the National Library of Scotland.

My new found second cousin and fellow *Titanic* author, Yvonne Hume, exchanged pictures and information with me, filling in many blanks about our shared ancestors. Charles Pellegrino, in his wonderful tribute to Jock in *Ghosts of Vesuvius*, opened my eyes to the important role of the band in preventing panic and thus saving lives.

But most thanks of all to my wife Nonie, without whose

patience and support I would not have been able to find the time to research and write this book in a year. Her tenacious picture research in the Nova Scotia archives in Halifax was also invaluable and produced many of the most shocking images in this book.

Readers can continue Ward's journey at www.titanic-band.com

∞ Picture Acknowledgements ∞

Author's collection: 1, 2 (middle), 3 (top left & bottom), 8, 11 (top right), 12, 15 (top & bottom left), 16, 168 (text). © akg-images: 6 (bottom), 15 (right). © Alamy Images: 14 (bottom). © The Art Archive: 11 (top left). © Christie's Images/ The Bridgeman Art Library: 24 (text). © Corbis: 11 (bottom), 43 (text). © Dumfries & Galloway Council Cultural Services: 2 (top & bottom). © Getty Images: 12 (text), 14 (middle right), 20 (text), 119 (text). © Glasgow Evening News: 14 (top left). © Mary Evans Picture Library: 7 (top left), 13 (top), 14 (top right). © The National Archives of Scotland: 13 (bottom), 201 (text), 223 (text). © The New York Times Archives: 7 (top right), 10. © Nova Scotia Archives and Records Management: 7 (bottom), 9, 154 (text), 156 (text), 158 (text). © Press Association Images: 4. © Science and Society Picture Library: 5, 6 (top). The Leandro Bisiach violin with Andrew Hume's name inset © Jonathan Woolston, Cambridge: 3 (top right).

Every reasonable effort has been made to contact any copyright holders of material reproduced in this book. But if there are any errors or omissions, Hodder & Stoughton will be pleased to insert the appropriate acknowledgement in any subsequent printing of this publication.